403/650

CW01024130

The Friendly Squadron

1772 Naval Air Squadron 1944–45

A STORY TOLD BY MEMBERS OF A NAVAL AIR SQUADRON AND MEMBERS OF THE FAMILIES OF THOSE WHO HAVE DIED

THE BOSS

This book is dedicated with great affection to
LIEUTENANT COMMANDER LESLIE WORT, D.S.C. RNVR.
by a bunch of guys who had the highest possible regard for him.
They were known as 1772 Royal Naval Air Squadron (Fireflies).

IN MEMORIAM

"Death is not putting out the light
But putting out the lamp"
Tagore

Those who live on remember those who gave their lives
in training and in war.

Rod (Steve) Stevens
Monty Baker
Jim Sloan
Harry Garbutt
Maurice Goodsell
Mike La Grange
Glen (Mac) McBride
Ken Neuschild
Glyn Roberts D.S.C.

We remember too those who have died since 1945

Les Wort D.S.C.
Eric Bramhall
Gordon Davidson
Geoff Gill
David Hebditch
Don Banks

The Friendly Squadron

1772 Naval Air Squadron 1944–45

A STORY TOLD BY MEMBERS OF A NAVAL AIR SQUADRON AND MEMBERS OF THE FAMILIES OF THOSE WHO HAVE DIED

Compiled and edited by Teddy Key

A SQUARE ONE PUBLICATION

First published in 1997 by
Square One Publications,
The Tudor House
Upton upon Severn, Worcs. WR8 0HT

© 1997 Teddy Key

ISBN 1 899955 23 2

British Library Cataloguing in Publication Data
is available for this title

*Typeset in 11pt TimesNewRoman by Avon Dataset Ltd,
Bidford-on-Avon, Warwickshire B50 4JH
Printed by Antony Rowe, Chippenham, England*

CONTENTS

In Memoriam ii

The Squadron Crest – Its story vi

Quotations of War Leaders viii

Prologue 1

The Cast of Players Assemble on Stage 9

The Main Prop – The Fairey Firefly 26

Early Rehearsals – The Players begin to learn their parts 42

The Company goes on Tour 68

Final Rehearsals – In Australia 74

A Vast New Scene – and we meet a huge new
Leading Lady 86

The Performance – A moderate run only 96

Farewell Oz – Thank You – Welcome Home,
Forgotten Fleet 175

Dramatis Personae – The Players speak their piece 192

An Epilogue – Review, even a Revue 286

Acknowledgements 292

The Editor 297

THE 1772 SQUADRON CREST

*The Badge. On a field per fess, red and blue. A Bow white.
String with arrow and flighted gold*
The Motto. **TENAX PREPOSITE**
*The first format was designed by Des Mullen, an observer from
New Zealand. He was an original member of the Squadron.*

From the Public Records Department, Kew

These records show that letters to the Admiralty Badges Design
Committee started on 25th July 1944 and it was not until 17th March
1945 that final agreement on the 1772 crest was reached. Communication was started by Lt. Cdr. A. H. Gough, CO, and after many letters
and being relieved of his command, the matter was finalised by Lt. Cdr.
Les Wort, the new CO. The early design with binoculars was rejected in
August 1944 and the Badges Committee redesigned it. The final design
was described thus; 'winged striking power over land and sea together
with long-range vision'. In the beginning the Latin motto had been
translated as 'Tenacious of Purpose'. Exchanges of letters finally
resulted in the translation, 'Steadfast of Purpose'. Their Lordships
described the motto as 'good Latin' but in the Public Records Office
the Latin reads, 'Tenax Prepositi' and not 'Tenax Preposite' as on the
final design. Another prang!

*Ken Hughes, Senior Classics Master, Tiffin School, Kingston upon
Thames, Surrey*

'Tenax Preposite' doesn't make good Latin, I'm afraid, so I think you
ought to ditch that one! It sounds to me as if the original motto-
makers were, as so often, plundering Horace (aka Quintus Horatius
Flaccus) for their inspirational words: Odes Book 111, no. iii, line 1
is 'iustum et tenacem propositi virum', meaing 'the just man who
holds fast to his purpose'. I think I prefer 'tenacious' to 'steadfast',

but either is a perfectly acceptable translation, I think.

I hope a little exposition is in order. Horace published these three books of Odes as one volume in 23 BC. They are lyric poems (originally intended to be sung to the lyre), a mixture of love poems, light-hearted social comment, literary allusions and political/moral poems. At the heart of them are Odes i–vi in Book 111, usually called the 'Roman Odes'. They are longer than the others and heavily political/moral. They contain Horace's contribution to Augustus' attempt at the moral and political regeneration of Rome after the long Civil Wars. The 'just man who holds fast to his purpose' does not get blown off course by pandering to public opinion or political opposition, or indeed by anything at all. So a pretty suitable motto for you . . . I'd say!

Who would say now that Latin does not have a place in our educational system? One is quite certain that the above is not lost on that bunch, still known as 1772 Squadron. It has always been a well-known fact that 1772 usually liked their data, nice and clean and ship-shape.

QUOTATIONS OF WAR LEADERS

Lives of great men all remind us
We can make our lives sublime,
And, departing, leave behind us
Footprints on the sands of time.
Longfellow.

'I think we have done well. There's one thing we envy you and that is your British tradition. It's the one thing you've got which can neither be bought nor sold.'
Admiral Chester Nimitz
Commander-in-Chief Pacific Ocean Area

'It is likely that Kamikazes will attack the Fleet as a final fling. Any ex-enemy aircraft attacking the Fleet is to be shot down in a friendly manner.'
Admiral William F. Halsey
Commander South Pacific

'I would suggest that each will be able to say to himself, 'I fought in the Third Fleet under Halsey,' and so saying face up with greater courage to whatever tomorrow shall bring.'
Vice Admiral Sir Bernard Rawlings, KCB, KBE
Second-in-Command, BPF

'I feel sure I can rely on you to do as well in peace as you did in war and get down to this gigantic task so that we can all just return to our homes as soon as is humanly possible, feeling that we have done a good job.
Admiral Lord Louis Mountbatten
Supreme Allied Commander SE Asia

'The blazon of the RNVR deserves to be commemorated in every sea and ocean in the world, for wherever the Navy went, there also went the RNVR. The Navy was proud to have them as friends and comrades and to the traditions of the older service a host of gallant newcomers added some glorious new chapters of their own.

Admiral Lord Cunningham

Captain aboard HMS Formidable after being bombed, signalled Flagship: 'Little yellow bastard!' Admiral Vian made the memorable reply, 'Are you referring to me?'

Vice Admiral Sir Philip Vian KCB, KBE, DSO
Flag Officer Commanding 1st Carrier Squadron BPF

'I hate war as only a soldier who has lived it can, only as one who has seen its brutality, its futility, its stupidity.'

Dwight Eisenhower
Late ex-President United States

'Whilst the armistice may still be a few days away, today, the 12th August, is the end of the British Task Force as we know it. I have no hesitation in saying that it has written a memorable page in the history of the British Navy. In the time coming, when many of you will be returning to shore life, but to both those who leave and those who remain in the service, I would say two things. Firstly that you will carry with you throughout life a feeling of pride in what you have done out here. And the second, that you will realise that I am profoundly grateful to you all.'

120236. Vice Admiral Rawlings. CTF 37. 12/8/45

'Let the story speak, our past becomes the weaving of the loom for our future.'

Inscription on the Cenotaph, Whitehall, London

PROLOGUE

*'An event has happened upon which it is difficult to speak . . .
impossible to be silent.'*   Burke

That event happened over 50 years ago. In its broadest context it was
World War 2 and in its more limited context it was 1772 Naval Air
Squadron's battle at sea and in the air against one of the cruellest
enemies known to the world in this century. We ran the gamut of
emotions in our magnificent youth, from extreme excitement to plain
and unashamed fear. It was but a few weeks in the three score and ten
years, which we now all claim to be a very real part of our sagging
frames and fading memories. We spent a good deal of our service careers
in training, for such was the nature of learning to become aircrew in the
Royal Navy. Since then 'The Friendly Squadron' has kept together in
the usual way, annual reunions. The Squadron has not died, though
several of our colleagues lost their lives in training and in action and
some have died since the war. This humble little book is a tribute to
them, – our toast whenever we meet is always, 'We Remember Them'.

We have celebrated every year since we 'broke up' in Sydney in
September 1945 and in 1995 with the rest of the 'Forgotten Fleet' we
celebrated the 50th Anniversary of VJ Day. The previous year we had
celebrated the 50th Anniversary of our formation at RNAS Burscough,
HMS Ringtail, on May 1st 1944. After all those years it seemed to be
a logical thing to pool our memories and put the whole story between
one set of book covers.

And so, at breakfast on Tuesday 5th September 1995, that was the
answer to the question, 'Where do we go from here?' Why not put all
our very scratchy memories together; why not commit 'our story', which
existed in bits and pieces in several books concerning the Pacific war,
to paper. Encouragement was forthcoming from Stuart Eadon, whose
epic works, 'Sakashima-and Back' and 'Kamikaze' had laid the
foundations of much of the detailed story of the Pacific War. Graham
Mottram, Curator at that time of the Fleet Air Arm Museum at
Yeovilton, now with the demise of HMS Daedalus at Lee on Solent,

the undisputed spiritual home of all Fleet Air Arm members, wrote to the Squadron, 'I have long tried to support any genuine attempt to produce chronicles of FAA activity. Without them the story will always be skeletal and lacking the flesh of human experience. I can well imagine that 1772's history will be one of the more readable and entertaining.'

Support is of course strong within the Squadron. Chris Maclaren says, 'The story of 1772 Squadron needs to be told. It is a piece of the history of World War 2 and tells of the formation of a flying unit right from the start, with all its attendant problems, until it developed into a squadron to be proud of.' Croose Parry emphasised that our role was, 'a very small one in a huge war . . .' Sammy Samuelson, ever the enthusiastic patriot, said, 'The story has to be written, because we *were* forgotten . . . we *were* unique.' Johnny O'Driscoll feels that 'the story would, in a small way, illustrate how we fitted into that enormous and ultimate assault on Japan.'

We were in fact the third squadron to be equipped with the Fairey Firefly and even whilst our two predecessors, 1770 and 1771 Squadrons, were distinguishing themselves in action and we were trying to overcome some difficulties in our 'working up', this Firefly aircraft was killing test pilots. Among its problems was the catastrophic effect of the pilot canopy becoming detached in certain altitudes and hitting the tail plane unit. The rear observer's cockpit and hood was also not without its problems. Observers lived with the dread of baling out. Ian Darby claims that when he baled out over Japan with his pilot Burnie O'Neill he was the first to make a successful evacuation of the rear cockpit.

How small was our war? We all took quite a time to train. We came from Canada, Australia, New Zealand, South Africa and the UK and between us must have covered a wide section of the planet in our training. Our forming up at Burscough took over 8 months and the journey to the Pacific another 2 months. Our final Squadron training at Schofields in NSW Australia lasted over 2 months and our active service about the same time. We took about 6 months to get home and be demobbed. Teddy Key says that he notched about 600 hours of flying time throughout his war service and landed on a carrier about 30 times. Many Fleet Air Arm aircrew can make this record seem quite puny, but it was about average for most of 1772 Squadron.

There are those among us who feel that we should have written this story many years ago. George Trollope has said that our memories would have coped a whole lot better than they do now, for we are all now clocking in at 'three score and ten'. That is very true, but it is only now that we can bring a much greater sense of wisdom and a sense of proportion to this story. As a group of people who have maintained this unique bond of friendship, we add up to a fragmented heap of seemingly disconnected memories. Each one of us claims to remember 'this' and to have no recollection of 'that'. Would it be possible to muster all this information without distortion of the facts and the truth? Airmen can be like the proverbial fishermen and just once in while stretch the truth just a teeny bit! Another way of saying, 'shooting a line'. In each other's company the truth and the tragedy, the fun and the madness do emerge. We have always seemed to generate lightness and laughter when in each other's company. The title of the story, 'The Friendly Squadron' seemed to emerge in an instant and not one of us has so far offered an alternative.

What sort of story would it be? We would have no pretensions about its publication size; it would be a limited edition for members and relatives and a copy would be donated to Royal Navy archives as suggested by Graham Mottram. It would be a corporate diary of a group of chaps who grew up together when they became 1772 Squadron. It would tell the individual stories of how they arrived at the Squadron and what has happened to them since Sydney 1945. It would be a story of their memories. Certainly it would be a mixture of anecdotes and incidents as only the individual saw them. Obviously it is a 'War Story'. It will be a story of tragedy and sadness because not all of us survived: we lost friends and we remember them with great love and admiration and a sense of real loss. There is drama in the story. Sometimes one is confronted with the feeling, 'Did it happen?' 'Was I there at the time?' 'I don't believe it!' Our history of a conflict was but brief, extremely brief in the sense of history, but in terms of our young lives it was 'one hell of an experience'; a most significant part of our education at an impressionable age. Sometimes we reached a level of 'Pantomime' and certainly we created a degree of 'Farce'. We had a demon king, comics and knock-about clowns. We gained a bit of a reputation for producing some bizarre types of landing an aircraft, taking off and even pretending to take off! Whatever happened 'then' seems to be quite different from how we see it 'now'. Charlie Chaplin said, 'Life is a tragedy when seen in close up, but a comedy in long-shot.'

It is not easy to define the conception of 1772. We know about its delivery date; May 1st 1944. We were the third in quite a long line of Admiralty Firefly intentions and plans; their intentions stretched well beyond 1945. Indeed, after September 1945, 1772 Squadron did carry on, 'showing the flag' in HMS Indefatigable, to New Zealand and South Africa, before it was finally disbanded. WE however terminated OUR story in September 1945. One thing we are absolutely certain about, is that 32 Royal Navy pilots and observers and a very large company of maintenance crews gathered together at HMS Ringtail in May 1944. Of the aircrew there were two RN officers but the majority of us were RNVR. We had an RAF Flight Sergeant and a Fairey Representative to guide the ground crews through early teething problems. The Firefly was still that young and the Navy did not seem to be capable of raising a senior maintenance NCO. The first C.O. was not a success but his replacement, Lt. Cdr. Les Wort, D.S.C. RNVR was altogether a very different type of man and leader. He remarked early in his command of 1772 that he would change us from a slap-happy squadron to an efficient . . . and happy one. This he did. The beginning of self-respect and a sense of pride soon became evident. As time went by the complement changed, for a number of reasons; sadly, tragedy sometimes caused the replacement of aircrew and there was the occasional 'fair wear and tear'. The squadron, postwar, evolved slowly after disbandment in Sydney; reunions began to fill the gaps in time when we felt the need to see each other again and recall old times and keep each other informed about what we were doing with our 'civvy street' lives. Reunions 'took on board' the ladies, wives and girlfriends, and we joined the larger Indefatigable reunions held in Birmingham. These were of course much larger affairs and we even enticed Agnes Stevens, Steve's widow, and Ian and Ngaire Darby to England for the first one. We made contact with some of the ground crews but sadly, despite the energetic efforts of chaps such as Gordon Macrow and Harry Russell, their number had remained awfully low. The post-war 1772 became an extended family and loyal supporters of our meetings included three widows: Dorothy Wort (Les died after the war), Agnes Stevens from Canada, and Linda Gillingham, Glen McBride's widow travelled from New Zealand. They were all in attendance at our VJ celebration at Sherborne and Yeovilton in September 1995. Les Wort's two daughters Sue and Jenny were also among our welcome guests. Joan Wright, Glyn Robert's sister, remains in contact with us and has written for this book on her 'cavalier brother'. Alan Gittins, Glyn's nephew has also been in constant contact with us. Glyn and Glen were shot down over Japan and Alan has spent a good deal of time researching their deaths and of course trying to confirm the nature of their last resting place. It has not been an easy objective for Joan and Alan, but they have been very determined to discover the truth. Agnes too has since 1945, investigated the nature of Steve's final moments. Their stories are told later.

The 1772 family has remained a compact one. That has been its strength. From that point in time at the end of 1945 when it became a part of the 'Forgotten Fleet' it has remained, 'The Friendly Squadron'. It is to be assumed that as we all disembarked about that Christmas time 1945, we were only too eager to join the 'real world', now a slippery concept, but then, something uppermost in our minds.

Will there ever be a definitive statement on 1772? We are now content with our own judgement on ourselves. What else have we left? Above a certain standard in almost anything, one is not really better or worse. We were a trifle careless to start with; perhaps we were 'slap-happy'. Maybe we were 'Little Tin Gods'; but this too is another story. We did weather some indifferent leadership in the beginning and we had some rotten luck, which seemed to set us back. In the end we did very well. Our record in what must have added up to about 300 deck landings in our Fireflies, was very good, except for one catastrophic morning off Jervis Bay in Australia. Against a still fanatical enemy which was running out of the essentials of a warring machine, we had commendable success.

Sometimes in our lively reunions of casual banter and reminiscence we wonder whether it was real or maybe, are we making it all up? Was it just a play, something which happened to other guys; a time when we put the real world 'on hold'. Was this play a drama, a tragedy or maybe a farce? Something of everything, one now supposes, for now the stark reality of our mature years merges with the weird patches of memories in our heads. Pinch me! Did it really happen?

On May 1st 1944 the story begins with a group of idealistic and adventurous young officers and men who came together at HMS Ringtail in Lancashire. All the world was to be their stage . . . they were to be but 'merely players'.

How had these 'merely players' arrived at Burscough to form 1772 Firefly Squadron? By several routes, would be the correct answer, but there were common elements.

The FAA flyer had first submitted himself to a regional Royal Navy Board as a volunteer under the 'Y' Scheme. A challenging interview and a searching medical stood in the way of acceptance. A sudden question was thrown; 'If it is half as many minutes to eleven as it was past ten, three quarters of an hour ago, what is the time?' Failure or success would not necessarily depend on the correct answer but one supposed, upon how you answered the question, how you stood, and the brightness of the eye! The British equivalent of the American 'right stuff' was OLQ. Call-up at the age of 18 meant that you arrived at such a reception camp as HMS Royal Arthur at Skegness, formerly, Billy Butlin's Holiday Camp. The sign above the gate still proclaimed, 'Our true intent is all for your delight'. One had become, finally, a 'jack'. The sailor's rig was smashing with its unique 'flies', collar, silk and lanyard. A slimming body stocking when you had starved sufficiently!

The collar required special help when putting on a great coat, such as a Wren to slide her arms under yours and hold down the bottom corners! No cryptic account this . . . unless of course you were never a sailor. There was a whole new language; ossifers, killicks, snotties, subbies, jaunty, God Walloper, pusser, chokha, knackered, crashing the swede, scrubbed, growing skurs . . . and eventually at the depressing end of the spectrum of navy flying slang . . . pranging and cashing your chips.

The white band on 'the lid' meant, potential officer material during those rigorous initial 8 weeks training at HMS St Vincent at Gosport. All will mention St Vincent or RPO Willmott! Elementary Flying or Training Schools introduced our specialist ambitions. The pilots then moved on to Senior Flying Training School in either Kingston, Ontario or Pensacola in Florida; the Observers went to Arbroath or Trinidad. Back in 'blighty', proud of our commissioned rank and wings, Midshipman(A) or Sub Lieutenant(A), we were to be convinced at either RNC Greenwich or Portsmouth, that we needed some polishing and refinement and reminded that however we regarded ourselves, we were in the first place, naval officers. This was known as the 'Knife and Fork' course. An apocryphal story of Portsmouth went thus. An RN lecturer emphasising a particular point, told the story of the large splendid Wardroom early one breakfast time. Only one seat was occupied, by a very senior officer buried deeply in his newspaper. A young 'subbie' arrived, sat down, stretched hugely, scratched himself, stuck a finger in his ear, and belched. The newspaper descended slowly and a deep voice said, 'Now fart', and the face returned behind the newspaper. The reader will discover that we all did various things after our training such as Fighter School at Yeovilton where we flew either Seafires or Hurricanes. These postings were loosely known as 'stooging', ferrying all sorts of aircraft or flying in a Fleet Requirement Unit where one towed targets.

The ultimate goal was, of course, after all this lengthy training, to become a member of an operational squadron . . . 'merely players' in a play, which in the case of 1772 never reached the level of a long-running West End triumph; it was, however, to play a significant and exciting part of our lives. 'More than enough excitement to last my lifetime', said one player!

> *Oh I was like that when a lad,*
> *A shocking young scamp of a rover,*
> *I behaved like a regular cad.*
> *But that sort of thing is all over,*
> *I'm now a respectable chap.*
> *Trial by Jury.*

The Steering Committee of ex P's and O's at the Duke of Wellington, East Horsley, Surrey. L to R: Alan Rowlinson, the Reluctant Chairman, Standing, Geoff Rham, Croose Parry, Sammy Samuelson, Teddy Key, Johnny Coles, Johnny O'Driscoll and Wally Pritchard. (Absent, Gordon Macrow).

. . . above us is inscribed the Duke's message. 'Publish and be Damned.'

> Why bother? I hear you say
> To tell old tales, oh so crusted;
> Why not put to peaceful rest,
> Comrades olden . . . or long-dead?
> Why relate the pride and shame
> Of right or wrong in times of dread?
> Has squalid war become your joy,
> Have you no other thoughts in your head?
>
> Oh. yes! So many dreams
> Of what we did . . . nonsensical,
> Though chiefly in the span of war
> When we were serious and most clinical.
> We did, simply what was necessary
> Against an enemy . . . diabolical.
> For us the memories are very real,
> Perhaps we sense . . . therapeutical.
>
> We will not permit the memories
> Of those, now long-since gone,

To fade . . . their lives to mean so little;
This group of pals you see, was as one.
For those who live, why inter
Those high old times, in formation?
I'll tell you straight, we'll not lose
The memories of a 'Friendly Squadron'.
Anon

THE CAST OF PLAYERS ASSEMBLES ON STAGE –
RNAS BURSCOUGH

All the world's a stage,
And all the men and women merely players:
They have their exits and their entrances,
And one man in his time plays many parts.

As You Like It

Our stage from May 1st 1944 to January 1945 was at different times a dustscape and a mudscape. Royal Naval Air Stations were defined as 'camps', the alternative naval establishment being known as 'barracks' and all of us, had at some time, known the virtues and otherwise of these two naval 'resting places'. In the case of the latter, we had all endured the Victorian monster known as HMS St Vincent at Gosport. On balance the Fleet Air Arm 'type' preferred the 'camp'; it was closer to aeroplanes and just a little less prone to 'bullshit'. The Royal Naval Air Station at Burscough near Ormskirk in Lancashire was to be our home and the place where the 'Friendly Squadron' was formed . . . and 'came of age'. Noting the above solecism it was a place where we could express ourselves in our own way. Therein lay the first problem; perhaps a trifle more discipline might have been what we needed!

RNAS Burscough or HMS Ringtail was sometimes quite a bleak place and with the pressures of making a success of 1772 we were occasionally guilty of some incompetent and stupid actions.

Wardroom accommodation was quite reasonable if one accepted a tolerance for living in a Nissen Hut in the alternating extremes of heat and cold. We lived in these huts; about ten to a hut. There were aggravating Tannoy speakers in each hut and at least one of these was ripped from the wall . . . in sheer frustration. It was a costly thing to do; thinking about it now, very silly. There was an occasion when someone felt a little hungry and decided to explore the Wardroom kitchen refrigerator and another incident which resulted in 1772 being tagged with the title of 'Little Tin Gods'. But such stories belong to our idiot

9

fringe. At the time, they seemed to be 'one hell of a good laugh'.

On the serious side of our lives, the backcloth widened beyond these narrow parameters. We took to the air in our new aircraft, the Firefly. We were confronted by a huge new stage; one of great beauty and excitement.

The greens of Lancashire farmlands and the grey-greens of the sea, often speckled with white, were beautiful and doubly so on a fine day. The sea for us, stretched beyond Liverpool, Southport and Blackpool and north of the Welsh coast. We flew beyond the Isle of Man and to the coastline of Ireland. Here we did our 'Navexes' or navigational exercises. These were the times when all the skill belonged to the 'looker' and pilots fulfilled the role of taxi-driver.

'The Firefly was an aircraft which was to grow in our estimation, generally speaking, for it was a fine new Royal Navy flying machine. The scenery which unfolded before us and below us was fantastic and beautiful in all its moods, such was our euphoria; land- and seascapes, all sky and sea, fields and cities.'

'I did not realise at the time of so much action and excitement that one day I would be flying that machine with destructive intent. Such thoughts belong to the end of my part of the 1772 story, meanwhile the Burscough experience was "really something". Whatever the period of my wartime flying I would look back and realise that I had begun a fellowship and phase of my life that would last a lifetime, though I had at almost every part of it to "screw my courage to the sticking place".'

From the pilot's point of view there were those times when you had a chance of taking a plane up for a test flight, after some maintenance. That was super free-flying time.

For quite a while we were earnestly committed to the task of forming a squadron. We were keen, we had ended our training and 'stooging' and had at last become part of a potential front-line Naval Air Squadron, flying this quite new Naval aircraft. We were happy to learn how to live with each other, work with each other and begin those friendships which were in many cases to last so many years.

We were full of confidence and the conceit such confidence engendered. We did however have to live with others. We linked up with other Squadrons who were 'on board' and of course there was, 'the station personnel'. We had to work with the maintenance organisation of Burscough as well as many other units, such as parachutes, photography, flying control and communications. The basis of a Naval Air Squadron was its mobility. In other words 1772 had to be not only a competent flying unit but able to 'pack up' at any time and transfer itself to another base, to a transport ship and on to a carrier. A basic part of our organisation was that every aircrew member of the Squadron had another responsibility besides that associated with flying and officer duties.

There were the duties of Senior Pilot, Senior Observer, Staff Officer, Divisional Officer, Engineer Officer, Armament Officer, Compass Officer, Radio Officer, Parachute Officer, Photographic Officer, Sports Officer, Stores Officer, Squadron Diary Officer and even the Squadron Line Book Officer. All these duties brought the flying personnel into varying degree of contact with the station personnel. Who in 1772 did what will evolve as the story progresses, but from necessity the duties did change frequently. Pride of place in the station personnel had to be the female of the species, namely that magnificent body of women known as Wrens!

It is an old cliche that every sailor had a girl in every port. In terms of the Wrens, Burscough was a very well endowed place. This was a port, of sorts, and we were sailors, of a sort! It has already been told that our story has many facets, so why shouldn't it also have the element of the 'love story'. Not every story can be told, of course; we were and still are, gentlemen, and in any case who is going to tell . . . now! Burscough could be a very dreary place and a lovely girl was a very welcome moment of company.

Ex-Wren Jackie Cockrill (now Raleigh) was a Radar Wren. She tells us the following. 'Did you know that on those occasions when you were told to keep out of the circuit, the reason was that trials were being carried out for what eventually became known as G.C.A? There were endless complaints from pilots wondering why they should be kept waiting when all they could see was a small aircraft doing what appeared to be "circuits and bumps". The pilots never seemed to notice the vehicle at the end of the runway bristling with aerials or to wonder who the men in civilian suits were who occasionally appeared in their mess. E. K. Cole sent a team of scientists to Burscough to help in the development of "Talk Down" R.D.F. and we R.D.F. Wrens (later known as Radar Wrens) played a small part in this work. I am not aware of how much of the work carried out at HMS Ringtail contributed to G.C.A. as we know it today, but it all seemed to be very intense and important at the time.'

The inconvenience is not remembered and one pilot has said that you never kept him waiting! Remember? 'Navy time was five minutes before time.'

Joan Simonsson, once Wren Joan Hanson, of Flying Control, says that writing a story which includes Burscough, brings back a flood of memories and she too is depressed by the apparent decay after 50 years of neglect which is the current site of HMS Ringtail. She says, 'How well I remember cycling past that row of little white houses which led down to the main gate and one cheeky sailor who was usually on guard duty. I remember the muddy camp with all its Nissen huts bringing back thoughts of black coal-stoves; such devils to light and so easily going out. I remember bunk beds and trips outside to the ablution blocks in all weathers, but I also remember companionship, laughter among friends, camp entertainment and cycling to a nearby golf club for cups of coffee.'

Sue Tupper who was a Wren Officer, and was Sue Tonks at Burscough, remembers 1772 arriving at Ringtail , 'flying your frightfully modern aircraft,' where, 'their ancient "stringbags" and Anson "Classrooms" seemed rather outshone.' She hoped that they did a good job training the seagoing types to work 'their new-fangled radar.' Both Suzanne, (as she was called at Ringtail), and husband John, (also ex-Burscough), came to know about 1772 through a photograph of 1772,

Third officer Sue Tonks.

published in the FAAOA News Sheet. About which they wrote, 'Who's this lot?' Well, we politely informed them, and they in turn politely remembered us. We have it on authority from these Wren contacts, that sadly, we did have a reputation, the nature of which will unfold, in due course. Apparently it was often the cry. 'Oh no! 1772 again!' And really, all we had done was, prang another aircraft!

Burscough was a very important part of our lives; the essential ingredients being its aircrews and its maintenance crews. Again one must emphasise that relative space in this book given to those who flew the Firefly and those who maintained it, is very unfairly loaded in favour of the aircrews. The value of the maintenance guys who laboured under some most difficult conditions making it safe for us to get into the air, carry out our tasks and return safely, cannot be over-estimated. Chris Maclaren writes: 'Our ground-crews were excellent and supportive in every way. I cannot speak highly enough of them, particularly when one considers the atrocious conditions under which they had to work sometimes in order to keep the aircraft flying.' It has been difficult to obtain a large response from

'The aircrew in May 1944 outside the familiar tin Nissen huts known for our duration as '1772 Dispersal Huts.'
The first photograph, May 1944. Back row, L to R: Teddy Key(P), Foret Millar(O), Geoff Rham(O), Des Mullen(O), Rhys Heaven(O). *Harry Garbutt(P), *Glyn Roberts(P), *Glen McBride(O), Croose Parry(P), Ian Darby(O), *Ken Neuschild(O). Middle row: *Steve Stevens(P), Knocker White(O), Johnny O'Driscoll(P), *Monty Baker(O), Lt. Cdr. Gough CO(P), Shiner Wright(P), *Mike La Grange(O), Rollo Moon(P), Burn O'Neill(P). Bottom row: *Maurice Goodsell(P), Jimmy Haslam(O), Stu Jobbings(P), Jackie Ramsden(P), Sammy Samuelson(O), *Eric Bramhall(P), Johnny Coles(O), Johnny Palmer(O), *Don Banks(O), Pete Kingston(P).
*Deceased.

13

the ground crews; the photograph of the whole unit shows how large a mobile squadron could be, but few have responded to any number of advertisements in Naval journals. Our total complement was 32 aircrew and nearly 100 groundcrew.

The Boss, CO. 1772 Squadron from November 1944.
Lt. Wort RNVR on the right, who with Sub. Lt. Fleischmann-Allen, on 1st December 1943 shot down an FW200 Condor whilst flying a Martlet launched from HMS Fencer in the Western Approaches on convoy protection duties.

Sixteen crews including the CO. Lt. Cdr. A. Gough formed the original squadron and right up to the very end, when we were searching for and caring for POW Camps on the mainland of Japan and carrying out armed reconnaissance, we received our final replacement crew. In July 1944 Geoff Gill(P), Gordon Davidson(P), Don Randle(P), Paul Douet(O), Roy Melville(O) and Alan Rowlinson(O) joined us. In October 1944, Bob Scott(P), Ronnie Bramhall(P), Rollo Norman(O) and Wally Pritchard(O) were with us. It has not always been possible to pin-point all the dates of the comings and goings, but Roy Hubble(P) and Val Bennett(O) also joined about this time. The replacements had been due to the loss of three crews due to fatalities in flying accidents. Not the least was the mid-air collision of the CO. and Senior Pilot. Both received new postings! The most significant addition in November

Val Bennett(O)

Geoff Gill(P)

George Trollope(P)

Ronnie Bramhall(P)

Ray Battison(O)

Roy Melville(O)

Chris Maclaren(P)

Don Randle(P)

Alan Rowlinson(O)

Paul Douet(O)

Les Wort and Robin Henderson(O)

Wally Pritchard(O)

Rollo Norman(O)

Gordon Davidson(P)

Bob Scott(P)

15

1944 was the new CO. Les Wort. In January 1945 we acquired a new
Senior Observer, Lt. Robin 'Hank' Henderson and another observer
joined as we passed through Ceylon: Ray Battison, who had known the
CO. in earlier days and became his observer. Chris Maclaren(P) joined
us from 1770. Vin Redding(P) and John Prince(O) were the very last
arrivals, from 1771. The history of those who left us is more vague.
Des Mullen left us on health grounds and we cannot be certain to this
day what became of Haslam, Moon and Ramsden. Before we sailed to
join the Pacific Fleet we lost, temporarily, 4 crews to 1770 who took
part in the Sakashima operation and we lost 2 crews on a more permanent basis to 1771. The 1770 crews returned to the Squadron for the
final show. How did we react to all these changes? Somehow they
seemed to disturb us very little and in our callow youth our training and
social life must have progressed as usual.

Slowly the characters began to emerge. The unfolding of the story
will bring out these personalities. They were a happy breed; but what
was the breed? In short, apart from the regular officer, the one with the
straight rings on his arm, the bulk of the 'A' Branch was RNVR. In
1939 the RNVR constituted about 1000 of the 7000 men in the Navy.
In 1945 this number had been boosted by 88% and at its peak, there
were 48,000 officers and 5000 ratings. Not all of these were flying
personnel but a very large percentage were pilots, observers and air-
gunners. We, the majority, who with some arrogance regarded ourselves
as 'wartime custodians' of the Royal Navy, were . . . 'Branch Types'.
We wore our 'wings' with pride and we had an 'A' in our gold wavy
loop. It is possible to compose a more or less standard portrait of a
Branch Type. As written by a senior officer it might go thus:–

'He is young, probably has just passed his 18th birthday; the raw
material of the young blade, one who is often very young for his age,
yet has, in many respects, matured beyond his tender years, by the fact
that he has escaped family ties and has been given some expensive
flying machines to play with. His nature appears to have roughened,
just a little. Nevertheless he has talent and engaging charm; has a strange
mixture of devotion to duty and an almost reckless disregard for rules
and, occasionally, law and order! He tends to trade on this sense licence,
since he regards himself as someone who is currently leading a
dangerous existence. He adopts the attitude, for the duration of
"hostilities only", that he has joined a very advanced type of "sixth
form". As such, he is aware that he has become part of a very real
paternal society and that he is, as a Naval Officer, responsible for the
welfare of others and must set an example. The Branch Type, as he

likes to be known, comes from a public or grammar school and as such, has acquired a reasonable School Certificate and demonstrated to a board of senior Royal Navy Officers that he is capable of leadership. In the Squadron under question, 1772 Fireflies, he could have originated from one of many breeds. The Squadron contains Scotties, Brummies, borderline Cockneys, Kiwis, Canucks, Yorkshire Tykes and even a Springbok. It is quite a melting pot! It is a cheerful, if sometimes, careless group of arrogant young men who enjoy each other's company, much as they do the company of our Wrens. A few have found time to be married and possibly sow the seeds of a family. Most importantly, the Branch Type is devoted to the art of flying his aircraft: hedonism is not his sole pursuit! In this basic area of his commitment to the Royal Navy, he is something of an expert; his attitude is generally, very professional and indeed a few are undeniably "aces" in the making. He had been trained to the highest possible level of leadership and flying skills. He is an officer and a gentleman, capable of any task put before him. He is often described, especially by his fond parents as "being resplendent in his uniform". He can be conceited and self-opinionated, but, overall, a nice chap. He has an insatiable appetite for fun and laughter; for the most part he is a moderate and self-controlled imbiber. He enjoys his social pint and generally handles it well. He is moderately fit considering his life-style, is devoted to his current girl-friend and if not married, "would die for her"! I can only say that the Branch Type as seen in this Squadron is a most worthy being, trustworthy, an expert in his field, courageous and quite handsome. He has a "present", but only time will tell about his future. A fellow senior officer has dismissed them as "line-shooting little bastards". Another colleague referred to them as "Little Tin Gods". I repudiate those judgements and I wonder what posterity will make of them . . . 50 years from now'.

True, there were characters and as in any group of people it is dangerous to generalise. In 1772 there were serious ones, there were genuine clowns, those who had little fear, those who were most fearful. There were abstemious ones, (not many mind you), and many with a healthy appetite for living, rather than dying. In 'our play' there were many types. We even managed a 'demon king'. We had a magician of a pianist who played the piano beautifully; much the worse for drink . . . even lying on his back! His name was Forêt Primrose Millar. Now, there is a sense of theatre! Sammy Samuelson, recalling our Nissen-hutted world, where 'the food was not too bad' and 'the beer must have been cheap', says that as a Snotty he claimed his pay packet was less than a Subby and he was always having to borrow. He says that he always enjoyed the 'Bull and Dog' and a little further down the road,

'The Red Lion'. There, Sammy recalls the little room behind the bar where there was a piano for Forêt. Johnny O'Driscoll remembers happily, as he should do, his marriage on Trafalgar Day, 21st October 1944 to Madge, a Wren he had met while at Fighter School at Yeovilton. He, Teddy Key, his best man, and George Trollope travelled to London for the occasion on 20th October and back across London on the 21st in an air-raid. He tells how they honeymooned in Torquay, (one train per week from London). He adds, that to give the CO. Gough, his due, he did grant them a 48 hours extension of leave.

On many occasions however 'the parties' were essentially stag. It was never really finalised as to what set off a 'session', the name given to a good evening's drinking, but, they happened and they were unplanned; they had a fairly riotous element to them and were too often somewhat undisciplined. It was part of the bonding process one supposes; even essential to the 'forming up' process of 1772, or indeed any squadron. The spirit of the Squadron, after a few weeks did subside, so at times we tried to escape. Part of the rebirth of that spirit was concerned with the change-over of COs. When Les Wort took over the command of 1772, things did improve in a most profound way. He was known to remark, 'If I cannot drink with a man, I cannot work with him'. Such a remark might now be understood as rather shallow but those of us who lived with him until the Squadron disbanded in September 1945, know that his arrival was a significant point in the life of 1772.

Johnny Coles claims that the Nissen huts seemed to be quite a fascination for some. Harry Garbutt for example can be remembered, wheeling a solid-wheeled wheelbarrow up and over the roof. Probably a dare, but sadly Harry will never deny it, for it must have been a short time after that, he was killed in a flying accident. Johnny further notes the squadron's fascination for pyrotechnics, in the way that they enjoyed dropping flares down chimneys and even making crude rockets out of cycle frames, flares and Koffman cartridges. There was only a moderate degree of success and there is one story more to tell, later on, which relates to stolen flares.

The airfield at Burscough was once a 650 acres potato field and as HMS Ringtail, was commissioned on September 1st 1943. It now seems incredible that it was a very young development when we arrived and that when we left in January 1945 it had still not reached the degree of development envisaged by the Admiralty, way back in 1941. Whether we made damning judgements of the place is now clouded in time; I suppose we all made disparaging remarks about Ringtail at some time or another. Strangely, we now remember it with some affection and a

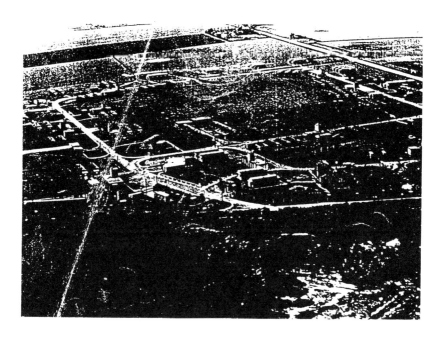

An aerial photograph of Camp 2 showing the main gate and the Wardroom. The site is now a sports field but the transition between Fleet Air Arm and playing fields was a slow and very messy time for those who lived in the environs of the old airfield.

Photo by Jack Freestone of Ormskirk.

few of us still manage 'a buzz' when we return. Therefore let some worthy citizens of Burscough help the storytellers to remind us of what happened then and what has happened since then.

Mrs Maureen Riding (nee Reid) tells that her little school had to be moved in order to build the airfield and she is very certain that the present derelict flying control tower marks that spot. Many farm homes had to be removed and much land was requisitioned. Much of the land was owned by the landlord of the Bull and Dog, Walter Gorst.

She recalls how the sailors' collars were touched for good luck as they walked along the little road between the 'Bull and Dog' and the Main Gate. She implies that other wishes accompanied such 'touchings' but she is a little vague on such matters! Beyond the gate, the road which was once a runway was taken up eventually and the track sometimes used by groups of amateur artists. Camp 2 across the road

1772 Flying Dispersal, showing hangars and crew quarters. The Bull and Dog is bottom right and Camp 2 is at the very bottom of the photograph.

Photo by Jack Freestone of Ormskirk.

The first photograph of the whole squadron. The photograph will not show a high degree of detail but it does give some idea of the numbers involved in a mobile Naval Air Squadron.

Johnny Coles claims that we had quite a good rugby team.

. . . note the Boss setting the tone, bottle in hand. He led from the front –
always.
. . . or were we playing soccer against the 'troops'?

from the Bull and Dog which was once the site of the Wardroom became
a TA training school and developed into an eyesore known by the local
residents as 'grot spot'.

George Brown after serving at Ringtail as a Wardroom Steward
settled in Burscough and owned a cafe down near the locks on the

canal. His daughter, Beryl Arkwright responded to an advertisement in the Ormskirk Advertiser and kindly told us about this connection. She says that her father remembered our Firefly squadron; he referred still to Camp 2 as 'the Bull and Dog' camp. Beryl sent a copy of an article published in the Sunday Observer in 1976 which bemoaned the 'perpetual reminds of WW2 outside the village of Burscough' which remained an area of decaying huts and Nissen Blocks, 'the remains of the Fleet Air Arm Training School'. Nothing much over the years had been done to clear the mess, which years of indifference had bequeathed to the area. The obscure and confusing laws governing planning matters and it would seem, some casual attitudes by Liverpool leaders, were the reasons given.

Philip Pearson still lives adjacent to the airfield and cycles frequently around the relics of buildings and space that once were 'Ringtail'. Being an ex-RAF engine fitter he is interested in aircraft restoration. He is currently building a Spitfire cockpit complete with instruments. He sent an article from the 'Fly Past' magazine which proved to be full of useful information. Before the airfield reverted to a mixture of farming land and dereliction it had been used for crop-spraying aircraft, sport parachuting and microlight flying. The design of the airfield, as 1772 knew it, was apparently typical of Naval Air Stations at the time, namely 4 runways, 3 of which were 1,000 yards long and the 4th, aligned with the prevailing wind, 1,240 yards long. Their width was 30 yards compared with the RAF standard, which was 50 yards. A standard 3-storey Control Tower, plus 32 Mainhill hangars, mostly 60 × 70 feet made up the basis of the airfield structures. On the north side some larger hangars were installed in that major servicing area. After the station was commissioned in 1943, it was adapted to many uses, day fighter, night fighter, torpedo fighter, radar training and it was used as a Fleet Requirement Unit. Forty squadrons used the airfield. Of the Fireflies 1771 preceded us and they left in June 1944, a month after we arrived: 1770, the first Firefly squadron and the one 1772 relieved on HMS Indefatigable, arrived at Burscough in July 1945 and were disbanded. Our original Mark 1 Fireflies were handed over to 766 Squadron at Inskip after our deck landing exercises on HMS Empress. We, according to the magazine, received Fireflies with long-range tank facilities. 1790 Squadron, night fighters, formed up on January 1st 1945; they left on June 24th but the War was over when they arrived in the Pacific area. 1791 night fighters were also too late and were disbanded on August 18th 1945. The RAF Station, Woodvale, was taken over as a satellite – in naval parlance, a 'tender' – and became HMS Ringtail on April 7th 1945. On February 18th 1946 a Firefly of 825 got

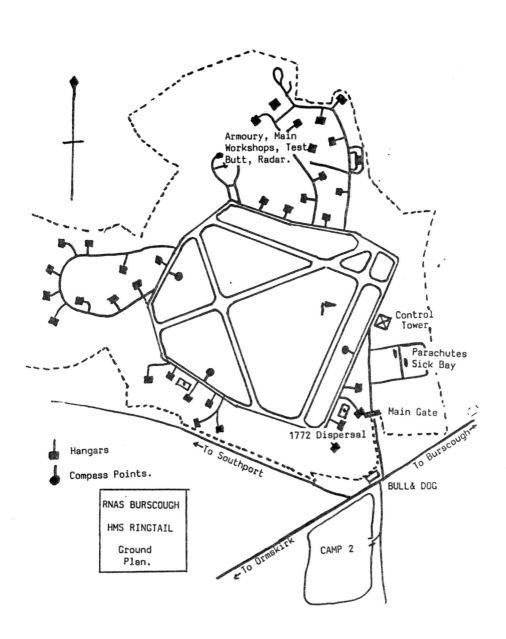

Armoury, Main
Workshops, Test
Butt, Radar.

Control
Tower

Parachutes
Sick Bay

Main Gate

1772 Dispersal

←To Southport

To Burscough→

Hangars

Compass Points.

RNAS BURSCOUGH

HMS RINGTAIL

Ground
Plan.

BULL& DOG

←To Ormskirk

CAMP 2

RNAS Burscough HMS Ringtail Ground Plan.

24

into trouble above the clouds. The pilot baled out and the aircraft crashed in Bootle, Liverpool, killing a child in the street*. After January 1946, RNAS Stretton took over Burscough as a sub-storage site. The Royal Navy finally relinquished the site about 1957. A Ringtail Road provides a link today with that name which was Burscough's wartime history.

Mrs Ruth Baxter and her husband have been interested in the local history of the war years and she refers to a book about the history of 'Ringtail' which her father owned, though this copy is, sadly, missing, much to her regret. She has been in contact with Yeovilton and they have sent her a brief history of 'Ringtail'. Copies of this limited issue book are difficult to trace. She tells too of the gravestones in St Johns Churchyard of aircrew who died whilst serving at Burscough. They are mainly the resting places of flyers from overseas. She remembers the noise of aircraft and members of the family who once owned farmhouses on the site.

We are very grateful to these people who have taken an interest in our story. Today one wonders if we were an awful nuisance at the time. I bet we were!

Burscough was our home and now it is a place of pilgrimage for us. Far from attractive, it does however represent a part of our lives when we really began to grow up, in spite of doing some daft things and overstepping the mark of reason. To accomplish that, our chief prop was the Firefly, another Fairey product for the Royal Navy, but was it any good and ultimately . . . were we?

> Sigh no more ladies, sigh no more,
> Men were deceivers ever.
> One foot in sea and one on shore,
> To one thing – constant never.

Much Ado About Nothing

* There is no evidence in the record of this crash, that an observer was on board. It was probably a pilot-only flight test.

THE MAIN PROP... THE FAIREY FIREFLY

'They flew through the air with the greatest of ease... those daring young men...'

It wasn't always with the greatest of ease and we don't suppose that on every occasion there was a maximum degree of derring-do. In Bill Harrison's definitive book on the Firefly, he claims that the aeroplane had an enviable record for a new fighter, despite being classified as 'mainly suitable for escort duties'. The Firefly had shown that even in its most unenviable role as 'a supportive and flak suppressive aircraft, it had really come out with flying colours as the Fleet Air Arm's most formidable all-weather aircraft, due in no little way to the courageous crews that flew her'. Well, it is nice after all these years to be told that, along with 1770 and 1771 squadrons, 1772 was held in some regard.

The Fairey Firefly entered service in 1943 flying alongside fabric covered biplanes. When it retired 23 years later, the Firefly had witnessed the development of jet-engined fighters capable of flying at Mach 2. Even the Firefly in its varied development had had a jet engine fitted to it! Few aircraft in naval aviation history have remained operational through such a period of change.

The Firefly was conceived in 1939 when the Air Ministry proposed circulating requirements to a number of firms, for a single-engined, two-seater fixed gun fighter, for use in the Fleet Air Arm. Specifications and modifications seemed to ebb and flow in that Admiralty pattern, customary when developing something new. The Admiralty was of course involved and eventually a number of firms were busy considering these specifications and submitting tenders. The 'Firefly' could have been a Blackburn, Boulton Paul, Gloster, Hawker, Vickers Armstrong or even a Westland. But then of course ... it would not have been a 'Firefly'! During its life, a great deal of invention went into deciding what it was really going to be: many versions were produced. 1772 followed close upon the work of the test pilots and whilst the three Firefly Squadrons were working up or flying in action, the Firefly was still being test-flown, and was killing test pilots! With regard to the

engine there didn't seem to be many alternatives, though the Fairey
Queen, Bristol, Taurus and Rolls Royce Boreas were considered. The
Rolls Royce Griffon, capable of a speed at sea level of 236 knots and a
ceiling of over 31,000 feet was finally chosen as the best engine for the
Firefly. The evolution of the Firefly through design and tender was a
complicated one. The details of this growth of an aeroplane have been
brilliantly chronicled in Bill Harrison's book on the Firefly, to which
several members of 1772 have contributed.

*The Firefly had the most pleasing lines. This is one of 1772's Mark 1's over
Burscough. Marks 1, 4, 5 and 7 were essentially different designs since
during their evolution considerable changes were made. Note the inward
retracting undercarriage.* (Photo by: Val Bennett)

A view in formation flying. Note the long-range tank.

Val Bennett

In 1940, an Admiralty specification N5/40 found its way to H. E. Chaplin, Chief designer of the Fairey Aviation Company. He saw in it the possibility of creating the first relatively high-performance aircraft produced for the Navy by a British firm. He therefore set the ball rolling for an aircraft that was to have 13 years of service in 9 guises. Chaplin, quite logically known as 'Charlie' to everyone at Fairey, was involved with the early designs of the Swordfish, Albacore and Battle. Just before the war he had been involved with the project design of the FC-1 airliner and he was responsible for the 'droop snoot' used on the Fairey FD2, later incorporated into the Concorde design. Chaplin was confronted by a number of specifications. His aim was to produce an aircraft with a 'clean design, few projections, the highest possible obtainable speed, yet, capable of standing up to the rigours of flying from and landing on a carrier deck in all weathers, folding wings and the strength, great enough to withstand being catapulted'. The Firefly had to be very robust and not susceptible to corrosion in a salty atmosphere. Chaplin had to consider the visibility from the cockpit in a carrier approach in bad weather conditions, as well as the ability to handle the aircraft in confined space, such as a carrier hangar. A very serious condition which he had to face was whether this aircraft could be put into production within two years! The problems of development multiplied and multiplied. Ideas such as modifying other aircraft were thrown into the complex equations; they even toyed with the idea of modifying the Spitfire to meet most of the specifications. In April 1940 the Admiralty put in a requisition for 200 Fairey fleet fighters, the engine incorporated to be a Rolls Royce Griffon. They were asking for a speed of 330 knots at 20,000 feet. In 1941 the first three Fireflies were hand-built at the Hayes Experimental Shop, an early site of what is now Heathrow Airport. Early production machines were delivered from July 1942 and on 17th July the Fairey Firefly Mark 1 was released to the service. 200 Fireflies were put on order and in the same year the first deck-landing trials took place on HMS Illustrious. The Firefly was at last assuming the role which those of us in 1772, following upon 1770 and 1771, were to develop further as an operational aircraft in the Fleet Air Arm. In its development it had been considered as a single seater fighter, an RAF night-fighter among many other suggestions . . . and even fitted with a 'Whittle' type jet unit.

Trials were still being advanced into 1944 with night deck-landings, different armaments and new equipment, including radar, into 1945. In some respects the Firefly proved more than capable of holding its own with single seater fighters, it could out-turn conventional fighters, even the famous Japanese Zero. This was achieved with the very special Youngman flaps which were fitted to the Firefly: they not only improved the turning circle but were of great value in lowering the landing speed. The stalling speed could be as low as about 70 knots, indicated airspeed. The Youngman flaps were so well designed that they never spoiled the very pleasing shape of the Firefly. The Firefly, through 1770 Squadron which had been formed up at Yeovilton on 1st October 1943, was in operation against the Tirpitz and night flying Fireflies had attacked German Condors. It served against Heinkel 111's which were intent on launching V1 Flying Bombs. The Firefly then graduated in the Pacific alongside the huge American Fleet. Its final act with the 3rd. Pacific Fleet was to locate POW camps in Japan and drop essential medical supplies for them. The other task was to police the mainland airfields and to ensure that peace agreements were being obeyed. The Dutch used the Firefly against rebels in the Dutch East Indies and the Mark 5 became a redoubtable aircraft, as an all-weather strike weapon.

Official documents refer to the 'handling' qualities of the Firefly. Summarised, that judgement is as follows: 'The Firefly is pleasant to handle and is stable about all axes. On take-off there is a strong tendency to go to the right. The stalling speed is between 66 and 85 knots, indicated airspeed. Intentional spinning is prohibited, but recovery is straightforward. The maximum speed is 370 knots (425 mph). There are some visibility problems when in the tail down attitude of deck-landing. A curved approach is required. The aircraft is rugged and ditches well. Generally quite docile and it has adequate power to do its

Navy's New Fighter

Firefly With A Sting

*An early publicity release of the Firefly during WW2. Note the more
spacious pilot cockpit compared to, say, the Seafire. Big men could fly the
Seafire but it was a tight fit. The rear cockpit was another problem
altogether. It was difficult to eject from this and the problem was destined
to remain one of the observer's nightmares.*

Reproduced by kind permission of the RAF Museum in whose collection it resides

Ref. No. 6010-15.

job. It carries four 20 mm Cannons or sixteen 60 lb Rockets. An alternative armament is a 500 or 1,000 lb bomb.'

The development of the Firefly was not without its tragedy. On 26th June 1942 Chris Staniland, a very experienced chief test pilot, was killed. His Firefly going through phugoidal oscillation tests went into a steep dive from about 10,000 feet and never recovered. Evidence from the wreck showed that the cockpit cover was missing and that part of tailplane had failed. The fabric-covered elevator was subsequently strengthened. Another accident had shown that some problems existed on a small area of the elevator and on a previous flight Chris Staniland had lost a cockpit cover. These and other factors were beginning to slow production. Minor accidents occurred during spinning trials. In June 1943 Lt. Cdr. Brown had a narrow escape when his open canopy draped itself round the leading edge of the port tailplane.

1770 Firefly Squadron formed up at Yeovilton on 1st October 1943 under Lt. Cdr. P. Godfrey RNVR. Later Major V. B. G. Cheesman RM, took command. 1771 Firefly Squadron formed up at Yeovilton on 1st February 1944 commanded by Lt. Cdr. Ellis DSC., DFC., RN. The second test pilot disaster took place on 1st March 1944. Wing Cdr. Peter Webster DSO., DFC., a member of the Performance Test Squadron of A & AEE took off to undertake 'rate of roll' tests. Fifty minutes into the test, Z1839 spun into the ground. He had completed about 30-plus quarter rolls and the final roll was at 310 mph. The finding was that the starboard wing had 'failed in upload'. Undercarriage problems persisted and CO_2 contamination was still a possible problem in the rear cockpit in the few months before 1st May 1944. Rate-of-roll tests were discontinued!

1772 Firefly Squadron formed up at Burscough on 1st May 1944. In 1945 tests were still going on. 1770 were then involved with Operation Iceberg and 1772 was within one month of leaving to replace 1770 in the British Pacific Fleet. The problem of the cockpit hood still remained and there were to be two more fatal test accidents related to the Firefly's cockpit hood problem. On 13th October 1945 Fl. Lt. John Seth-Smith crashed just after take-off. Above the cloud cover he lost his empanage and starboard wing-tip and had crashed close to Putney Bridge at the Ranelagh Club at Barnes. Had there been any records of hoods detaching on active service since 9th September 1944? There were, as far as it is possible to tell, 5 cases of hood failures; 4 had been torn off inadvertently and in one case the hood had struck the fin and rudder and lodged there. Pete Kingston, 1771, lost his on one occasion over Japan. On 27th November 1945, Fl. Lt. Colin Evans test-flew a Firefly Mark 1 PP463, a new aircraft. After rolling on its back and going into a 30 degree dive from 7,000 feet, the hood had become detached. There were structural weaknesses and suction together with high speed caused the ultimate collapse. Redesign of the hood followed and the sad saga of the Firefly hood was virtually over. It had caused the death of two test pilots for certain, and maybe two others.

We, pilots and observers of 1772, were largely ignorant of much of this during our time flying the Firefly, and probably for a good many years after the war. The Firefly was liked, respected and apart from operating and service-in-action hazards, was an aircraft with no nasty habits. Or were some of us just fairly ignorant or kept in ignorance? In any case, so much is owed to those who gave their lives in order to make the Firefly a better aircraft to fly and as safe as was humanly possible.

At more or less the same time 1772, unwittingly, was doing its best to 'bend the Firefly! One of the exercises at Burscough was an oxygen climb to maximum altitude. On 4th August 1944 S/Lt. Gordon Davidson with Johnny Palmer as his observer did such a climb. At 33,000 feet, as far as Gordon could climb and still have some semblance of control, he decided to do a fast descent. Down he went on full power, the speed quickly reaching 400 knots. They were then in a terminal velocity dive: the controls locked solid. With the use of the elevator trim he pulled out. Corrected airspeed for compressibility and atmosphere gave a true airspeed figure of 600 mph! As Bill Harrison reported, 'the other young bucks of 1772 were so impressed that most of them had a go too'. Stu Jobbings managed to tear off his undercarriage fairings in the process. Johnny Coles telling his story of such a climb with Eric Bramhall, the pilot, puts on record that the Fairey Representative, (the aircraft was still a new one and the maintenance crews needed an expert at times) almost had an apoplectic fit when he saw what they had done. Teddy Key says that he can't recall the height and speeds he reached, but because he was stupid enough to fly a trip such as this with a head cold, he was destined to suffer from sinus problems all his life!

But what did the pilots think of the Firefly?

Major Cheesman, 'Cheese' to all who knew him well, a Firefly pilot who might easily wear the title 'Mr Firefly', because he was CO. of the pioneering Firefly squadron 1770, had previously flown Hurricanes and Seafires from carriers. In this respect he found the Firefly to be ideal. He said that it was not a true fighter because it was a trifle heavy, but with its Youngman flaps, it could out-turn anything. 'With her new Griffon engine, she gave us the power we needed and her broad undercarriage was superb for deck landing'. He considered the

20 mm cannons to be a bonus but they were 'not good enough to sink the Tirpitz!' He pressed authority into providing rockets as another form of armoury and the Firefly became an ideal attack aircraft for attacking precise targets particularly in oil refineries such as Palembang in Sumatra and Pankalan Brandan, a very vital 'cracking plant'. He goes on to say, 'On returning home, somewhat weary, she was a pleasure to land, even if you ran out of gas.' Cheese had a special story to tell about its landing qualities on water . . . known as ditching. On 2nd January 1945, on arrival 'home' to find that Seafires had made 'a balls-up on the Flight Deck', he was ordered to orbit and wait. That is quite a simple thing to do . . . if you have sufficient petrol in the tanks! He was registering 'zero'. He alerted his observer, Desmond Wilkey, to 'stand-by to ditch'. He says the thought, 'don't panic', flashed across his mind. 'We will do this absolutely right and not even get our feet wet' . . . 'get out your ditching notes Desmond'. Orbiting at some 400 feet, suddenly, the engine cut. Silence. 'Break formation, into wind, open hood, unplug R/T, tighten straps, drop speed to stall, tail down, down, down. Tail in. Splash. Stop . . . Good Girl!' They clambered out and as she settled, the panel on the starboard side wing opened and out popped the dinghy, hissing like mad. 'Bless the maintenance boys' I thought. Alongside the dinghy and in jumped Desmond. They pushed off and down went the Firefly. Five minutes later the Destroyer HMS Wakeful was alongside the dinghy. Their feet were still dry and they celebrated with a gin in the wardroom. What could be better? A tribute to another quality of the Firefly . . . and the Major's flying skills.

Major Cheesman splashes down! Such performances could enhance those moments of boredom which did exist on board. Is the Batsman signalling the Major to 'switch off his engine?'

There had been problems of high fuel consumption in the Firefly. The ditching of Major Cheesman in January 1945 as well as another Firefly at the same time, had alerted 1770 Squadron to this situation and particularly Lt. R. O. Steel who was Squadron Engineer Officer. Like 1772, 1770 Squadron had specialist Fairey and Rolls Royce engineers attached to the Squadron for such teething problems, especially of the relatively new advancement of the Merlin, the Griffon. Tropical flying suggested the need for modification to the needle valves which had remained, 'as for European flying conditions'. The situation had to be resolved since fuel consumption was at such a high level and unless 1770 and Rolls Royce got it right, 'the Firefly would be inoperable in relation to the range of other aircraft'. To ensure that 1772 was eventually spared this problem it can be concluded that Major Cheeseman's 'dry' ducking had not been in vain. He didn't run out of deck space, just juice!

The Firefly followed its predecessor the Fulmar as a ladylike plane to fly, especially if one had a limited amount of experience. The Seafire had its glamorous image but was difficult to put down on a carrier. The Corsair, huge, strong and very powerful – its engine power was daunting to say the least, was not a plane for the young and inexperienced or those of a nervous disposition! It had a few unfortunate tricks too. Rumour had it that one could actually have a situation where one could select 'fold wings' in flight! The Hellcat was a reasonable compromise and was less frightening to the average young 'A' Branch flyer. As one has read the story of other Fleet Air Arm aeroplanes one is forced to conclude, 'thank you Mr Fairey'.

Let 1772 aircrew have their say

Ian Darby. 'I quite enjoyed flying with Burn O'Neill in the Firefly. I found it to be very effective for the minor role it was allocated over Japan. American politics, I suppose. We demonstrated its firepower and speed and I think its robustness with the undercarriage helped enormously with the deck landings. As we discovered, it was not the ideal aircraft for the observer to bale out from but as we had planned, if the aircraft could be rolled, the crew was ejected most satisfactorily by pushing the stick forward in the inverted position. Well, Burn and I didn't hit the tailplane when we had to leave in a hurry!'

Don Randle. 'The Firefly had no vices and it was very strong. It was a very good looking aircraft and in my opinion if an aircraft does not look good, then it won't fly very well.' Was Don thinking of the Barracuda or the Spitfire when he penned that remark?

Croose Parry. 'A plane without any vices, a pleasure to fly and extremely reliable. As far as I can remember there were no accidents caused by faults in the plane or the engine. Its role as a fighter reconnaissance plane was outdated by the time it entered service; it was more effective as a ground attack aircraft where small specific targets were available.'

Burn O'Neill. 'A very gentlemanly aeroplane to fly. It was safe and predictable. I would have enjoyed the chance to dogfight something nippy just to prove that those Youngman flaps were something special.'

Teddy Key. 'I flew the Firefly for about 200 hours and the engine was always ticking over nicely at the end of every journey. Sammy and I could say with total honesty that 'She was great; perfect for us.'

Implicit in these comments is the gratitude the pilots and observers had for our maintenance crews . . . the fact that we never had a single airframe or engine failure of any serious dimension is indeed a remarkable record. It has been a source of regret felt by those of us who put our trust in these guys that we have been unable to get a larger number of them to join us in our reunions over the past 50 years. Gordon Macrow, Harry Russell and John Price are but three regulars. Tom Alcorn and Don Turner are 'out there' having found us late. Maybe one day we'll meet them.

Gordon has done as much as anyone to remedy the situation through advertisement in naval publications. It is not surprising that most of those mentioned above relate to his Radio Section led by Petty Officer Stanworth. He was a survivor of HMS Eagle which was sunk in the Mediterranean. Petty Officers such as Gordon, Tom and Don did radio repairs and of course the all-important daily checks on equipment were handled by them. Gordon says that often heavy deck landings caused problems in the 1161 when the tuning wheel would be dislodged. A refit was usually required after every deck landing.

The important Homing Beacon was a very reliable instrument. Ian Darby, who was initially the Officer in Charge of Radio followed later by Wally Pritchard and Ray Battison, according to myth dreamed up an idea of increasing the VHF range by a device which added to the Firefly's 'Stringbag' impersonation. Even he admitted that the idea was a flop!

One small feature which made 1772 a little distinctive, was the coloured airscrew spinner. It is known that this innovation was the work of Lt. Cdr. Gough, the first CO. Fireflies did not normally carry any specific markings. Individual aircraft were identified by using different coloured spinners. There were four sectional colours, white, green, blue and yellow. The white leader, for example, would have an all-white spinner. Number 2 had a white spinner with a red tip, number 3 had a white spinner with a red band and number 4 had a red band at the stern end of the spinner. These colours remained until after the Empress deck-landings when we were equipped with new aircraft.

Johnny Coles does, however, remember a couple of maintenance hiccups. He and pilot, Eric Bramhall, had to put into action their 'Mayday' procedure when their navigational aids went u/s during a simple, local night-flying exercise on 28 July 1944. They became hopelessly lost in quite foggy conditions. The RAF saved them! On 2nd October, the same year, they had to make a wheels-up landing when the hydraulics failed, again during night flying. Who said 1772 was perfect?

Chris Maclaren, another Seafire type, was originally posted to 1770. On his first flight he had some trouble starting the engine. Somewhat embarrassing, but a helpful Chief Petty Officer put him right and explained a few things. Then having arrived at the end of the runway, he remained in some doubt about 'trim settings'. What does an arrogant youth, (Chris's judgement of himself), do then? Admit to further ignorance and taxi back? Never. With Seafire settings, he took off and spent some difficult moments fighting an aircraft with a will of its own. Airborne, common sense of his training enabled him to settle down. He considered the Firefly to be smooth and comfortable to operate on the ground, but as with anyone used to the unique lightness of the Seafire, found it slower to respond and heavier. He found that with more flying hours under his belt the Firefly had some very good points, not the least its turning circle. 'I had the opportunity to prove this whilst flying with 1770 Squadron in the Pacific. Flying alone on Sub. CAP. duties the oil seal on the propellor suddenly started to leak throwing oil all over the windscreen. At this precise moment 'the submarine' called me to say that Bogeys were approaching fast. As they were flying at 10,000 feet and I was at 2,000 feet, I proceeded to climb as rapidly as possible and at about 5,000 feet I broke through the cloud to see two Zeke fighters (the naval version of the Zero) dropping their belly tanks. They had obviously spotted me coming up through the clouds and were about to attack. One peeled off into a diving curve. Telling my observer to keep his eyes on the second Zeke, I pulled my Firefly round to make his chances of getting a shot at me more difficult. This made it impossible for him to bring his guns to bear and he shot past and dived into the cloud. Meanwhile his No. 2 had started to attack. However, by making use of my Youngman flaps I was again able to avoid being hit. He followed his No. 1 into the cloud and disappeared. It must be appreciated that to try to 'dog-fight' with oil smothering the windscreen, is not to be recommended, so I decided against following.

Whether they were on some special mission I know not, but they were obviously only going to try one pass and didn't wait to get into a scrap . . . for which I was truly grateful.'

As a Naval aircraft the Firefly had been developed on the lines of the Fulmar and had good landing capabilities on the deck with a wide span to the undercarriage. It certainly had no vicious faults from a flying point of view. Once on landing back on board after an attack on Matsushima airfield in Japan, where the A.A. fire had been particularly severe, the aircraft was considered to be too badly damaged to repair and was pushed over the stern of the carrier. Yet she had handled perfectly throughout the 200 mile return journey to the carrier and through the landing.

As with all aircraft there was room for improvement in specifications and the later Marks included many of these. In my opinion another 30 knots on the maximum speed would have made the Firefly one of the most formidable aircraft to come up against. She had tremendous firepower carrying our 20 mm cannons and when used as an attack aircraft could carry 8×60 lb rockets or even carry bombs. Flown sensibly she could stay airborne for well in excess of 4 hours. These made the Firefly one of the most versatile aircraft in the Fleet.

Mention should be made of the post-war record of the Firefly in winning the Boyd Trophy for deck-landings and there were several sequences when 1,000 landings were made without a blemish. Cappy Masters, the Senior Deck Landing Officer on the Indefatigable does however record with justifiable pride some of his team's (Peter Broome and David Bryce-Buchanan) Seafire landings-on. They outshone many an American carrier in landing a complete squadron of Seafires in remarkably little time compared with the much-vaunted sturdy fighters such as the Hellcat and Corsair.

The first Firefly 'kill' went to Lt. Levitt the senior pilot of 1770. He shot down an Oscar and another Jap later.

Croose Parry claims the unofficial record of being the first Allied plane to land on a Japanese airfield, maybe still a hostile place. Not a lot of people know that – until now.

A chance meeting with Lt. Cdr. Birch RN(Ret) conveyed something of the role of the Firefly in the post-war years. He thought that perhaps the Sea Fury could have done the work of the Firefly and saved one crew member! '1771 Sea Fury Squadron' would have deprived us of our beloved 'O's! He stated that the Firefly was a very popular aircraft and was capable of some excellent 'land-on' records in the Royal navy Light Fleet Carriers; the old Fleet Carriers of WW2 had of course, gone to scrap. He thought that she was never the fighting equivalent of the Seafire . . . in the air, but then we knew that. Admiral Vian's judgement of the Seafire was of course another point of view and no doubt the heavier Corsair and Hellcat were both versatile in air-to-air combat and air-to-ground attack. Only one of 1772 went on to fly later marks of Firefly, our Senior Observer, Robin Henderson, since he was a regular RN Officer. 'Not a bad aircraft . . . not great . . . but not bad', was the final judgement of George Birch.

In 1945/46 a British fleet of about 50 carriers was reduced to 5 light fleet carriers. During the Korean war there were 12 Fireflies in 827 Squadron; HMS Theseus had Furies and Fireflies. Firefly Mark 5's were also aboard HMS Glory and HMS Ocean. During the 3-year conflict ending in July 1953 there were several periods of plus 1,000 accident free deck-landing sequences among the 6 Firefly Squadrons on the 5 Light Fleet Carriers. Just over 1,700 Fireflies were made, half of them Mark 1's; there were 9 Marks of Firefly. Marks 8 and 9 reached what to many in 1772 would have been regarded as the death-throes of a great aircraft; they served as trainers, an honourable state, target towers and unpiloted targets. Teddy Key, curious about a list of Z series Fireflies which had 'died on the baking tarmac' in Ethiopia, (published in Harrison's book), cross-checked the numbers in his flying logbook and discovered that two of them had been flown by him and Sammy Samuelson in 1944 at Burscough. These two Fireflies had been used by the Canadians and then as a deal with Ethiopia, had been used against rebels along their borders. What surviving records showed, was that these aircraft had 'died' before their time. Such waste! Those aircraft had been the joy of our young lives and they had been left there to rot!

How many Fireflies of the 1,700 produced, remain? The Royal Naval Historic Flight has a later mark than the ones we flew and it has a different engine. At Yeovilton in September 1995 we watched this machine take off, climb at a steeper angle than any of us can remember and go straight into a climbing roll! The Naval Aviation Museum in Ottawa, Canada has a Firefly made from two FR 1's. Its registration number is DK545 and it has a Rolls Royce Griffon 11B engine. It was manufactured in 1945 and spent a great deal of its time as part of 826 Squadron and No. 18 Carrier Air Group. In 1954 it was struck off the RCN strength and sold to Ethiopia. In 1993, two Fireflies, still in RCN colours, DK545 and PP462, were donated to the National Aviation Museum and the Shearwater Aviation Museum. Since October 1993 this Firefly has been an exhibit at the National Museum. 1772 at one time, had a few DK Fireflies. The museum at Duxford has rebuilt a Firefly Mark 1. A few years ago Chris Maclaren was invited to attend its 'rolling out'.

A classic Charles E. Brown study of the Firefly 1. She could look as pretty as a Seafire with its very similar semi-elliptical shape of the wing.
Reproduced by kind permission of the RAF Museum. From the Charles E. Brown Collection (RAFM) Ref. No. 6010-11.

They 'flew through the air . . . on their flying trapeze' – to be correct. The Firefly was a sturdier vehicle for airborne antics but like any aircraft, she needed respect . . . and a firm hold and understanding of all the relevant bits and pieces.

> There were young men in 'Seventy Two',
> They played around in World War too,
> Their Firefly with cannon guns,
> A gentle lass, early Mark Ones.
> From Indefat. to Tokyo . . . they flew.
> *Anon.*

Some facts on the Firefly Mark 1

Fuselage	Semi monocoque	
	Folding wings. Manual	

Fuselage   Semi monocoque
Folding wings. Manual

Fuel tanks.	Main	145½ gals
	Total	191½ gals
	Drop tanks	45 and 90 gals
	Total	371½ gals (max)

Engine   Rolls Royce Griffon   V12 liquid cooled (the end of the family succession Kestrel, Buzzard, Merlin and Peregrine)

37 litre capacity   (Similar to Rolls Royce 'R' which had powered the Mitchell Schneider Trophy aircraft in the early 30's)

Consumption	2400 rpm	85 gals per hour.
	1800rpm	40 gals per hour.

2750 Bhp
2 magnetos. Total of 24 plugs.
Variable pitch propeller.

Armament   4 × 20 mm Cannons.
8 × 60 lb rockets.
or
2 × 500 lb or 2 × 1,000 lb bombs.

Handling   Quick response from stall (66 to 85 mph. Indicated Air Speed according to load).

Recommended speeds	Roll	210–250 mph
	Loop	300–335 mph
	Roll off top	335–345 mph
	Upward roll	345 mph

Max. Speed at S.L.   247K   277K at 17,000 feet.
Intentional Spinning prohibited, but recovery easy.

Landing.	Engine assisted	100 mph
	Glide	115 mph
	Glide, without flaps.	127 mph

History   'Conceived'   1939
Entered service   1943
First squadron to form up
1770   1943 (At Yeovilton)
1771 formed up   1944 (At Burscough)
1772 formed up   1944 (At Burscough)
1792 formed up as a Night Fighter Squadron. It was regarded as an 'excellent prospect in this role'.

Features of WW2 Service.

Attacks on Tirpitz

Attacks on German Condors

Attacks on Heinkel 111's launching V1 Flying Bombs.

East Indies. Operation Iceberg. Attacks on Palembang oil installations.

Pacific Fleet with Americans. In action to end of war, 1771 and 1772.

Korea. July 1950 to July 1953. Mark 1 Fireflies were unsuitable. The Korean War was as far as Fireflies were concerned finished with Mark 5's. 6 Firefly Squadrons played a part on 5 Light Fleet Carriers.

Malaya. 1954. 825 Squadron attacked terrorists. This was the last operation when the Firefly fired its guns in anger. At the end, the Firefly, was involved as a trainer, a target-tower and as a target itself . . . an unpiloted drone.

1956. The Firefly's 13 year service ends. (This is not a complete story by a long way. That story is written so well, in Bill Harrison's book.)

EARLY REHEARSALS ... THE PLAYERS BEGIN TO LEARN THEIR PARTS

'A little learning is a dangerous thing'   *Pope*
'I sank by my levity, – my brother, contrary to the laws of
nature, had risen by his gravity.'   *Sydney Smith*

The cast foregathers, or most of them; others were to complete the team throughout the squadron's lifetime. Burscough had welcomed us and we knew our way between camps and the aerodrome and we discovered that providence has placed a great little hostelry half way between the airfield and the wardroom! The 'Bull and Dog' was to become a lifelong symbol of friendship. Croose Parry says that he arrived on May 1st 1944. Two days later he adds that, 'it was his 21st Birthday, so a party was started and we all got to know each other in the best possible way.' Or was it the Red Lion further down the road? That place was always a very good first reserve.

Alan Rowlinson remembers arriving at Burscough, late one evening, to find an almost empty bar. He says that he retired early, somewhat dispirited, but the next morning, having met his pilot, Geoff Gill, and his other colleagues, he remembers a wonderful sense of elation 'having joined a truly friendly squadron'. He had arrived at a time of a 1772 boycott of the Wardroom bar. Alan remembers the extraordinary speed at which he settled in and discovered that real spirit of 1772 as well as finding a most compatible pilot with whom to fly.

Burscough was our world for quite a while; the wardroom Nissen huts, the Bull and Dog, time-off in Southport, the Burscough Wrens and several other joys. But we came to Burscough to try to become an operational squadron. There was still enough war left for us to join in and we knew this without any doubt. Training began within days of becoming 1772 Firefly Squadron; our first task was to meet our CO., get to know our Fireflies, form crews and become aware of our other squadron duties and responsibilities.

Within the first month we were learning section and patrol formations and carrying out navigation exercises with wind finding flights to give

Early in May, just outside 1772 crew HQ.

the Observers plenty to keep them busy. We did some low-level cross-country flying, cloud flying and that most vital of practices for deck landing, ADDLs or Aerodrome Dummy Deck Landings, that typical tail-down technique of Naval flyers. Within that month we had been

43

kept extremely busy. The ever-friendly Johnny O'Driscoll, writes, 'There were these interminable ADDLs and wind-finding exercises, a secret ritual carried out by Observers without any understanding by the Pilots . . . and very often, little understood by them.'

By June we were adding more variety to our flying. We began to use our guns; having fun with what was called 'splash firing'. We practised slow flying, a basic skill closely allied to deck landing skills. We practised aerobatics, a flying exercise not enjoyed by all 'lookers'. This was married to 'dog-fighting' and aerobatics in pairs. We improved our ability to fire our guns in the right direction by using camera guns, mounted in the wings; quarter attacks figured frequently in our log books. We all attended a Naval Instrument Flying School at Hinstock during the months of June and July. This comprised about 8 hours in Oxfords. They were really flying classrooms and we did a whole series of navigational exercises.

Johnny O'D returned from his course at Hinstock and described it as memorable, if only because it nearly ended in tragedy. 'Croose Parry picked me up in a Reliant. There was one other passenger, probably Glyn Roberts, on the morning of 29th July. We had covered about two thirds of the journey back to Burscough when the engine faltered and eventually failed. After a hair-raising interlude and a struggle with the dead engine, Croose managed to put us down at Inskip. What a relief!'

'Glyn shows the others how to do it. Burn is dubious, Mac smiles good-naturedly having already heard all Glyn's lines and Gordon Davidson probably knows better.'

(Johnny Coles)

July came and again a very busy month. The infamous shambles of a new patrol formation, beacon exercises, air-to-air firing on drogues towed by Martinets, dummy forced landings and dusk and night flying. It was all very exciting; we were actually beginning to learn how to use the aeroplane as a destructive agent. Every day provided another challenge. Wally Pritchard provides an observer's view of those first few months. 'Having arrived directly from training to my first (and only) squadron, it was a very exciting time with every day producing some new experience. Roy Hubble was my pilot for most of the exercises but I also crewed for the CO., Shiner Wright, George Trollope, Bob Scott and Stu Jobbings. Some of the more enjoyable times included low-level flying, a trip to Belfast and back, "shooting up" a company of the East Lancashire Regiment at zero feet. I loved pair cloud flying – always exciting – and squadron formation flying with 12 aircraft.'

Sammy Samuelson. 'I usually flew with Teddy Key and that was fine though I didn't care much for the "dog-fight" exercises. Some of the other pilots I flew with were a bit scary. I remember flying with Glyn Roberts once along the north coast of Wales, which looked beautiful. Glyn then turned inland and said, "I'll show you my home". We flew at zero feet up a narrow, steep and rocky valley. I think he must have slid back his cockpit hood and pointed *up* at the hillside, to one spot. Anyhow, he said, "There's home. UP there." I remember too that once we were returning to Burscough from a night navigation exercise and someone had landed before us with the undercart up (probably Eric Bramhall and Johnny Coles). This put Burscough out of action for a while. We were told to land at an RAF station, (most probably Woodvale) and as we came into land, I looked out of the rear cockpit and things did not look right. I said to Teddy, "I don't think this is the runway". He said something like, "Crikey, I don't think it is" and off we went again to the real Woodvale. I think we had tried to land on the EAST LANCS HIGHWAY".

Summer began to fade and in August in particular, we flew almost every day, sometimes making two flights each day. We did pair flying, learning to lead and to follow. We discovered the ham-fisted secrets of corkscrewing in 2's and 3's. This was an evasive technique in which you applied the rudder in a very heavy-footed way. It was a method of evading the bullets which could one day be directed in a far-from-friendly way, up one's stern. Still more ADDLs, more formation flying and the oxygen climb. Sammy reckons that Teddy Key and he topped the 30,000 feet mark. Ian Darby recalling the great skills of his pilot, Burn O'Neill, particularly his 'immaculate formation flying' and almost every other aspect of his flying skills over the 18 months they flew together, tells of the many exciting moments they had. He remembers the crinkled wings after the oxygen climb. He claims proximity to the speed of sound and a few popped rivets. In the chapter on the Firefly aircraft, mention was made of Gordon Davidson's and Johnny Palmer's rapid descent at a speed which, when corrected, was very close to the speed of sound.

Into September there was more of the same. Exercises called 'Fighter Affiliation' and Operation 'Stuffit' appeared in the log books. Nobody is absolutely sure what they were, other than exercises with other squadrons at Burscough, not the least Avengers, with which aeroplane we were destined to operate over Japan. There was more night formation and more exercises with our armaments, chiefly air-to-air.

Ian Darby. 'We had a few exciting misses especially when taking off in formation. Our wing tips cut the grass on several occasions. On 16th September I was flying with Glyn Roberts over the Irish Sea. We were on a night navigation exercise when he demanded that we bail out as the engine sounded a bit 'iffy'. I had to laugh . . . eventually! But it was serious at the time. On 23rd a few days later, again with Glyn as pilot on an air-to-air exercise he complained that the aircraft undercarriage would not descend! He said we had to bale out. "Getting to be a bit of a habit!" I thought. I told him he was an idiot and on return, he flew low over the control tower, who informed him that 'the undercarriage appeared to be down'. Glyn then 'cranked up' by the manual hydraulic pump and from thereon he was unbearable. I told him to stick his head outside because he sounded quite woosey. We landed, but the tail wheel didn't come down. Strange? Free drinks were provided by the MO.'

Croose Parry, never far behind in some of our more exciting episodes: 'I remember landing at night with wheels retracted which surprisingly felt like a very smooth touchdown, although there were a lot of sparks flying around!' Once up before the Station Commanding Officer for low-flying over Blackpool pier, I soon discovered that I could not talk my way out of it, as my plane number had been take by RAF Provost Marshalls. I remember the CO was most understanding about both these misdemeanours and I only received a mild rebuke.' Croose was a fine pilot and his skill in getting that Reliant safely back on the ground is fair testimony. He recalls how amusing it was, in retrospect, that in the cockpit three pilots were trying to undertake emergency procedures. He did conclude by saying that he was grateful to find Speke airfield below him. He played a leading role in the famous three aircraft pile-up on the runway one day. He was however always something of a romantic and remembers a navigation exercise across the Irish Sea and seeing in the distance the lights of Dublin. 'Another world', he thought.

On another aspect of 'lights', Burn O'Neill was over Liverpool when all the lights came on. He recalls that it was most thrilling and because he had left his transmitter on the Burscough Wrens heard everything. It is not recalled whether the conversation was wholesome for generally sensitive ears but Kiwi 'lingo' could be impressive and expressive when excitement took over, whether from gentle Burn or effusive Ian.

October was a very quiet month from a flying point of view. Teddy Key says that he flew only twice. However there were courses to attend, and a spot of leave. Major Cheeseman has written that to run a front line mobile squadron, every officer, besides handling his flying duties, must undertake a ground duty. Lt. Cdr. Gough, our first CO followed this idea and besides a senior pilot and senior observer there were other duties which have been mentioned already. We attended courses in some instances, related to our extra duties, though we all had to attend the Rolls Royce engine course. These duties did change round a little but a number of us held the same post during the lifetime of the Squadron.

Johnny O'Driscoll. 'I also attended an engine course at Rolls Royce at Derby, since I had been appointed Aero Engines Officer and ought to know something about the Griffon engine. We had a Fairey representative with us, Robbo Robinson by name, and I believe one other such expert. We also had Flight Sergeant Fryer from the RAF as our senior maintenance NCO. All very fascinating, but too technical for a layman in such a short time; I was never aware of being at the forefront of engine technology! There were of course many problems to be solved. One day during ADDL's two or three pilots were involved with one aircraft which was on each occasion reported as running roughly. After each pilot handed over the aircraft to the next one, the problem was mentioned but none could put an explanation to the cause. On return to the flight apron on the final trip, after about 6 landings, the engine cut out. It was then discovered that each propellor blade was missing 3 to 4 inches from the tip. The "woodwork" was found splintered over the runway tarmac. ADDL's could be very severe on tyres but in a situation where the whole technique is to land in a tail-down attitude, the mind boggles slightly as to what pilot and batsman had to say about it. There is no other record of this affair.'

November was special because we did our first deck landings. We flew to HMS Empress in the Irish Sea, did our five or so deck landings and returned to base.

Johnny O'Driscoll. 'On 25th November 1944 in Firefly D for Dog, Z2022 I flew to HMS Empress for deck-landing experience. I landed on successfully, but when my hook hit the deck it bounced up, locking back into the fuselage. I went through the barrier and finished up causing minor damage to the aircraft parked forward of the barrier. D for Dog was a write-off. Naturally I was a bit shaken but even more so when summoned before the Captain. I was asked why I had not closed the throttle and avoided gouging a long groove up the wooden flight deck. He was far more concerned about his ship than my welfare, about which he made no comment!'

As far as records go, we did quite well. But then about this time

Johnny O'Driscoll landed 'differently' on HMS Empress. Nothing to do with him, 'the hook bounced up'.

(Johnny O'Driscoll)

there was a wind of change. Les Wort was with us. Things were changing and Bob Scott says it well. 'I had just joined 1772 and had done my first deck landings on the Empress on 26th November. Les Wort had just joined us and I have two memories. After lecturing us, he drank us all under the table that night. The next day after what seemed a very prefunctory look at the Firefly, he took off, threw it about and landed it, as though on butter. And he didn't say "follow that". From then on he had my vote'.

The thing one remembers most about November, December and January was 'mud'. There seemed to be an awful lot of it about. The fever of the early training seemed to have calmed down and the weather was not conducive to the volume of flying we had done in May, June and July. There was a feeling that things were beginning to drag; we all wanted to move on from Burscough and perhaps leave behind some of the less happy memories. Burn O'Neill . . . 'Just why did it take us so long to get into the action from May 1st onwards?'

The answer had to be 'leadership' and the chapter of events; some stupid and careless accidents which reflected on all of us. The change of Commanding Officers, as already related, was profound. We had not responded to the over-zealous, gung-ho style, for Lt. Cdr. Gough was a 'press-on' type of regular (an epithet provided by an outside observer of the squadron). There are many types of leadership; we had nurtured between us a monumental incompatibility.

There is not much else to say on that matter, except to describe some of our performances. A good many accidents in flying are concerned with some sort of contact with the ground, usually accidentally. And we seemed to have some trouble . . . with the ground; even travelling across it, before we came airborne!

The details of our 'prangs' at Burscough are listed below. They arrived in this set of records via the infamous A25, a report completed after an accident. This table came to light in 1995, when during our 50th celebration of our 1st May 1944 'birth' day, Graham Mottram, the Curator of the Fleet Air Arm Museum at Yeovilton, during a conversation about our accidents, disappeared and came back with the full printout.

DATE	A/C TYPE	SERIAL No	UNIT	ACCIDENT LOCATION	NAME INITS	RANK	SERVICE
6.06.44	FIREFLY	Z1979	1772	BURSCOUGH	JOBBINGS	SH S/LT(A)	RNVR
LANDED WITH U/C RETRACTED							
29.05.44	FIREFLY	Z1986	1772	BURSCOUGH	KINGSTON PB	S/LT	RNZVR
STALLED,STBD WING DROPPED							
8.06.44	FIREFLY	Z1962	1772	BURSCOUGH	KINGSTON PB	S/LT	RNZVR
FORCEDLANDING,CRASHED SHORT OF RUNWAY							
17.07.44	FIREFLY	DK415	1772	BURSOUGH	GOUGH AH	LT CDR	RN
Engine trouble, forced landed							
19.07.44	FIREFLY	Z1951	1772	BURSCOUGH	PARRY AC	S/LT(A)	RNVR
LANDED WITH U/C RETRACTED							
29.07.44	FIREFLY	Z1956	1772	BURSCOUGH	WRIGHT MJC	LT(P)	RN
COLLIDED WITH Z1958,PARACHUTED OUT, LT SLOAN KILLED							
29.07.44	FIREFLY	Z1958	1772	BURSCOUGH	GOUGH AH	LT CDR	RN
COLLIDED WITH Z1956							
11.08.44	FIREFLY	Z2023	1772	BURSCOUGH	JOBBINGS SH	S/LT(A)	RNVR
GROUND LOOPED, U/C COLLAPSED							
13.08.44	FIREFLY	Z1946	1772	BURSCOUGH	O'DRISCOLL JT	S/LT	RNVR
LOOSE THROTTLE LEVER,GROUND LOOPED,U/C COLLAPSED							
11.09.44	FIREFLY	Z2038	1772	BURSCOUGH	WRIGHT MJC	LT(P)	RN
ENGINE FAILED,LANDED IN FIELD							
09.44	FIREFLY	Z1945	1772	BURSCOUGH	ROBERTS GD	S/LT	RNVR
BROKEN HYDRAULIC PIPE,TAIL U/C WOULD NOT LOCK DOWN							

A printout provided by Graham Moffatt, the Curator of the Yeovilton Museum. This is just the Burscough chapter!

A few of the prangs . . .
. . . and the prangers.

Our past had finally caught up with us! The causes more-or-less speak for themselves; a fair amount of carelessness, one engine failure (we do not remember the final judgement on this) and perhaps the odd bit of . . . being just a trifle rash. There were however three very serious accidents.

On 26th June 1944, Harry Garbutt, pilot, and Ken Neuschild crashed just off Blackpool Pier. Sammy Samuelson, observer to Teddy Key, comments. 'They were in the habit of flying upside down, just for fun. I think Harry tried to pull out by doing the second half of a loop, as it were, but was just not high enough. When we went to Ken's funeral which was at Preston or Fleetwood, we went through Blackpool on the way there and back. Blackpool has held no attraction for me since.' Teddy Key who watched the whole thing too: 'The memory of seeing that crash into the sea is most clear, still, in my mind, confirms Sammy's story.' He was however asked to go and identify Harry's body in a

Harry Garbutt

Ken Neuschild

S/L Harry Garbutt and Midshipman Ken Neuschild, on top, who were killed in a flying accident on 26th June 1944.

Fleetwood mortuary. The two and a half ringer doctor who drove Teddy to Fleetwood was to give the police a most royal 'bollicking' for submitting a young pilot to such an experience. Teddy recalls that on return to Burscough the Lt. Cdr. and he got very 'high'. The awfulness of it was that it was not Harry lying there, very damaged, but Ken; and there were documents on Ken to prove that it was Ken.

On the 29th July 1944 Lt. Cdr. Gough and Lt. Wright, the Senior Pilot, collided in mid-air. Lt. Jimmy Sloan and Lt. Monty Baker, the two observers were killed. Lt. Cdr. Gough had planned a particular type of patrol formation. There were two such formation trips and Teddy Key had recorded in his flying log-book after the first one. 'Shambles'. On the second one the collision occurred; the day after. Wren Joan Hanson (now Mrs Joan Simonsson), a Flying Control Leading Wren writes, 'The incident concerning 1772 Squadron ended with fatal consequences. Having scrambled some of the Squadron I watched two planes, chasing each other, then to my horror they collided and went down, out of sight. Holding my breath, I waited but all too soon, a plume of black smoke could be seen rising up, indicating that the worst had happened. Although two survived I do not remember seeing a parachute'. Two planes chasing each other does not marry up with the nature of the exercise and the report of the crash says that Lt. Wright baled out.

Left: Lt. Jimmy Sloan RN Senior Observer killed 29th July 1944.
Right: Lt. Monty Baker RNVR Observer killed 29th July 1944.

*The triple prang in the fog, 25th October 1944. The bicycle is thought to
have had no bearing on the accident!
(Agnes Stevens – but every member of the Squadron possesses this one.)*

On the 25th October there occurred one of the gems of taxiing
accidents. Perhaps not truly a taxiing prang, though all three aircraft
were on the ground at the time of impact . . . and they had no intention
of leaving the ground! The exercise was organised, if that is the right
word, to fill in a bad day. Visibility was down to 200 yards so what does
a 'press-on type of CO' do? Lt. Cdr. Gough planned a carrier deck-
ranging exercise in which aircraft tucked themselves in closely at the
end of the runway, as is usual on the more restricted area of a flight
deck. The idea was that each aircraft, on a signal would move into a
position on the 'centre line', open up, roar off at take-off revs and then
throttle back. Subsequent planes would follow on in the same manner.
The long nose of the Firefly is not as inhibiting to vision as with a
Seafire, but nevertheless, the nose is long, and in a tail down position,
the vision was not good. And so all is ready for what in the Branch one
would have called 'a monumental cockup'. The three aircraft concerned
are described in the 1772 list of prangs; a busy day for A25's. Aircraft
4Z failed to throttle back, overtook 4M, hitting it with the port wing
tip. 4M groundlooped. The process was repeated on 4J. They all
groundlooped and they all lost their undercarriage. The exercise
was abandoned and the new CO arrived on 1st November! If it hadn't
been so ludicrous and so embarrassing we would have laughed. Now

53

Leading Wren Joan Hanson in 1944. Now Mrs Joan Simonsson.

we can and for the very good reason, that nobody was hurt. Let Leading Wren Hanson have the last word on this incident; after all she was in a fine position up there in flying control, with a front seat. 'The other incident happened right in front of the Tower before our very eyes. On a day when the weather was closed-in and there was no flying, manoeuvres on the runway were taking place. We had been informed there would be no aircraft taking off, just "deck parking exercises". Not having seen this before I was watching with great interest to see what was involved, little guessing the horror that I was about to witness. The aircraft taxied round the airfield and came to form up in front of the Tower in offset pairs, with engines running. They came to a standstill. Suddenly one aircraft started accelerating forward while the others were still stationary; it collided with the aircraft to its side and ahead, with the propeller slicing through the fuselage between the pilot and observer and with a third aircraft being involved and the skies seemed to be raining metal. From a scene of complete orderliness, in a matter of seconds, we were viewing devastation. It all happened so quickly, yet seemed to be in slow motion. We were extremely shocked as we could see it happening, but were powerless to stop it. Great was the relief when we saw that miraculously the crews had escaped . . . but what a shambles.'

Croose Parry, an innocent character in this performance, on seeing the wreckage claimed that it had been a miracle that Knocker White, his observer, had not been injured. Alan Rowlinson, the intended observer in the fast-moving aircraft, had just before the event, reported sick. Maybe he always had a strong insight about survival, for he is still with us!

Our record of prangs has been a source of some chagrin but one way of getting the whole thing into perspective is to read other stories of Squadron activities, in the air and on the ground. A very good palliative in a sense, for any 1772 ex-aircrew is to read that eminently readable book, 'Carrier Pilot' by Norman Hanson. The pages are smothered in tragedies in training and operations on HMS Illustrious as a Corsair Squadron worked up and went into action in the Far East and Sakashimas. A good many things went wrong in Norman Hanson's world. One hazard was the Corsair built-in 'bounce'. An over violent oleo system in the undercarriage was sending the Corsair over the wires and into the barriers before a remedy was found, but that gremlin had cost some lives.

There was of course a lighter side to life at Burscough, though many of the memories have dimmed; probably because of brain-cell

Only one of the quintet was a Burscough Wren, second left, Jackie Cockrill, representing the 1948 Air Command Fencing team at Olympia. The charming picture confirms what a fine body of Wrens can look like.

(Jackie Cockrill)

deterioration or perhaps because some of the memories and antics are best forgotten. Southport provided about the best evening outing other than the two pubs, for the single guys who loved a Wren, then Southport was the place to dine.

Both Johnny Coles and Wally Pritchard remember the return journeys, minus a lady friend of course, when they travelled back to Burscough on the footplate or even on the front bumpers! The fact that one had made the last train was providential. Wally enjoyed the weekends when he would visit the Carisbrooke Hotel and be entertained by local girls and WAAFS. He is greyish and retired now and he is not specific about the memories! Johnny O'Driscoll has long wondered if those journeys on the footplate qualified him as a member of ASLEF. Sammy Samuelson loved the Wrens. He thought the photography Wrens were very helpful in developing our films. We were often there ascertaining the results of our camera gun air-to-air firing. The dark room no doubt had some underlying mystery, but the memory fades, darkly! Sammy continues, 'The Gunnery Wrens used to dash around the countryside in their Tilly (pick-up) vans looking for drogue targets. For this they were allowed to wear bell-bottomed trousers which were most attractive and reminded me of the "beach pyjamas" which the smart girls wore in the South of France in 1937/39'. Sammy was a man of simple, healthy good taste. He loved cycling the lanes of Lancashire, traffic-free in a perfect summer. He enjoyed the country pubs, good ale and good food. Eton and family had trained him to be a first-class hedonist. He enjoyed the Farmers' Club in Ormskirk and in Liverpool would enjoy the concerts in the Philharmonic Hall. He remembers the concerts conducted by 'Flash Harry', the affectionate name of Sir Malcolm Sargent. He remembers too the evening 'sessions' in Southport where the main challenge was to get to the amusement park by walking in a straight line. That would include rose gardens and bowling greens. In retrospect, we have much to be ashamed of. And who was it who was once spotted standing on top of the roller coaster, hands raised triumphantly above his head? Some mad young aviator, one supposes. Madness could reign supreme sometimes; one can at this late stage (like 50 years later) put it down to the release of tension or just another way of getting over a squadron tragedy. Croose Parry recalls the highly successful home-made rocket manufacture that went on during the quiet hours. These were made from starter cartridges. A major achievement he remembers was when one actually pierced the cloud base. Another story goes that one nearly pierced the CO . . . Lt. Cdr. Gough. Alan Rowlinson remembers 'baling out' practice which was carried out on the tarmac. At the drop of an arm, the pilot was supposed to shout 'Bale Out, Bale out, GO GO!' He would then open the cockpit cover and arrive outside the plane at the same time as the observer. In his case, the arm dropped, the pilot's cockpit cover crashed back, Geoff Gill, the pilot splattered out and down the wing, turned and saw him sitting quietly in the rear cockpit . . . waiting. 'Oh God', he said, 'I forgot to tell my looker.' Alan has always attributed to Geoff a gratitude for the way he helped him to integrate. 'I liked to think we clicked as a crew', – Alan has always insisted. Maybe in the end they did get their act together, but it was Alan's misfortune to be deprived of Geoff, when the latter was posted to 1771. They became very close friends and were in time each other's Best Man.

We did have a bit of a reputation for being just a trifle self assured; maybe a euphemism for arrogance. As the attractive ex-Radar Wren Jackie Cockrill has said, 'There was this feeling about 1772 and when something went wrong, the cry went round the station, "Oh No! not 1772 again!" ' Alan tells the story of 'the Little Tin Gods'. 'At some time near the end of June 1944, entirely by accident, a member of the squadron was wrongly accused by the Station Commander of helping himself, after hours, to food from the Wardroom fridge. The reaction was to declare a boycott on the bar which accounted for the increase in trade at the Bull and Dog and the Red Lion. In the Autumn, Burscough was honoured by a visit from ENSA which included Canadian Wrens dancing in the chorus line with never-before-seen black nylon mesh tights. Apart from the fact that it was a very good ENSA show, the decision was made that since all the cast were to be entertained in the Wardroom after the show, this would be a very good night to break the boycott. We all reckoned it was a "good party" so we were slightly surprised to be ordered next morning to appear, "forthwith", before the Station Commander. The exact wording of the tirade cannot be recalled but the following phrases represent the gist. We do remember, after walking into the room, he started, "Don't get up gentlemen," (we were sitting around in a somewhat slouched, hung-over way), "be yourselves, spit on the deck if you want to. When guests are invited into the Wardroom, officers are expected to be civil, to communicate, to offer hospitality, to entertain, etc. etc. But you",' he had reached a shouting mode, "you must think you are 'little tin gods', but you will certainly have to improve if you want to escape possible restrictions". Thereafter we certainly improved, but on odd occasions we did wear as a badge, a figure cut out of sheet tin, closely resembling the little black figure found on Robertson's marmalade jars. On the whole it was a dubious memory and long after, we tend to want to

H.M.S. "RINGTAIL"

PRESENTS

"LITTLE BY LITTLE"

A Revue of Station Talent,

WEDNESDAY and THURSDAY, May 17th and 18th, 1944,

in the Cinema, Camp II,

at 20.00 hrs.

Produced by Lieut. J. HARRIS

A revue put on by the Burscough Station personnel.

Burscough Wrens display some of their charms in the Can-Can.
Wren Doran, Wren Livock, Wren Peters, Wren Ludlow, Wren Michelmore,
Wren Starling, Wren Cockrill, Wren Girling, Wren Waine.

(Teddy Key)

remember the Canadian Wrens' dance routine in those black stockings.' HMS Ringtail was capable of staging its own shows. These were jolly shows with some good audience participation. A good evening, watching the chorus line of our own beautiful Wrens, would end in a sensible manner with a quiet drink maybe in the Wardroom and we slept peacefully in our Nissen hutted beds and dreamt of their Can-Can.

That men drank a little during the war is no great secret. That a sailor, whether at sea or on dry land was not averse to a 'wee measure' is undeniable. That flyers, in order to ease their tensions were prone, not only to the odd bout of social drinking or capable of the most impromptu party or sessions, as it was known, is also common knowledge. It is not surprising then that we naval flyers enjoyed an 'odd sherbert', a soothing and palliative jug of ale, or in Oz, a tube of Fosters. In such a session, true, the ale did flow and sometimes to accelerate the process, we had our chug-a-lug pot. This was an inscribed chamber pot, decorated by our own tame war-artist, Val Bennett, and it was capable of holding a fair volume of liquid. Individuals would be challenged to sink the pot, at least two pints, in one go . . . or pass it round. This custom was practised and probably still exists, at such occasions as 'Bump Suppers' in Oxbridge, and is known as 'sconcing'. The victim would be challenged in the Wardroom because he was deemed to be dodging his drinks, or in other words, he was guilty of 'piking'. He would then, purely out of pride sink this lot to the chant of, 'Here's to . . . he's true blue, he's a piker through and through; meant to go to heaven so they say, meant to go to heaven, but went the other way,' . . . and then, 'Chug-a-lug-chug-a-lug-chug-a-lug' . . . Later in our singing sessions – it was always good singing beer – the message of, 'Good night ladies etc' would clear the wardroom of the Wren Officers. There were some good station types who would join the aircrews in their boisterous self-entertainment. The Wrens having retired to their chaste beds, the nature of the songs would become a trifle rabelaisian. Certain songs were quite wholesome and always fun. Suffice at this point to recall the best known of the lot which relates to pranging an aeroplane. Pranging was our private nightmare, so we made light of it. But we never got drunk! The discipline remained. We had been made to realise from the beginning that our role as aircrew was superseded by the fact that we were first and foremost, naval officers and gentlemen. Boisterous we may have been, noisy we most certainly were. We did things we should not have done. But we did our duty and we did not, 'drink and fly'. You'd better believe it!

We played poker a lot in the crew room because there were boring

*The Chug-a-lug Potty. Artwork by
Val Bennett.*

(Teddy Key)

times waiting to fly or just waiting for the weather to break. We carried out our other duties and sometimes we played healthy outdoor games. Johnny Coles is convinced that we had a first class rugby XV. Our squadron side took over Burscough's fixture list, which it discharged with distinction. 'We had several excellent players,' he said, 'not the least Mike La Grange who was close to Springbok international standard. Mike knew all the tricks of the trade and taught us quite a few. A very simple one, and one of his favourites, was to show the forwards how, by rolling up your shirt sleeve and pushing the ball under the feet of the opposition, you could obtain an immediate penalty. Quite innocent today when one considers the modern game.

There was romance, sometimes serious, occasionally intense and no doubt sometimes 'just for the duration'. Steve and Agnes were married and lived in a small house on the Southport Road. Teddy enjoyed putting his feet under that particular table. It carried very good fare. Johnny O'Driscoll married his Madge. They had met at Yeovilton during Johnny's Fighter School training and Madge was a Wren Steward. The other affairs must remain a secret.

Those 'early rehearsals' had to end at some time; the learning process now under Les Wort had more purpose and we were growing up. The 'sixth form' attitude had to go. We had learnt a great deal and we were no longer as dangerous to others or ourselves as we had been way back in the summer of 1944. On about January 28th we left Burscough for the Clyde. The aircraft were flown to Belfast and craned on to HMS Ruler. Most of us went by rail with all our stores and bits and pieces.

Away from the prying eyes of senior officers of the station we would 'hive off' to the 'Bull and Dog' barn . . . probably windowless. Here we drank away a happy hour or so with the maintenance boys. The sing-a-long always featured strongly. 'Through music,' it was once said 'we discover a great deal about ourselves.' Ho! ho! . . . or was it the Red Lion on this occasion?

*Two 21st Birthday sessions . . . on a no-flying day of course. One is Pete
Kingston's and the other Teddy Key's!*

A Burscough Ball. Peter confides in Mac. – Steve and Agnes were Mr and Mrs – and Agnes was pregnant?

(Agnes Stevens)

The 'company' of 1772 was on its way to a war zone – East Asia or Pacific? We became a touring company, and though Burscough had been on the whole, one great experience, we wanted the whole of the damn play to move on before we became, well, just plain stale.

There were songs – and songs. A poem entitled 'Lydia Pinkham', written by 'Anonymous', became the basis of a boisterous song.

> Then we'll sing of Lydia Pinkham,
> And her love for the human race;
> How she sold her veg'table compound
> And the papers publish'd her face.
>
> Oh, it sells for a dollar a bottle
> Which is very cheap you see,
> And if it doesn't cure you
> She will sell you six for three.

Anon.

There were songs sung to all sorts of tunes; Bless 'em all, Rum and

Geoff Gill and Alan Rowlinson. A crew that should never have been broken up. Geoff was posted to 1771 Fireflies as a replacement pilot. Alan went into action with Dave Hebditch as his pilot. Geoff and Alan had formed a friendship which stretched into post-war years until Geoff died. Alan remains in touch with Delphine, Geoff's widow. Their separation as a crew was a great blow to both of them.

(Alan Rowlinson)

Coca-Cola, John Brown's Body and many others, but the real favourite was always 'A25'.

The A25. Air. 'Charlotte the Harlot'

They say in the RAF that the landings OK,
If the pilot can get out, and still walk away,
But in the Fleet Air Arm the prospect is grim,
Of landing's piss poor and the pilot can't swim.

Burn the Batsman'. He was very good and we trusted him. Didn't we?

Chorus. Cracking show. I'm alive.
         But I've still got to render my A25

           I fly for a living, and not just for fun,
           But I'm awfully anxious to shoot down a Hun,
           But as for deck landings when done in the dark,
           As I told Wings this morning, Stuff that for a lark.
           Chorus.

I thought I was coming in low enough . . . but,
I was fifty feet up when the batsman gave 'CUT',
And loud in my ears, the sweet angels sang,
Float, float, float, float, float, float, float, float, float . . . PRANG.
Chorus.

           When the batsman gives 'lower', I always go higher,
           I drift off to starboard, and prang a Seafire,
           The boys in the goofers all think that I'm green.
           But I get my rake-off from Supermarine.
           Chorus.

As I sat on the booster, awaiting the kick,
Amusing myself by rotating the stick,
Down went the blue flag, the thing gave a cough,
'Cor Blimey', said Wings, 'He has tossed himself off'.
Chorus.

They gave me a Firefly* to beat up the Fleet,
I polished off Rodney and Nelson a treat,
But forgot about the masts that stick out from Formid.
And a seat in the Goofers was worth fifty quid.
Chorus.

As I rolled down the deck in my Wildcat Mark Four,
Loud in my ears was that sweet engine's roar,
Chuff, clank, clank, chuff, clank, clank, chuff, clank, clank, clink.
Away wing on pompom, away cab in drink.
Chorus.

When you come o'er the rounddown and see Wings frown,
You can safely assume that your hook isn't down,
As a ruddy great barrier looms up in front.
You can hear Wings shout . . . 'Switch off, you silly . . .'
Chorus.

Now I come to the last ruddy verse
And to all sprog pilots I really am terse,
Keep your eye on the batsman, the clock and the deck,
And you'll carry on flying and not break your neck.
Chorus.

Thanks to Johnny Palmer for help in sorting this out . . . and cleaning it up!

Some heretofore less familiar verses related entirely to 1772 Squadron. There are others it is believed, which are considered to be libellous. These verses do relate to specific crew members and the answers will be obvious to those who have over the years and the span of this text, paid some attention.

The batsman stood there with his arms open wide,
But I stalled on approach and went over the side,
My shiny new Firefly sank like a stone,
Just as well that I was flying alone.
Chorus.

* Seafire and Firefly were interchanged occasionally depending how we felt at the time.

66

The day it was foggy you could not see a thing,
But our aircraft were ranged there, wing to wing,
Down went HIS flag and off went the race,
The Fireflies were spread all over the place.
Chorus.

I knew that I was coming in fast,
The batsman gave 'wave-off' and stood there aghast,
I arrived in the barrier with my eyes shut tight,
I still dream about it . . . every night
Chorus.

We had an observer an ace on the keys,
In his kilt you could see he had knobbly knees,
To the 'Water of Life' he was very attached,
But at the piano he couldn't be matched.
Chorus.

One worthy pilot wearing a frown,
He was never quite sure if his wheels were down,
He thought that the Firefly flew on fresh air,
But the end of the runway wasn't quite there.
Chorus.

oOoOoOo

Brother, we sit, ready to go,
Thinking of things we think we know.
Dreaming of deeds we mean to do,
Maybe now, or a minute, – or two.
Something noble and grand and good.
Won by merely wishing we could.
Now we are going to . . . No! There?
Brother, our tale, now hangs . . . anywhere.

Apologies, belatedly to Rudyard Kipling.
From his poem about the Monkey People.

THE COMPANY GOES ON TOUR

'And now I call upon you for a true account of your
wanderings; to what parts of the inhabited world did you
travel? What lovely cities did you see, what people in
them? Did you meet hostile tribes and lawless savages or
did you fall in with some friendly and god-fearing folk?'

Homer

The Squadron was split into two groups for the journey which took
from the end of January to the middle of March, when we arrived at
Sydney, Australia. One group sailed in HMS Ruler and one in HMS
Activity. Both had crowded flight decks though the 1772 Fireflies were
on board HMS Ruler. Accommodation was uniformly very crowded
and both Escort carriers had become cargo and troop carriers.

Firstly some 'Ruler' lines;

Johnny Palmer. 'About six of us were accommodated in the Barber
Shop below the flight deck. It was very warm when we reached the
Tropics. We took it in turns to sit in the barber's chairs.'

Johnny O'Driscoll. 'An overnight storm in the Bay of Biscay resulted
in an attendance of 3 officers at Wardroom breakfast . . . I can bear
witness. We arrived at Gibraltar on 3rd February 1945, departing early
am on the 4th. There was a showing of "The Desert Song" in the cinema
but many were still suffering-from a party the night before! The ship's
Barber Shop housed 8 aircrew during the entire voyage; it was rather
confining. Another storm in the Mediterranean made several of the
aircraft, which were lashed down, become very unstable. Glyn Roberts
led the rescue operation: there was no damage as far as I can recall. We
had revolver firing practice from the stern of the 'Ruler' and equally, I
cannot recall ever hitting the target. Aircrew participated in Watch
Duties at night on the bridge: the Officer of the Watch would go below
saying, "call me in the event of difficulty" and I cannot remember the
private thoughts of the Helmsman. The storm had damaged the rudder

and propeller of the ship, so we put into Alexandria for repairs. I remember the "garry" races back to the ship after an evening run ashore, a game of rugger under the sweltering sun on a sand baked pitch that was as hard as concrete. I remember exotic cakes and cream at Pastroudies and drinking brandy and ginger ale (medically recommended) at the Services Club. In Ceylon, more brandy and dry ginger, or pink gins, in the luxury of the Hotel Galle Face; what a smashing hotel, on the ocean water front! There was Mount Lavinia, a few miles south of Colombo, which boasted a super swimming pool. It was in this pool in which we delighted in keeping cool, that I lost my wedding ring. After a great deal of panic we managed to "clear" the pool and through the settled water I saw the ring on the bottom. Extraordinary good fortune. Ray Battison joined us in Colombo.'

Ian Darby remembers much of this and recalls the pleasures of Alex and Colombo. 'I seem to remember some aircraft falling over the side of the Ruler. It was a tremendous storm and stayed with us all the way from Gibraltar to Alexandria. It was quite scary on deck at night trying to tie down these aircraft, which were crashing into each other.'

Robin (Hank) Hendersen. 'I remember the Boss grilling us all one day because he thought someone had squeezed a bit of his toothpaste.'

Teddy Key. 'I suppose that I was as pleased about getting a vast amount of Squadron equipment from Burscough to our new base at HMS Nabthorpe or RNAS Schofields just outside Sydney, without losing a nut, as I was about anything, on a journey which was devoid of creature comforts. But then I had a first-rate Leading Seaman (Stores) looking after me. We kept fit physically; a particular sparring partner of mine being the ship's doctor, Jimmy Steeds, a Cambridge rugger blue and international scrummager. We used to battle away in a series of exercises which defied the limited space on the flight deck. Spiritually, we were not very fit. We gained a reputation with the ship's CO for skipping Sunday Divisions. The poor old Boss was lumbered with the problem of persuading us to support him. Of course we did, though I remember little of those "divine" Sundays. I do remember one in our midst saying to the Boss, "I'm doing this for you Boss, not the bloody Navy or this God of theirs". Just one little example of the fractious atmosphere our indifferent conditions managed to produce. The stopovers were fun; for me the hotel at Mount Lavinia was very special. I cannot remember with any accuracy my companions though the memory of that sea and sand lingers still. And that little Sinhalese woman on the beach who peeled a whole pineapple with the most lethal macheté, with but a few strokes! We ate them, holding them by the rough end, like ice cream cones. But the streets of Colombo were not paved with gold, just a few billion "goblets" of betal juice, the little red berries the Sinhalese seemed to chew for ever and ever. They smiled their blood-red smiles and spat! Chewing gum is a beautiful and aesthetic pursuit, by comparison! We arrived at Sydney in the middle of March and as we leant over the side of the Ruler, there on the quayside in khaki shorts were the distinctive legs of Geoff Rham. We had arrived and the Squadron would soon be reunited. Why do such silly memories linger when I am certain that more important ones have dissolved? We sailed out almost immediately, having unloaded stores and we flew off the aircraft. The deck length ahead looked very limited; one was very rusty in terms of flying familiarity and Doc Steeds said he'd love to be my passenger. Sammy was on the "Activity" but it was good that Doc had such confidence in me. Or was he, like most of us, desperately keen to get off the Ruler?'

Some 'Activity' happenings

Gordon Macrow. A real stalwart of Navy memorabilia and reunions, was a member of our excellent maintenance crew. Gordon was a senior Petty Officer whose responsibilities were to see that our radio equipment was in tip-top condition. His job therefore was to see that we had every facility in working order to ensure that we did "get home"! 'Having left Greenock and sailed into the Atlantic in heavy seas I had to take a working party, those who were not seasick, to secure aircraft on the flight deck. "Activity" survived the storms in the Mediterranean unharmed and while the rest of the convoy put into Alexandria for repairs we continued unescorted through the Suez Canal into the Indian Ocean and to Fremantle in Western Australia. I recall the Indian Ocean was like a mill pond and we were able to stop and pick up survivors from USS Sylvester which had been sunk by a Japanese submarine. On arrival at Sydney we berthed at Woolloomooloo and disembarked for Schofields to await the remainder of the squadron.'

Sammy Samuelson. 'I was in the Ruler for, I think, one day. I didn't like the Wardroom.' (Did one have a choice of ships?) 'I was transferred to the "Activity" which was fine, except that with its deck cargo of aircraft and narrow beam it seemed a bit unseaworthy. Also the food tasted slightly of diesel oil. During the bad Atlantic weather we had only a corvette as escort but from Gibraltar we were to be on our own. We stopped at Port Said for a day; my only visit to Africa to this day. It was quite sufficient for my lifetime. The ship's officers were all RNR and were a splendid lot. We used to play Tombola in the Wardroom and the Chiefs and PO's joined us. We played liar dice which were sticky

Leisurely inertia on Ruler.
(Johnny Palmer)

. . . and little activity
(Val Bennett)

. . . and a little madness.
(Teddy Key)

HMS Activity.

objects because we drank port a good deal. We lived four to a cabin, a very small one where some joker had rigged a "roll indicator" on the bulkhead. We stopped over at Fremantle and went to Perth but I remember little except that it was very spacious and very old-fashioned. The trams had big hooks on the back for prams.'

Croose Parry. 'I volunteered for duty as Second Officer of the Watch, which was interesting and one learned how the other half of the Navy went about their duties. During the storm in the Bay of Biscay the Captain faced a point of decision and gave the command to alter course 180 degrees in order to ride out the storm with more safety and not the least, a little more comfort for everyone. His sudden increase in physical girth was due to the fact that he was wearing his lifebelt under his duffle coat. With the huge deck park we were a little top heavy. The "cruise" finished beyond Port Said in more balmy conditions than those in Biscay and the Med. Wonderful sunsets, flying fishes. Steaming across the Australian Bight we were escorted by an Albatross, soaring above our wake. We "tied up" under the shadow of Sydney Bridge.'

Wally Pritchard. "I spent a good deal of my time as Second Officer of the Watch. I enjoyed the children on the banks of the Suez Canal shouting interesting phrases in Anglo/Arabic. When we picked up the message that there was a ship's boat in the vicinity, I was required to advise the Captain. I entered his cabin after knocking, and shook him.

The response was immediate and positive. He gave me one big rocket for "touching the Captain". Apparently this was a course of action that a lesser man than the Captain did when there was a mutiny. I celebrated my 21st birthday ten days short of Sydney and the bar was dry. We drank Van der Hum with brandy, – unusual, but a welcome substitute for champagne. One of the first things I did on arrival in Sydney was to buy a large bunch of bananas.'

Alan Rowlinson. 'Travelling to Greenock from Burscough via Largs I was billeted for one night aboard a 200 year-old wooden sailing ship . . . called HMS Indefatigable! We all turned to, when the first storm hit us and we all did one-hour stints, lashing down the aircraft which were difficult to hold down. I was on duty about mid-morning with two ratings and I lost my nearly-new cap over-board into the Atlantic. One just didn't have time to think about being sea-sick.'

Bob Scott. 'The "Activity" was a sort of flight deck popped on top of a merchantman. They called these things Escort Carriers; the forward and after welldecks were open to the elements. An abiding memory is of playing poker for six weeks . . . and winning! We played sometimes well into the night. We would then go into the galley for corned beef sandwiches, first of all brushing off the cockroaches. The "crossing the line" ceremony was a welcome relief; a great occasion.'

It had been an adventurous few weeks. Things to do, much time to waste and sometimes so much frustration and boredom. Time passed and we were in another world and often felt so very far from home. The Squadron united at HMS Nabthorpe or Royal Naval Air Station, Schofields, an aerodrome on the outer fringes of Sydney and beyond Parramatta. We were to take our time again, in preparing for action and for a number of reasons we were to be broken up again before we eventually went to war. Our final rehearsals were imminent and we looked forward to flying in this new land of Oz. Our youthful optimism drove us forward and in the end we finished more or less intact; even 50 years later.

> I knew a lad who went to sea
>   and left the shore behind him.
> I knew him well, the lad was me
>   And now I cannot find him.
> Away, away, away. He went to salty waters.
> Away, away, away. He went and left the shore behind him.
>   American Ballad.

FINAL REHEARSALS . . . IN AUSTRALIA

I had else been perfect,
Whole as the marble, founded as the rock,
As broad and general as the casing air,
But now I am cabin'd, cribb'd, confin'd, bound in
To saucy doubts and fears.   Macbeth

We will let the words of Les Wort, The Boss, set the scene. He wrote these a brief time before he died. 'We had been severely inhibited during a very long sea voyage. A few days out from Sydney we were informed that the aircraft were to be flown off the ship. This news produced frenzy of activity on HMS Ruler by both the Hellcat and 1772 Squadrons in preparing the aircraft for flight; replacing radios and other equipment, degreasing guns and generally getting back to normal. Ruler returned to sea on 18th March and we flew off to RNAS Schofields (Monab 3), about 20 miles west of Sydney. When we arrived, conditions were somewhat primitive. There was still a great deal of building work going on and the finish of the Wardroom was still far in the future. In the meantime, the bar consisted of planks resting on barrels in a small hut. The Aussie building workers asked us if we had any British pennies which we gladly handed over. Later we discovered that such coins fetched very high prices because they were thought to be better balanced than Australian pennies and therefore were more suitable for the universal Australian gambling game called "Two-up", which seemed to go on all night on the camp, under footlights. At least it made a change from the blackout we had left behind. The next four months were spent in further working up with the emphasis on rocket firing, for which we usually flew to Monab 5, which was at Jervis Bay. Here we carried out a great deal of airfiring, rocket firing on the range nearby and lots and lots of ADDLs at Schofields. Our destiny was becoming much clearer; we were coming to terms with our future role as a Squadron. Working up included a few deck landings on Ruler, which was still in the offing. One such a landing by a Sub Lieutenant, who shall be nameless, reduced my own particular aircraft to three separate pieces with the result that I had to fly back to Schofields from Jervis Bay the next day in another plane. We celebrated VE Day at Schofields and a special menu was provided. On the evening of that day we decided that we ought to go into Sydney to celebrate. There was a railway running into Sydney, with Quakers Hill station just outside the camp, but on that day of all days, the railways went on strike. Not to be outdone we loaded the troops into our three-tonner, the officers into the 15 cwt and we proceeded to Sydney where we found a "ghost" town; no pubs, no cinemas, everything closed down. We split up into small groups and went our several ways. I found myself with about half-a-dozen chaps one of whom had a standing invitation to visit a family named Cox but he couldn't remember the address. We pooled our pennies and repaired to the Post Office, which was open. We began to phone the not insubstantial number of Cox's in the book. We succeeded at the third attempt and then proceeded to their house. The Cox family rose to the occasion quite nobly and we had a splendid party . . . in fact, a boomer.'

The acronym MONAB strikes one as odd because its substance, for all its jerry-built qualities, as Ian Darby referred to it, was reasonably fixed to terra firma. It meant, one has to conclude, that it was a wartime emergency airfield, solely built for Naval Squadrons which were mobile, and 1772 had proved that, in arriving there! It was a heap! Windows appeared in huts after quite a time. There was always the threat of nasty spiders and the likes and we were advised to shake out our boots in the morning because simply anything could have climbed into them overnight. We slept in mosquito nets, not because of any danger of

23.03.45	Firefly	MB389	1772	Schofields	Scott	J S/LT	RNVR	Stalled at 25 ft
28.03.45	Firefly	DV147	1772	Schofields	Hubble	RP MTO	RNVR	Swung off Runway to Stbd on landing
6.04.45	Firefly	MB378	1772	Schofields	Jobbings	SH S/LT(A)	RNVR	Stbd Wind dropped, crashed over Stbd side
6.04.45	Firefly	MB380	1772	Ruler	Hubble	RP MTO	RNVR	Crashed into Round down
10.04.45	Firefly	MB396	1772	Schofields	Trollope	GBS/LT(A)	RNVR	Selected up before being airborne
18.06.45	Firefly	MB383	1772	Schofields	Parry	AC	RNVR	Tyre burst, swung off runway, B/C collapsed
19.06.45	Firefly	DK439	1772	Schofields	Key	EA S/LT	RNVR	--do--
3.07.45	Firefly	DT979	1772	Schofields	Roberts	GD S/LT	RNVR	Collided w/Seafire & Firefly MB3948 on take off
3.07.45	Firefly	MB398	1772	Schofields	Parry	AC S/LT(A)	RNVR	Seafire throttled back damaging mainplanes

A 25's were not so numerous as at Burscough but that is partly due to the fact that several prangs escaped official records . . . it would seem! The Boss said that the Subby who shattered his aircraft shall remain nameless. We don't suppose that Roy Hubble, was ever without a name!

malaria, but just to fend off the nasties and prevent a few days of the effects of nasty bites. Sammy Samuelson says that Monabs were named after imaginary British towns or villages beginning with NAB. Johnny O'Driscoll even remembers that the Wardroom had a beamed roof and was entered by four or five wooden steps, leading to double doors. Even more remarkable is that he recalls that one of our Aussie outback neighbours regularly rode his horse up the steps, round the Wardroom and rode out again. Who needs neighbours like that? It ought to find a place in some TV Soap. Sammy further recalls that some of the Seafire pilots enjoyed a game in the Wardroom which required circumnavigation of the room without touching the floor. He remembers the cold of Australian nights; it was Autumn in the months of March and April. The only heating was by two little electric fires: the Captain stood in front of one of them and the Commander stood in front of the other. This is a prime example of pulling rank – one supposes. Sammy enjoyed the noise of frogs and crickets in the evenings. It reminded him of France. What a delightful chap he always was; just a wee bit eccentric maybe, but he noticed things and he cared about people. He was even known to dig drainage ditches around the troops tents during and after heavy rain. He had learnt the "craft" on his father's farm!

In March we went through our whole flying repertoire with the emphasis on 'the rockets'. We did more formation flying, we cork-screwed and did pair attacks and we came into contact, not too literally with some 'Boomerangs'. The Boomerang was a small Aussie fighter and a squadron of them were stationed not far away at Menangle. One day, a challenging gauntlet descended from one of these Boomerangs on to our dispersal. The challenge was for a dogfight over their base. Bob Scott records, 'I have in my log book "Beat up of 83rd RAAF (Boomerangs), Menangle airfield on 22nd March. Were there two affairs and did I miss the first?" Even to this day, Bob, a great scrapper, would appear to regret missing out on something really good! It was great fun. Wally Pritchard claimed it to be 'most exciting and showed the excellent manoeuvrability of the Firefly. The Boomerang was remarkably mobile but they didn't reckon with our Youngman flaps. We gave them a good show.'

There were many incidents in this final stage of our working up. Not all of them are recorded and some prangs are omitted from the official records. Probably just as well.

Bob Scott. "On 23rd March, the first time with rocket rails under the wings, I spread my Firefly on the end of the runway. The Boss left it there for days. Was he trying to tell me something?'

Ian Darby. 'Burn and I did some cannon and rocket firing against a

NATIVE WEAPON: Official secrecy still forbids anything like a useful description of the first single-seater fighter to be designed and produced in Australia, namely the Boomerang. But from the picture showing a line-abreast formation of them high above their native land, their resemblance to the Wirraway trainer (Australian version of the Harvard trainer) will be noticed about the wing design, while the fin and rudder resemble those of the NA-25.

Type of engine (beyond the obvious fact that it is an air-cooled radial) performance and armament are not disclosed, but it is said to be heavily armed and to possess good manoeuvrability. Long-range drop tanks can be carried under the fuselage. Under threat of invasion early in 1942, the prototype took the air 14 weeks after design was started.

A press release statement on the Boomerang, from an Australian source. On another occasion a challenge was offered by a resident Corsair Squadron. One Corsair crashed, killing the pilot. It is an unpleasant memory, because most of us in 1772 have happy memories of our scraps at Menangle.

concrete filled tank (WW1 variety) on top of a hill. Burn fired the rockets and then the cannon, the shells went up the rear end of the rockets blowing them apart. Great chunks of solid propellant smashed through the wings and a great lump lodged in the propeller spinner setting up a fearful vibration. Burn "rang" me up and said I may have to bail out as the aircraft was difficult to control. However he managed to get it back to base.'

Wally Pritchard. 'Continuing to fly with Bob Scott we had some very active exercises, particularly with air-to-ground firing. On one occasion shooting up tanks, we were so low that splinters made three holes in the wing and splintered the windscreen. What a line! – not very surprising since we had fired 8 rockets at it, plus four cannons! Another interesting moment was a W/T Range Test and fuel consumption test to Brisbane and back. I was again with Bob as pilot. As the Squadron radio officer I was required to make a formal report of our achievements which were then sent to the Admiralty and C-in-C, by the Boss. In addition to Roy Hubble and Bob, I was crew for the Boss, Croose Parry, Steve Stevens and Pete Kingston, until I flew with my new pilot, Chris Maclaren, on 21st June, and I continued with him for the rest of my Squadron flying. With Chris I had an inauspicious beginning and put up a big black. On our first navigation exercise I had applied the compass variation the wrong way. It is different in the southern hemisphere! We managed to land three hours later with a pint of fuel remaining. A reception committee of an anxious Boss and a Flying Control Officer, on overtime, welcomed us home – and there was much rejoicing!'

An ADDLs prang resulting from the Schofields 'wheel gremlin'. Hot tarmacadam runways plus ADDL's equalled havoc. We became desperately short of wheels and other spares.

(Teddy Key)

The 'shorts' and the airfield tell us that this is Schofields. The legs look as if they belong to the Boss, but Burn O'Neill and Glyn Roberts did most of our batsmen duties.

In a way, all very normal and generally regarded as standard behaviour. Croose Parry tells of the time a tyre burst with the resultant loss of control. He went veering off the runway and on to the soft ground. The Firefly tipped up on to its nose before falling back to earth, partially breaking off the entire tail section. Teddy Key had a similar accident during ADDLs, resulting in the undercarriage being ripped off. He was photographed with the remains of the prop over his shoulder and smiling hugely. The Boss was not amused: it was his aircraft, again! Despite our fondness for him, we did seem to have a habit of bending *his* aircraft. We were though, by June, beginning to have trouble with numbers of serviceable aircraft; tyres were getting very sparse. Croose tells of a prang sequence which one supposes could fit into the category of 'a biggy'. 'We were to complete deck landings on HMS Ruler just off Jervis Bay. I was fortunate in being the first to attempt to land. On my approach, coolant liquid started pouring over the windscreen, so with limited visibility I returned to the landing strip where it was discovered that the filler cap had detached itself from the tank. Six aircraft were involved in this landing-on exercise. With my return, that left five. Soon after I had landed, four returned. Stu Jobbings had hit the rounddown, and gone swimming! The remaining four took to the air again to try their luck. Soon afterwards three returned to the landing strip. Another crash on the deck! I forget if this charade went on for a further time, but anyway it proved to be a very expensive exercise.' Wally Pritchard, continuing his story of his big collection of pilots, 'I continued to fly with Roy Hubble until April when he went to Jervis Bay and pranged an aircraft on HMS Ruler after which he was grounded and we lost contact.'

Teddy Key. 'I flew three trips on the 6th April. The first lasted one hour 50 minutes during which Steve, our senior pilot, barriered. My second trip was for 40 minutes when Stu Jobbings went into the sea after hitting the rounddown and the third lasted 1 hour 10 minutes when Roy Hubble also hit the rounddown. I have no record of whether in nearly 4 hours flying I ever did land on HMS Ruler. Two days later, George Trollope selected his undercarriage up . . . before he was airborne!' For all these reasons, it was sad that again the Squadron was fragmented. Two sections of 1772 were hived off to join 1770 and 1771 for the operation on the Sakashima Islands. If things had gone a little better, perhaps the whole of 1772 would have relieved 1770 on the Indefatigable much earlier than it did. Destiny was to decide that we wait a little longer to become operational as a complete squadron. 'Qué sera, sera!'

On the 10th April, Croose Parry went to join 1770. 'I suppose when

I landed on HMS Indefatigable it was my first deck landing in a Firefly'.
(Had he missed the landings on Empress in the Irish Sea?) He
remembers a distant glimpse of New Guinea and spending a few very
hot days anchored at Leyte in the Phillipines, passing the time of day
watching alarmingly large sharks circling the ship. In the evening they
would pipe, 'hands to bathing!' During his time with 1770, he took part
in various strikes against the islands of Ishigaki and Miyako attacking
ground targets with cannon and rockets. His fellow members from 1772
were George Trollope, Mike La Grange, Glyn Roberts, Val Bennett,
Knocker White, Gordon Davidson and Johnny Palmer. They were to
rejoin us on June 9th. On the 10th May, Stu Jobbings, Don Randle,
Rhys Heaven and Dusty Millar joined 1771 on HMS Implacable.

During this very unsettling period those who remained were sent on
a jungle training course with the Australian Army. This was intended to
prepare us for those occasions when we were shot down over rainforest
country. We would then be expected not only to survive off the land but
to endeavour to return to our unit, to live and fight again. In fact it
became quite a lark. In the hands of an imaginative scriptwriter this
little interlude could have been made into an early 'Carry on'.

There were 'bombs', or paper grenades, which were used on the
rainforest paths whilst one hid in the undergrowth. Sort of pretending
to hide from the Japs. Not a laughing matter for thousands of men who
had to take this sort of training very seriously . . . or die. With 1772's
appetite for all things pyrotechnic some 'bombs' were taken back to
Schofields where they provided some fun.

Robin Henderson. 'On this course at Canungra in Queensland just
"behind" Brisbane, where Australia possessed some genuine Malayan
type jungle, we came under the heel of Aussie Army instructors. I met
one of them the other day. He still had happy memories of our
"performance" up there'. Perhaps his memory is as bad as Robin claims
his to be. Robin on being asked to provide some of his thoughts of the
old days, could only comment, "Golly, was I really there?" '

Ray Battison. 'I doubt if I would have stood much of a chance
evading the Japanese. Some hopes. It was probably the toughest, most
strenuous two weeks of my life but the laughter overcame the tears.'

Alan Rowlinson. 'There were many periods during my service with
1772 that have been memorable, but the 14 days that some of us spent
at Canungra may well have been memorable but not very enjoyable. To
be greeted on arrival via the Sydney/Brisbane train and accompanied
by a mega-army of fleas, and an Army Sergeant, who recognised that
we were straight from the flesh-pots of Sydney, did not augur well.
That we might be introduced gently to some of the hardships, was our

Jungle training at Canungra, Queensland. No. 44 Cadre. L to R: Maurice Goodsell, Ray Battison, Bob Scott, Wally Pritchard, Geoff Rham, Alan Rowlinson, Roy Melville, (in front) Johnny O'Driscoll.

Stu Jobbings and Rhys Heaven

Dusty Millar, Don's Observer when on HMS Implacable.

Mike La Grange and Don Randle

hope. The reality of our welcome was that we had to do a gym-kit run up a 2,000 feet hill, in equatorial conditions, followed next morning by a march in full kit up the same hill, followed in the afternoon by a 'double march' in full kit, plus rifles, up the same bloody hill! The course was instructive and showed us how and why we should not sleep on the ground for example. They gave us reasons why we should not try to sling a hammock between some trees, with almost lethal leaves. The relaxation in the first week was a sports afternoon, the options being base-ball, cross-country running or rugby league. The enthusiasts opted for 13-a-side rugby and they quite enjoyed it. The biter bit came during the second week which was spent under simulated stark-realistic action conditions in the jungle. An Aussie Army NCO, myself and one other, (identity unknown) played in an Army area championship rugger match for Canungra. We won, and then we marched about 4 miles back to the jungle . . . and steaks for supper. Looking back we must have become much fitter, though I didn't feel it at the time. We had a farewell party, but the biggest buzz I had got, was the thought that I had represented a unit of the Australian Army at rugby.' Johnny O'Driscoll whose stomach has always had, and still has, a direct line to his brain, recalls with his usual good humour. 'One thing I remember about Canungra was a ditty, "Hurrah for Beetox, what a delightful smell" ' Crazy man!

Conditions were certainly spartan. One could be steeped in a damp cold misery and one way of alleviating that chagrin was to jump into a stream. Once we returned from the jungle bivouac only to attend Church Parade, wet, feeling awful and more than likely, stinking to high heaven. So often the behaviour of those commissioned to torture us, seemed to go beyond the realm of normal thinking men.

Johnny Coles. 'One day a farmer rode up on horseback to tell us that the war was over. An anonymous Pom was heard to say in a tired way, "Which war?". We were the awkward squad and it must have been heartbreaking for our instructors, who couldn't quite understand our attitude to training in jungle warfare. Somehow it didn't make sense and we could not foresee ourselves baling out, maybe with a Bren Gun and other ordnances strapped to our back.'

Those who were on this course missed the VE celebrations in Sydney. Instead they lived on Army 'tac'. Johnny O'Driscoll again. 'The Aussie Army made the nights very uncomfortable and they succeeded in depriving Maurice Goodsell of his Bren Gun while he was on lookout. This sort of thing was most definitely not Maurice's scene and one remembers him crying sadly in despair when he could not get a fire to light. Dawn excursions and mushrooming made pleasant diversions (food again!). I remember lecture 17, when we were presented with amended pamphlet No. 44, "Some hints on living off the land", written by Arthur Groom of Beechmont, Queensland. There were six pages on survival technique which finished with the words, IF IN SERIOUS DOUBT TRY ANOTHER PLANT. (Reading this with your tongue in your cheek, should help.)

Teddy Key. 'One forgets the bad things of life, so some say, yet they form part of the wisdom of life. One forgets toothache . . . in time! I remember the awful tea. Quite undrinkable, but you needed the bottom half to shave with. I remember a rifle inspection. The Aussie NCO looked down the barrel of one of our rifles and commented, 'Your rifle is dirty Sir.' This unremembered colleague slowly pointed the rifle to the ground and a little plume of dust gently floated to the earth. My God! We were awful soldiers.'

Bob Scott. 'Who doesn't remember Roy Melville and the parade ground triangle? In the dead of night he was caught banging away at this iron parade ground triangle. He was lucky not to be scalped by the Australian Army "brown jobs." Who doesn't remember the open air and very chummy latrines? I remember with horror the day we all went into the river after a very hot day and came out covered with leeches.'

The 'Melville Story' is a hazy series of disconnected facts. Roy was in fact, not scalped. He was brought back under arrest. He had a friendly escort, it is thought, with one of us as part of that escort. Back at Schofields it would seem that the Boss was too busy to deal with the matter and things just dissolved into thin air. The cause of all this nonsense was that one evening at Canungra had been particularly boozy: someone had found a couple of barrels of beer. The first had been consumed and the second was taken back to the huts. On the parade ground there was this "iron hook and a steel hoop". Was it a triangle or a hoop? Suffice to say that Roy, not well known for self-control after a session, went to town on this thing in the unfriendly hours. Roy was clad in just a shirt, his little thin legs protruding from the shirt. He went on and on and on! In front of the CO., Roy was met with, "You think you can come here and bash my clanger. How would you like it if I came to your place and banged your clanger?" Roy Melville, not long since an innocent young Midshipman, replied quite coyly. "I don't think you'd be able to find one Sir".'

Throughout the months of May and June and after the Jungle Course it was more of the same. Jervis Bay and shooting guns, low-level photography which was always good flying, and Air-to-Air exercises. We also had 10 days leave in the middle of May. The Squadron in pairs or singly or even in larger groups found solace with Australian friends. In June the 1770 'eight' returned to the fold and then on 7th July we left

(Agnes Stevens)

(Teddy Key)

The Indefatigable returned from the Sakashima operations and its squadrons came to Schofields, a mobile air base (MONAB). The usual nonsense of guys released from tension appeared on our 'flight board' and the Seafire boys put up a line-shooting scene . . . for the press. Dickie Reynolds is in the background bending Teddy Key's ear. They were in the ATC in Cambridge after entry to the FAA via the Y Scheme.

84

Schofields and joined a huge fleet carrier, HMS Indefatigable.

At last, the reality of why we were out here! The European War was over and here on the opposite side of the world there was something more to do in order to eliminate the 'nasties' from their territorial control. Was it our war? Did it not now belong to the Americans? They had one huge debt to settle, Pearl Harbour. The British Pacific Fleet was to be just a part of this completion of the Pacific War. Britannia did not rule the Pacific waves, but history will show that it still had a stinging tail. The scene now changes in a huge way: 1772 at last was going to put on a show. How long would it run?

> When Britain really ruled the waves
> In Good Queen Bess's time,
> The House of Peers made no pretence
> To intellectual eminence
> Or scholarship sublime,
> Yet Britain won her proudest days
> In Good Queen Bess's time.
>
> HMS Pinafore.

A VAST NEW SCENE ... AND WE MEET A HUGE NEW LEADING LADY

'I don't know what effect these men will have upon the enemy but by God, they terrify me.' Duke of Wellington
'War was once cruel and magnificent but now cruel and squalid.' Sir Winston Churchill

It is a characteristic of our advancing years – we are all now three score and ten years of age – that our fading and unreliable memories are causing us some embarrassment. It is a corporate memory which is the basis of this story and it is a fervent hope that those memories interlock in such a way that they reproduce a whole and coherent truth. It is possible to be flippant and to remember that our near-ultimate anguish, is that moment when standing halfway up the stairs you wonder what you are going up for or coming down for. Even more shattering is the terror, when you are not certain, whether you are going up or down! So at last, there is that word . . . 'terror'. It may not have been admitted at the time but it is certain that an overwhelming thought in our minds was the fear of the fearsome Japanese enemy. We knew a great deal about his base nature: we knew about his scant regard for an honourable style of a man, engaged in war. Yet the Japanese warrior was one who spoke and wrote about 'honour'. It was however a sense of honour we could not understand. In quoting the Duke of Wellington, one is aware that he was referring to his own men, so a little licence will be excused. It was the enemy who terrified *us*.

So, neither up nor down, we wondered, 'now that "our" war was over in Europe and Hitler had been laid to rest . . . in Hell – what were we doing out here in another war? This was American, Aussie and Kiwi space.' It was a thought which probably never occurred and if it did, it couldn't have lasted very long. We wanted some action after all the preparation and indeed, all the 'nasties' of the world had to be eradicated. Again on the flippant line, perhaps we thought as Oliver Hardy had often said, 'There's another fine mess you've gotten me into.'

But what about the Japanese? How had they 'gotten' to their state? A long history lesson does not follow; that has been dealt with at great length in many other places. At the core was the blind allegiance to the Emperor whose family had reigned for at least 1600 years. Their history had begun in 660 BC when the divine-born Emperor Jimmu ascended the throne. They had an inborn and profound respect for authority and decree. Ancestor worship made the family more important than the individual and the nation, a family of families, *the* most important. For them there was no life after death, it was quite natural to sacrifice themselves unhesitatingly for the parents or Emperor. Herein lay the germ of the Kamikaze mentality. Their lack of moral courage in the hands of ruthless dictators spelled one of the most horrific national catastrophes of all time. Their capacity for unprovoked attacks was well known, even before Pearl Harbour they had attacked Korea, Russia and China. There had for many years been a great deal of animosity between Japan and America: Japan had for a very long time felt that a conspiracy existed to check their unprincipled aspirations towards territorial expansion, convincing the Japanese that their Naval power must remain in an inferior and less prestigious state than the USA. The Americans took a strong lead in international politics denying Japan's right to colonial expansion. It is of some significance to note the ultimate demise of all Empires which began in island states. Like the others they were ultimately defeated by their greed and their inability to cope with a military force over an impossibly large area. They were ultimately stretched beyond their resources. It was in 1937 that Japan decided to enlarge its Empire. It was their natural cult based upon their mythology and posing under those divine qualities of the human pretender to the throne that they could not contain their will for vile projects of aggression. Before Pearl harbour the Japanese had been given three options. One, to accept Roosevelt's terms – and then die of shame; two, ignore those terms and be forced into blockade of all essential resources for a conquering armed might or in other words, seize up economically, and three, to reject those terms outright, go to war and take the oil and iron by force. They chose the third and so Pearl Harbour or the possibility of something like Pearl Harbour was always on the American agenda. Even to this day there are certain Japanese who still believe that it was the Americans who were the aggressors. In very simplistic terms, the Americans denied the Japanese the right to expand territorially. Japan never felt that she had committed any international crime and that is manifest in all their utterances at the signing of the peace and 50 years later in 1995 when the world celebrated the end of that particularly horrific era of Japanese history.

The horrors of Japanese warfare techniques were well known to the world by 1937, and particularly to China where acts of murder, torture and rape were rife in their armies. The world powers had demanded that Japan leave China but Hitler was pillaging Europe, why shouldn't they do the same to Asia? The Japanese are a highly specialised offshoot of the Chinese race and as such are not as closely related to the Chinese as is usually thought. The spirit of the Japanese was and is, summed up in the word 'Shinto', that divine worship combined with a compulsory obedience to an autocracy of military dictators. That, amounted to a fusion of state religion and undemocratic government. It was a contemptible philosophy of duplicity and treachery, but there were however conflicting forces at work in Japan. Whilst militaristic leaders clamoured for war, the Japanese Navy was apprehensive, and opposed to war as a solution to their problems. It is highly likely that the Japanese Navy could foresee some of the problems facing a navy stretched beyond its capacity to keep naval units supplied over the vast areas of the Pacific Ocean.

From all this evolved the brutality of the enemy. A Japanese acquired the licence to be monstrous in the face of his enemy. He could in fact do almost as he pleased without any consequences: his acts were carried out as one of 'the national family'. There was no place for moral courage, to distinguish between right and wrong. They were proficient and unscrupulous at killing in cold blood and their blind obedience was to be seen in the Kamikaze and other suicidal attitudes to fighting a war. Dickie Reynolds a distinguished Seafire pilot of 894 Squadron on HMS Indefatigable, who was questioned at Lee-on-Solent at the 50th Anniversary of DJ Day remarked that the 'Japanese enemy fought to die, WE fought to live.'

A cynical conclusion of one Japanese writer was that Confucious gave them their religion, but the Christian civilisation invented 'The Bomb'.

Teddy Key. 'I spent my childhood in Cambridge. Recently there, I came across a little book written by Michael Bentinck' entitled, 'My Dad, my Hero.' It was written by the son of a man Jim, with whom I had attended elementary school and we had been in the same Church choir. He was one of many who suffered under the Japanese yoke when he and most of the Cambridgeshire Regiment were captured at Singapore. Changi was to be his hellhole for a very long time. Jim died happily with his family in Cambridge having been repatriated after the war, but his health was always suspect. He died according to his son, with a prayer of forgiveness for his captors, though he never forgave the Jap who stole the engagement ring he had purchased for his girl! I quote briefly from his book to illustrate just one small part of Japanese brutality; 'Now that Jim could move about he was soon sent to Changi prison. He and others were forced to march to prison. Some of the men had suffered leg amputations and they were not at all fit enough for such a journey; those that could get along helped those that could not. One chap near to Jim fell down; he had suffered a broken leg and arm and broken ribs in the last few days of fighting. Jim bent down to help him and as he bent down he was kicked in the backside and fell over himself. As he looked round he saw a fat little Japanese guard glaring at him saying, "you no help him – he get up himself". Jim got up and stood back in line. As his comrade tried to get up, the Jap guard kicked him down again by actually kicking at his broken leg. The foul treatment continued whilst the other Japs just laughed. The situation was remedied to some extent by a British officer.'

It is not our intention to labour the attitude of the Japanese as fighting men; suffice it to say that we were aware of it and we were shortly to be flying over the mainland of a country now seething with loss of face, with the pounding that was being meted out by American bombers.

The might of Japan, to all intents and purposes, had been destroyed before we arrived on the scene of the very last act in World War II. In November 1944 saturation raids by B29's were raining down bombs on selected targets in Japan. Prisoners of war in Omori prison have recorded that on 15th February, they saw U.S. Navy planes overhead and on 16th February, Tokyo and Yokohama were bombed. Long before the A-Bombs disintegrated them, their agony had been multiplied by B29 loads of high explosive and incendiary bombs. Wave followed wave. By March 1945 the number of big-city targets had been increased. On the 16th March, Iwo Jima fell and the British Pacific Fleet had joined the Americans in the huge Pacific Fleet that was building up as one of the largest naval fleets ever. By this time it was estimated that the Japanese Navy consisted of 5 Battleships, 3 Carriers and 12 Cruisers: a small remnant of what had been a huge fleet with a very strong emphasis on Carriers.

After considerable success in Sumatra and the stirring raids on the Palembang oilfields on 24th January 1945, the Indefatigable returned to Sydney on 10th February. She sailed from Sydney on 27th February. Her operational base was Ulithi Atoll in the Caroline Islands and from March to May, Operation 'Iceberg' was in full swing. Her role was to be part of the BPF which was to be stationed semi-independently on the left of the Fifth Fleet battle line, off the Sakashima Gunto, southwest of Okinawa and part of the Ryuki Group, to prevent the Japanese staging aircraft reinforcements, through the Sakashima Islands. The targets were therefore airfields and shipping.

It was felt that at about this time Hirohito wanted peace at any cost, but he was merely a puppet of the Army chiefs, who in their particular fanatical way, were setting up a very large series of suicide groups. Evidence of petrol shortage was obvious by April and fewer Kamikaze raids had been observed. Their thoughts were set on the real possibility of invasion of the mainland. They must have known that huge American resources were building up in the Aleutians and the bombing by B29's was now supplemented by the U.S. Navy, whose carriers could operate closer to the mainland. The destruction from the air must have been horrific to the people of Japan. The Americans were cognisant of the 'blood baths' which had cost so much life on both sides in the battle for the Pacific Islands; this fact was also having a profound effect on the American people. The 'Manhattan Project' was there in the offing and it ultimately came to an end with 'Little Boy' falling on Hiroshima on 6th August 1945 and 'Fat Man' falling on Nagasaki on 11th August. From June to September the BPF added its strength to the huge American Fleet. It was as part of the U.S. Fleet 38 and BPF 37 that 1772 was to play its part in the Pacific Battle.

The United States Task Force No. 38 was composed of:

10 Fleet Carriers
6 Light Fleet Carriers
1191 Aircraft
8 Battleships
19 Cruisers
60 Destroyers
On 13 strike days this force destroyed 2408 aircraft
and sank 924,000 tons of enemy shipping

The British Task Force No. 37 was composed of:

4 Fleet Carriers
255 Aircraft
2 Battleships
6 Cruisers
15 Destroyers
On 8 strike days this force destroyed 347 Japanese aircraft
and sank 356,760 tons of shipping.

This task force rather resembled the British Army in Burma. It was almost forgotten!

The aircraft of the British Pacific Fleet were:

Hellcats   3 Squadrons 1839, 1844, 888
Corsairs   6 Squadrons 1830, 1833, 1834, 1836, 1841, 1842
Avengers   6 Squadrons 854, 857, 820, 849, 848, 828
Seafires   4 Squadrons 894, 887, 801, 880
Fireflies   3 Squadrons 1770, 1771, 1772
Walrus   2 Aircraft

This, one of the largest groups of Royal Navy aircraft ever to accumulate in one task force, was spread over 5 Fleet Carriers at one time or another and not all the squadrons were operational at the same time because carriers and squadrons were relieved from duty at specific times.

The 6 Fleet Carriers, which had been conceived in the 1930's as armoured-hangar aircraft carriers were:

Illustrious, Formidable and Victorious which were completed to the original design.
Indomitable which had been given an extra half hangar.
Implacable and Indefatigable, which had been modified with two full-length hangars of reduced height and consequently could not operate all types of American fighters: their folded wings were too high for the hangars.

The Squadrons on board the Indefatigable during the final assault on Japan were:

820 Avenger.   Torpedo Bombers with Pilot, Observer and Telegraphist Air Gunner, 4 machine guns in wings, belly and turret. 4 × 500 bombs or 1 torpedo.
894 Seafire.   Single seat fighter. 2 × 20 mm Cannon and 4 machine guns.
887 Seafire.   ditto.
1772 Firefly. Two seater fighter-bomber. 4 × 20 mm Cannon, 8 × 60 lb Rockets.

What of the huge new leading lady? She was in fact both monstrous 'diva' and a major 'prop'. She was a massive revolving stage with all its incumbent paraphernalia. She was HMS Indefatigable, Fleet Carrier. She possessed a sense of 'vastness', 'unfathomableness' and 'mystery'. Mystery in that one never really ever came to terms with her; one never understood her depth, her length and her girth. She was a magnificent power; she was the leading lady who dominated you, overawed you

HMS INDEFATIGABLE
For 12 years she was a magnificent fighting ship. It took two months for the British Iron and Steel Corporation to tear her into little pieces at the end of 1956.

with all her trappings, lifts and lofty ladders and gangways, trap doors, lights, ropes and pulleys, all in and on and below that treacherously knobbled and lumpy, vast 'flat-top' stage . . . Théatre vérité!

Sammy Samuelson. 'When I was at Arbroath on the 61st Observer's Course we went to Rosyth one day where the Indefatigable was in dry dock. We actually walked underneath it, little guessing that about 16 months later some of us would be on board. The Indefat. (the abbreviation usual in our casual language) was "VAST". I would never find my way about it. However, it was very seaworthy. I shared a cabin with seven others: it had been a gun room. There were holes in the deckhead above my bunk which were made there when the guns of an Avenger had gone off when its wings had been folded. A Sub-Lieutenant had been on the bunk and was killed. It was so crowded that we had to keep our gear outside, but it was a tough old ship and had weathered a Kamikaze crash on deck before we embarked at Sydney. Unlike the American carriers, our fleet carriers could withstand such a tremendous impact. The scars were still there when 1772 went aboard.'

Teddy Key. 'She was big, big; and in consequence a very impersonal place to live. I find it difficult to remember coming into contact with chaps I knew in the other squadrons. As stores officer I never really grasped the shortest route to the squadron stores office! The food was average but living in a Wardroom was at least civilised, except in the typhoon when absolutely nothing stayed in place. I remember that my cabin, shared with three others, was next door to the Royal Marine port side-stern gun turret. Even during practice it was hell to be in that cabin and nothing stayed in its place. I did however know my way to the covered quarterdeck just below the flight deck rounddown. To this cooler place one took one's folding camp bed to sleep at night; it was stifling hot in that cabin. Who were my cabin mates? It is just that sort of detail which now defeats me – and most of us, at times.'

The Indefatigable was built at John Brown's Shipyard, Clydebank. She was laid down on 3rd November 1939 and launched on 8th December 1942. She was commissioned exactly one year later on 8th December 1943 and completed on 3rd May 1944. Indefatigable had a complement of 1,700 ship's staff and about 800 aircrews and maintenance staff. She was designed for a speed of 32 knots and her sister ships were the Indomitable and Implacable. She was, at the end of her life, able to claim that she had been the first carrier to land on a twin-engined aircraft, the first to carry out refuelling astern of the oiler and take on bombs and ammunition. She was the first British carrier to be hit by a Kamikaze. The first deck landing on her was carried out by none other than Buster Hallett, one of the Fleet Air Arm's most distinguished flyers of WW2. The first Fireflies were under the command of Major Cheeseman RM. when they attacked the Tirpitz and the oilfields at Palembang.

The Indefatigable was taken apart at the Faslane Shipping Company on the Clyde. Four tugs took her from her mooring and she was cut up with efficiency and 'in an uncaring manner'. HMS Indefatigable was dead: the year, 1956. But before that, 1772 made her acquaintance, though most of us would claim that we never really came to terms with her completely; we knew little bits of her and we knew in varying degrees other men on board. Big was not always beautiful when it came to naval ships but the Indefatigable was majestic and powerful, and she was our home during a most memorable part of our youth. She withstood all that Japan could throw at her and her record of service was quite outstanding. It took one American pilot in a Hellcat to put her out of action. Thank you Yank . . . we live to tell this little tale.

We remember however our relative size in this huge Pacific gathering. Perhaps our story pales in comparison with other great squadrons of Avengers, Hellcats, Corsairs, Fireflies and Seafires. Carriers such as HMS Illustrious, at the end of 'Iceberg' returned to Sydney, jaded and worn out. Hers was a great story which had stretched over a long and distinguished career. Her personnel, whether Corsair pilots who had suffered many losses or squadron maintenance crews and the ship's company, had worn themselves out: the tiredness existed at every level. There had been the sometimes acrimonious relationship between U.S. and the British Governments and this was to continue between the

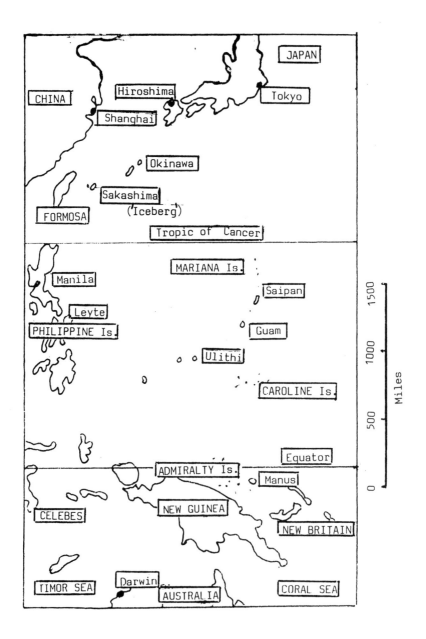

The Pacific Theatre . . .
. . . of War.

94

Admirals, to the final battle over the Japanese mainland. The end was never expected to be pretty, with the Manhattan Project in the background and the intense feeling of revenge which resided in the USA, regarding Pearl Harbour. It was not expected to be glamorous or indeed a great spectacle; just one hell of a slog; indeed, almost 'forgotten'. The next phase acquired some fresh, young faces among a few older ones. 'The "worn out" and "twitched" countenances would be replaced by a new enthusiasm and fearlessness.'

> Once more unto the breach, dear friends, once more;
> Or close the wall up with our English dead.
> In peace there's nothing so becomes a man
> As modest stillness and humility;
> But when the blast of war blows in our ears,
> Then imitate the action of the tiger:
> Stiffen the sinews, summon up the blood,
> Disguise fair nature with hard-favour'd rage.

Henry v

THE PERFORMANCE ... A MODERATE RUN ONLY

'By God, it was a close run thing.'   *The Duke of Wellington*

'History makes one shudder and laugh by turns.'

Horace Walpole

Our small part of the war was not really a close-run thing at all. The Japanese were finished; it was just a matter of time and tidying up the loose ends. The enemy was bound to be a divided one, but the fanatical element was still large enough to be a nuisance and a very real danger. The Allies therefore had to convince these people that they were finished, and that could only be done by invasion or battering them into total submission.

It was a close-run thing in that 1772 eventually arrived on board a Fleet Carrier with a job to be done. We seemed to have taken a long time to finish our training; we had been fragmented by the loss of aircraft and crews to 1770 and 1771 who were in action in the Sumatra and Sakashima battles. 1771 remained on Implacable for the final assault on the mainland. How close did it become before those with the big decisions to make decided that 1770 should stay in place on Indefatigable. They didn't and we had to replace a very fine performance. 1770 had a most distinguished record and from Tirpitz to the Pacific had won one DSO, 9 DSC's, 10 Mentioned in Dispatches. Two had been awarded posthumously. Under Major Cheeseman they had become a most competent squadron and we had to follow them. Anyway, our show opened "nervously", an apt word, because only a few of us had had combat experience. The CO. Les Wort, had followed a very distinguished course and he was a gentle but very firm leader. The 'Show' opened and many years later it was subtitled 'The Forgotten Fleet' – one of our worst reviews which stuck for 50 years, until a little revival and glorification in September 1995. What will 1996 and beyond produce? 'Which Fleet was that? Again please – I didn't catch what you said?'

The task of the British Fleet, together with its larger, American counterpart was to:

— Reduce Japan's naval strength and land force.
— Attack strategic targets on the Mainland.
— Investigate the strength of the Japanese in N. Honshu and Hokkaido. It was likely that ultimate plans to invade from the Aleutians would be centred on these northern islands.
— Destroy the merchant shipping strength.
— Provide air defence for the Fleet known as CAP, Combat Air Patrol. These activities would be carried out by escort duties, low level strikes, for the most part with dive-bombing Avengers and ground attacks by everyone.

On the 28th June, the British Pacific Fleet, (BPF) sailed without Indomitable and Indefatigable. We sailed out of Sydney later, on July 7th, and Chris Maclaren recalls landing-on on Indefatigable on that date. Admiral Vian went to Formidable and flew his flag from that Fleet Carrier and Implacable took over from Indomitable. On 10th July Task Force 38 began its attack on the Japanese mainland.

Eric Bramhall, Johnny Coles, Bob Scott, Chris Maclaren and Wally Pritchard recall a dummy strike with 820 on Finschafen in New Guinea. Teddy Key and Sammy Samuelson were involved with a 'throw-off shoot' by Indefatigable on the destroyer HMS Wakeful. Something must have gone wrong because it is recorded that Commander(O) on Indefatigable had sent the culprits over to the Wakeful to apologise.

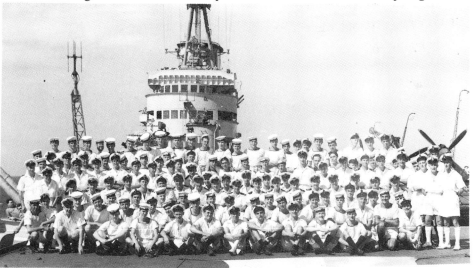

1772 Squadron aboard HMS Indefatigable.
. . . resplendent in tropical whites.

Teddy Key adds that his memory is a complete bank on this one and that it must have been two other fellows! Interception exercises were also carried out at about this time.

July 12th 1945

Arrived at Manus in the Admiralty islands. It was very hot and we were able to swim in the sea, with a huge steel net strung below us as shark protection. A less visible enemy proved to be the coral polyp and several managed to get 'coral ear'. We were now consuming our salt tablets and drinking plenty of lime juice. The heat in the cockpits when flying and indeed even on board was beginning to highlight the hazards of tropical life. We could have fresh water showers only at specific times. Sea water showers, one could have at any time. The shower line-up was something to see! Rows of tanned 'objects', but highlighted by gentian violet groins! The nasty little itches and blisters were beginning to be a nuisance.

July 13th 1945

We left Manus.

July 14th 1945

The first bombardment of the mainland by the BPF, but not Indefatigable.

July 15th 1945

We are involved in another practice strike and we are given the task of stern escort.

July 16th 1945

Admirals Rawlings and Vian are in control of the BPF whilst Admiral Halsey is in control of the whole Fleet. W. F. Halsey Jun. known as 'Bull Halsey', a sort of Patton of the U.S. Navy, was a very formidable character. The story of the relationships which existed between the British and U.S. Admirals would fill another book. It all seemed to work fine, though always there existed an undercurrent of 'feeling'. This had started way back in the discussions with Winston Churchill about the British role in the Pacific. Did the Americans really want us there? Nevertheless we were there and the 'power' men had to sort it out.

July 17th 1945

The British Pacific Fleet, Task Force 38, carried out its first strike on the mainland of Japan. 1842 (Corsairs), 1834 (Corsairs) 1771 (Fireflies) from the three carriers were involved. There were 37 offensive sorties and 153 patrol sorties. 9 aircraft were destroyed and 9 damaged. We were making our way north very fast, but found time to celebrate the 'Crossing the Line'. 120°F recorded in the Galley.

July 18th 1945

Airfields and other installations in Tokyo area attacked. First British aircrews were lost; 2 Corsair pilots.

July 19th 1945

The weather was very bad with typhoons about the area and Rawlings' Task Force was separated from Halsey's main fleet. One of the problems which began to manifest itself early on and was to be a constant problem for the men in charge of this huge fleet, was oiling. It would be safe to assume, that at the time, those of us at the bottom of the pecking order were unaware of these problems. The Fleet was still moving as fast as possible to its rendezvous under the command of Admiral Rawlings. The only flying was a CAP.

July 20th 1945

Today we arrived at our rendezvous and we joined the main fleet. 1772 was airborne and Croose Parry had some problems with hooks, wires and barriers. He has never made much comment on this incident except to proclaim his innocence. Deck landing of course has always been at the 'pranging face' of naval flying. Taking off is fairly easy; flying is not too bad. In these calmer and detached moments 50 years on, one can conclude that nothing was easy! Deck landings were a whole new ball-game. Our batsmen, 'Cappy' Masters, Peter Broome and David Bryce-Buchanan were very good and their records in speed-of-landing-on, were magnificent.

If most aircraft had problems with landing on, then the Seafire had even more, for two main reasons. One, the forward visibility due to the 'long nose' of that aircraft and the other, the rather fragile narrow chord undercarriage. The days to come saw frequent collapsed undercarriages. Batsmen lived with the pride of putting a whole squadron of Seafires down on to the Indefatigable without a blemish, in just over 30 seconds! The batsman signals translated to the pilots his judgement of the aircraft 'attitude'. They 'said' Go up, Go down, Go faster, Go starboard, Go port, Cut engine. The blow to one's pride was, 'Go round again! The worst one was 'Next time, put your undercarriage down!' There were 8 arrester wires for the pilot to catch on to, plus number 9 which tried to stop one going into the barrier. The 3rd wire was generally considered to be the best though they tried to get you on to numbers 4 and 5 if the ship was pitching.

Bob Scott, not long after leaving Sydney. 'Some of us, maybe only

The landing space could look exceedingly small . . .

me, were deemed to be short on deck landings. The Indefatigable and escorts turned off course and came into wind. My first deck landing was horrific, although accident free. I was paraded before Commander Flying for "strip-taking-off". Why not The Boss, I thought? Then in front of Captain Graham, the Commanding Officer of the carrier, I was given another wigging. He proceeded to tell me how to do deck landings, including putting the "Helm" hard over when passing the bridge down wind. Commander Flying was embarrassed! My embarrassment came later; the Fleet was turned off course again just for me.

Into wind once more, I took off twice and landed on twice.' Bob fails to record his or other's assessment of those two landings.

July 21st 1945

There were still some problems with typhoons about the area. Rawlings

'BB'... David Bryce-Buchanan says... 'you are fine... stay that way.'

'... but, not like that old chap.' NB. Nobody admits to this one.

was concerned that the refuelling problems would cause the Indefatigable to lose a day's strike. There was minimal flying on this day because of the typhoons. A meeting of top brass took place on the King George V Battleship. For the first time in this operation the chiefs of the two fleets were to meet. Halsey and his Chief of Staff met Admirals Rawlings, Vian, who was now in charge of the First British Carrier Squadron, and Rear Admiral Edelsten, commanding the destroyer flotillas.

July 22nd 1945

A day of little significance. There was some contact with units of the Fleet Train.

July 23rd 1945

We sailed to take up our flying position for the 24th, the day the American and British Fleets would commence the final destruction of the Japanese Navy whose remaining units were well camouflaged at Kure in the Inland Sea. As far as the Americans were concerned this would be final and complete revenge for Pearl Harbour. There were other political issues at stake and these were but a part of the Potsdam agreement. There were two Seafire prangs.

July 24th 1945

There was at this time some conflict between Rawlings and Halsey about the British role. The Japanese Fleet was in tatters; B29's from The Marianas, aided the U.S. Navy in this huge destruction. Although the BPF were not included in this 'revenge' operation, 1772 and other squadrons of Indefatigable, flew their first mission. The strikes started at 0545 and there were 15 strikes in all, 5 of them combined with Avengers, Seafires and Corsairs. The ship's company had a busy day; hands were closed up for 'Action Stations' at 0400 and 'Hands to Defence Stations' was signalled at 2100.

Teddy Key. 'Sammy and I did two strikes in the one day. We were airborne for a total of 7 hours. I remember breakfast as one of the most difficult meals I ever had to consume. The nerves were jangling and the Boss with more experience than me said that he too was just a trifle scared. Tokushima, the first strike, was at briefing described as being one of the strongest defended bases, with 200 plus guns. This airfield was very close to Kure and also in the Inland Sea. We were scheduled to do quite a complex operation with different angles of approach and therefore, a great deal of criss-crossing, coming in very low, escaping low before climbing to our rendezvous spot.

One Seafire and one Avenger were lost. Two Seafires from 887 ditched and one pilot broke his leg. Another Seafire from 887 had to belly-land on the deck. Other targets on the day were Masuda, Matsushima, Niigata, Takamatsu and the Japanese Carrier, Kaijo.

The Strike Report on Tokushima was signed by Les Wort who flew in Firefly 270. The following summary is based on a detailed report recorded under 1772 records at the Public Records Office at Kew.

Strike Report 24.7.1945 Tokushima

Tactical approach height	8,500 feet
Weather	Good
Wind	050/10
Angle of dive	45–50 degrees
Speed	300 knots
Rounds fired	600 per Cannon
Open and cease fire	6,000 and 1,000 Yds
Result of attack	Guns attacked ceased fire temporarily accurate (sic)
Getaway	Down to 0 feet. East to R/V
Flak	Phosphorous. Meagre. Inaccurate

The second strike of 1772 was on Takamatsu Airfield and Ajiri Saki Harbour. The Strike Report again signed by The Boss is summarised:

Strike Report 24.7.1945 Takamatsu

Initial Report	Nothing seen at airfield
Open and cease fire	2,000 and 1,000 Yds
Rounds fired	2,000. Results not seen
Damage inflicted	2 Luggers damaged
Getaway	Low-level jinking
Flak	Nil

Teddy Key and Sammy Samuelson. 'What were all those white puffs all around us?'

Among the targets of the day was the Japanese carrier, Kaiyo. The carrier was hit once, so one report claims. In fact all our four carriers claimed a share of the Kaiyo. Her back was broken and she was sinking. The Americans also claimed hits. Two frigates were also sunk as well as many minor vessels. 15 aircraft were destroyed on the ground and 30 damaged. Task Force 37 had flown 416 sorties for the loss of four aircraft.

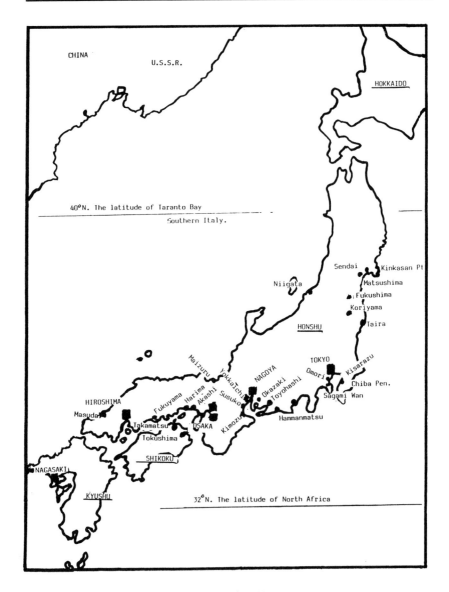

CHINA

U.S.S.R.

HOKKAIDO

40°N. The latitude of Taranto Bay
Southern Italy.

Sendai
Kinkasan Pt
Niigata
Matsushima
Fukushima
Koriyama
HONSHU
Taira

Maizuru
TOKYO
Kisarazu
Yokkaichi
NAGOYA
Omori
Chiba Pen.
HIROSHIMA
Fukuyama
Harima
Okazaki
Sagami Wan
Masuda
Akashi
Susuko
Toyohashi
Takamatsu
Kimozu
USAKA
Hammanmatsu
Tokushima

SHIKOKU

NAGASAKI

KYUSHU
32°N. The latitude of North Africa

Indefatigable and 1772 targets.

Tokushima
A briefing photograph.

(Val Bennett)

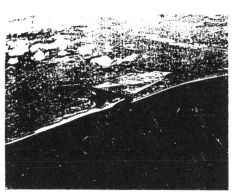

Tokushima Airfield
Approaching the target.

(Val Bennett)

*Croose
Parry and
his
Observer
Knocker
White.*

(Johnny
Coles)

*Teddy Key
and his
Observer
Sammy
Samuelson.*

(Johnny
Coles)

Croose Parry. 'Of the seven strikes in which I participated four were against airfields which entailed opening fire on the surrounds of the airfield hoping to quieten the ack-ack defences and then we would try to choose, as fast as possible, specific targets, such as aircraft on the ground and the hangars. Unfortunately more often than not these aircraft proved to be only dummies.' One does to this day wonder about the claims made by aircrews. Croose is recorded as one of the honest ones.

The dispersal of Japanese aircraft on the ground and among the neighbouring trees was not always known to us and too often 'the get in fast and get out faster' strafing method meant that targets only a short distance to the left or right of the blatantly phoney aircraft on the open areas of the airfield received too little of our attention. Subsequent evidence from aerial photographs showed these aircraft quite plainly.

It was on this first day that 1772 had its first casualty.

Teddy Key. 'Steve Stevens, our Senior Pilot and I were one of those pairs of aircraft which had become detached after our attacks. Flying back to the carrier in the most appalling weather, I was literally "glued" to Steve's wingtip. With cockpit hood back in conditions which made us bob up and down in a most alarming manner, the rain made visibility very difficult. There was a wicked red light in the cockpit, where it shouldn't have been! Steve knew where he was and had climbed steadily to get a homing beacon signal. We could hear the transmissions of one of our aircraft who was obviously lost but did not have the height. Steve called to him to "climb, climb". It was confirmed later that Maurice Goodsell was having trouble with his long-range tanks and was very short on fuel. They ditched and Maurice did not survive. Don

Don Banks

Banks climbed out successfully and lived to tell his tale. Three weeks later he was back with us and even flew again. His story will keep until the time he returned to the Indefatigable.

July 25th 1945

The bad weather of the previous day was still with us. The thermals were huge; it was awful weather for flying and several strikes had to be aborted. The enemy had made several attacks on the Fleet and Formidable's Hellcats shot down 3 Japanese planes. A torpedo bomber was also damaged. Targets included Tokushima airfield and harbour targets in Shikoku at Ajiro Saki. Some coastal vessels were sunk. On a strike, escorting Avengers, Peter Kingston and Glyn Roberts orbited a ditched Avenger crew until they were picked up by a submarine.

Ian Darby. 'We attacked targets of opportunity in Ajiro Saki and aircraft were destroyed on a Tokyo area airfield.'

Chris Maclaren. 'We attacked targets in Ajiro Saki in Firefly 275; chiefly, we strafed shipping. With Wally Pritchard in the back seat we were involved with one ship being sunk.'

Bob Scott. 'We flew two strikes that day, the first against Ajiro Saki and then a Tokyo airfield.

Strike Report 0730. *Tokushima*

Target	Harbour vessels
Weather	Down to 500 feet
Wind	Nil
Angle of Attack	10 degrees
Open and cease fire	200 and 50 yards
Speed over target	240 knots
Rounds fired	600 per cannon
Damage inflicted	2 boats sunk. One fire started.
Comment	20 mm OK but R/P would have been better
Flak.	Nil. Went round for another attack.
Conclusion	All equipment fine.
	Signed Lt. C. P. R. Stevens.

Strike Report. *Tokushima*

Target	Grass airfield
Approach Height	6,000 feet
Weather	10/10 at 8,000 feet
Wind	045/20k
Angle of attack	45 degrees
Open and cease fire	1,000 and 100 Yds
Bursts	3 sec . . . 2 sec . . . 2 sec . . . 4 sec.

*Gordon Davidson and
Johnny Palmer.*
(Johnny Palmer)

Speed over target	270 knots
Rounds fired	650 per gun
Flak	Heavy gunfire before and during attack. Light guns away. One hit in tail with 303. Signed Sub. Lt. Gordon Davidson and Sub. Lt. Johnny Palmer.

The prangs of the day included; two Seafires from 887, one breaking a leg of the undercarriage and the other Seafire bouncing over the wires and ending up in the barrier. Also two Seafires from 894; Sub. Lt. Gall was killed when landing on with an oiled-up windscreen. He came against the batsman's wave and hit the barrier, The barrier caught his head. The other Seafire hit the barrier but with less tragic results.

As the Indefatigable retired for refuelling there were the usual attempts to find us, by the enemy. One Jap was shot down by a U.S. plane and a parachute was destroyed by a Formidable Hellcat. Hanging on it was a black box; an attempt to locate the fleet position by a homing beacon. There had been at least 3 Japanese raids that day.

A sketch of Fireflies of 1772 Squadron attacking shipping in the Inland Sea. By Val Bennett.

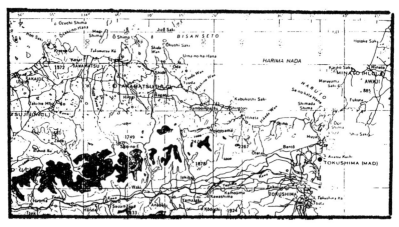

Takamatsu and Tokushima on Shikoku, were frequent visiting spots during the Fleet's stay in the area.
Takamatsu raid. 'As we strafed, close to the ground, the Avengers dropped their bombs ... a trifle ahead of schedule, for our comfort.'

Flight Sergeant Fryer.

Gordon Macrow.

Harry Russell.

John Price.

Some 'youngsters' who cared for our Fireflies and kept 'em flying.

July 26th 1945

The Fleet moved to a position where Admiral Fisher's Fleet Train was waiting to refuel us and many other ships. Oiling had become a very serious issue. Spares and provisions were very difficult to come by and maintenance crews had to use a great deal of wit and ingenuity to keep things going. Wireless chaps such as Gordon Macrow must have had a very pressing time because radio and radar parts were in very short supply. We were short on most things as well as food. The temperature was still very high with recordings well over the 100-mark. We received news of the Labour Party landslide in the UK. Thank you Winston for all your effort! Japan had suggested a negotiated peace. At Potsdam on 17th July the United Kingdom, the United States and China, offered unconditional surrender or prompt and utter destruction. Russia was not at war with Japan and did not join in the ultimatum. The first Atomic Bomb was beginning to be assembled.

July 27th 1945

The refuelling was completed with a reasonable degree of success with some help from the Americans. The weather had improved considerably.

July 28th 1945

The U.S. 3rd Fleet renewed its bombardment; the Japanese Navy virtually ceased to exist. Land-based bombers supplemented the American Navy attacks and the BPF were excluded for the third time. The Americans had made it abundantly clear that some of this Pacific War was in the nature of a personal revenge and the job was entirely theirs. Understandable in a way, but the British Admirals were not always pleased about the snubs. 1771 Fireflies started off the day by setting fire to a vessel in Sato Bay. At 0550, 1772 flew to Harima Shipyard in Oo Bay. Other targets that day were Akashi airfield and Fukuyama. 260 strikes both individual and combined, were launched. One of the individual strikes was sent off at 0740. Pete Kingston with Val Bennett as Observer set off to patrol and keep in contact with two downed Corsair pilots. At 1145, 1772 was again launched to repeat the earlier strike on the harbour at Harima and Habu on the Inland Sea. Ian Darby records in his log book, 'Attacked Harima Shipyard and sank 7,000 ton tanker.' Later he was to say in Stuart Eadon's Kamikaze, that there were six Fireflies involved in that strike all with 20 mm cannons. 'We were "shouted" a gin by Captain Q. D. Graham who seemed pleased with us.' Wally Pritchard, flying with Chris Maclaren, said that two 7,000 ton tankers and 3 MV's were left burning. Differences about what happened after our attacks were bound to happen. One went screaming down, aimed and then 'got to hell out of it' as quickly as possible. There was not always a lot of time just to admire one's work. Teddy Key says: 'Sammy sitting behind me, but now 50 years on, claims that he could not remember much in those conditions, he had his eyes closed; no doubt prayed a little and then waited his turn to do his bit, such as

Val Bennett, Pete Kingston   *Chris Maclaren and Wally Pritchard*

getting us back home safely.' There was a lot going on as Croose Parry says. 'On the occasion of the strike against Harima Shipyard, I remember as we neared the target being fascinated for a fleeting second by the different coloured puffs of smoke which were appearing around us, then realising what they were, quickly taking avoiding action.' the six crews on this strike included Steve Stevens/Mike La Grange, Teddy Key/Sammy Samuelson, Johnny O'Driscoll/Geoff Rham, Chris Maclaren/Wally Pritchard, Bob Scott/Rollo Norman.

A Reuter Report of the day was headed 'Allied Air Fleet hits at Tokyo'. 'Heavy bombers and fighters were steaming (sic) across Japan yesterday following the attack on 6 of the 11 cities which the Japanese had been warned were marked for destruction. Baron Suzuki, the Japanese Prime Minister, yesterday, according to Tokyo, told journalists "Japan will ignore the Allies' surrender ultimatum and will continue unswervingly in their efforts to prosecute the war". 'One of the main British carrier plane targets yesterday, the Harima Shipyard, was left a mass of debris and smoke, with the dock squarely hit and engineering shops destroyed. Shipyards at Habo and Shanosho were also heavily hit.'

The raid was of course one of the combined strikes, with Avengers, Corsairs, Seafires and Fireflies taking part. At last 1772 had reason to feel pleased with their effort; it had not always been thus in their months of preparing for just such an occasion: but it was not without a sad loss.

In this combined action, 8 aircraft had been lost, but only one crew, that was Steve Stevens and his Observer Mike La Grange. We had dived from 2,000 feet according to a strike report, quite steeply, before levelling out to 15° and a low-level getaway. The rendezvous was 3,000 feet, and to the south east, before setting a course of 163°(M) for home. 'One of our chickens was missing'. The dive was in a designated formation, but Steve did not join up with rest of us. Details were and still are sparse; it is difficult now, to ascertain for certain which of the two raids crews were on. One was at 0550 and the second at 1145. Each strike lasted a total air time of just less than 3½ hours. As far as one can conclude, Steve led one attack and Les Wort, the CO, led the other. Les Wort's strike report records 'meagre and inaccurate flak'. This was not the case with Steve's strike.

Admiral Halsey's signal was thus:

'Mark well the 28th July to Dumbos and Lifeguard, to CAP and men of the surface team, to the valiant British force on the right flank, well done. For the great flying fighters who fought it out over Japan to a smashing victory I have no words that I can add to the glory of the factual record they wrote with their courage, blood and lives.'

Information received from the South African Naval Museum adds the following: 'Mike La Grange's pilot, Lieut.(A) Rod Stevens RCNVR was leading 1772's Fireflies to escort a strike on 28.7.45 by Avengers against Harima Shipyard, Honshu. They arrived over Oo Bay about 1500 hours. The pilot was last heard of on the R/T, ordering the escort to attack its designated target, a tanker in the bay. On leaving the target the flight split up to strafe a number of luggers individually. It was at this point that Steve and Mike's Firefly was last seen, as the flight split up at not more than 500 feet. Their grave is unlocated. La Grange's name is commemorated on the Plymouth Naval Memorial, Panel 95, Column 1. On the day of his loss the BPF flew off 155 sorties, 118 making attacks in and around the Inland Sea. Strangely, most published British sources refer to only one aircraft, an Avenger, as having been lost. They also say that the Harima strike was in the morning and not the afternoon. It might be noted that his loss may have been due to AA fire, enemy fighters, the Corsairs met a few, or the weather which began to deteriorate later in the day.'

July 29th 1945

Bad weather most of the day. The Battleship, King George V and 3 Cruisers joined the U.S. Fleet in the bombardment of Hammanmatsu on Honshu. Two of the cruisers collided in the fog. Remember that

Rod (Steve) Stevens
(Agnes Stevens)

Mike La Grange.
A Sketch by Val Bennett.

three of us had done such a thing in the murk of Lancashire many months earlier. We wonder who signed their equivalent of the A25 'prang report'? The bombardment was not one of the great bombardments in naval history but apparently it did have yet another effect on the declining civilian morale. The only flying of the day was 'Seafire patrols'.

Another 894 Seafire did a spectacular bounce over the arrester wires, hit the island and the No. 3 barrier. It disintegrated in quite a spectacular way. Those not flying would choose to go to that edge of the flight deck known as 'the goofers'. In retrospect it seems a ghoulish habit, like the modern morbidity of wanting to gaze on a road accident. It was a happy day for the pilot, he was quite intact and who cared about another Seafire; who ever ran a war at a profit?

July 30th 1945

Despite the weather which promised typhoons in the area, strikes were again the order of the day. 336 sorties were in fact carried out. Among the targets were airfields on south west Honshu and shipping at Maizuru

A spectacular crash on the day. An 820 Squadron Avenger went over the side and was left dangling by the arrester wire, still attached to the Avenger's hook. The crew climbed to safety.

Seafire prangs could be spectacular

and Nagoya Bay. 1771 were given the shipping target at Maizuru harbour. At 0535, 1772 accompanied Avengers on a strike against Susuku airfield. Cloud was 10/10 over the target and the Avengers bombed through the clouds. Les Wort led the Fireflies below cloud to strafe the airfield. 'We saw very little, for the weather was indeed very bad.' The surface ships continued their bombardments of shipping: even small craft received scant respect. It was always possible that even the most innocent craft could have been a suicide vessel.

The second 1772 involvement: the planes were launched at 1145 to attack shipping at Yokkaichi on the Ise Wan. Ian Darby records that when attacking Susuko airfield they too had had little success with the strafing but had chased an enemy aircraft which disappeared. Chris Maclaren and Wally Pritchard attacked the oil depot and refinery at Yokkaichi. Bob Scott took part in both raids on this day. Two strikes on one day were exhausting and we all had a share of this. There was not

A fairly typical Japanese target designated as 'targets of opportunity'. Japanese Communications had been reduced to small coastal freighters.

117

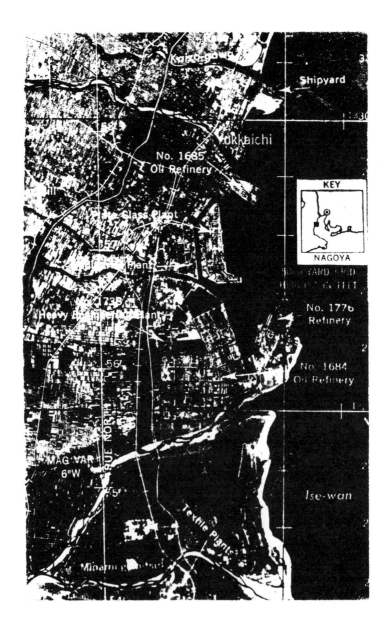

The target area . . . Yokkaichi.

(Val Bennett)

Bob Scott and Rollo Norman

a great deal to report with regard to damage. Perhaps by this time most of Japan had given up and only pockets of activity literally, 'soldiered on'.

It was not a good day for 887 Seafire Squadron because they lost a popular Kiwi pilot in Lt. J. D. Alexander. He was shot down on the Nagoya raid. He had run in to one of those pockets of accurate anti-aircraft firing. Enemy planes were now very thin in the air, but the Japanese light ack-ack was something to be feared. Ian Darby with Burn O'Neill as pilot was launched to search for their compatriot, Doug Alexander, in the mouth of Nagoya Bay. They sighted a long-range tank floating in the harbour but Doug had been killed in his plane and hit the sea.

The sea was quite heavy and an 887 Seafire buckled his undercarriage on landing. Claims that day were 6 enemy aircraft destroyed and 6 damaged besides a number of different types of small shipping. Two Seafires and a Corsair with their pilots were lost to flak over the targets. The enemy aircraft shot down were 'bogeys' which were attempting to get to the Fleet. They were dealt with by the patrolling Seafires and Corsairs. It is surprising now to recall in the hugeness, not only of the Fleet, but of the carrier, that we seemed to exist with little knowledge of all these details. Today a Kamikaze had done a lot of damage to a U.S. carrier some way from our fleet and killed many on board. It was known that the Kamikaze force was being developed into a very big threat.

Johnny O'Driscoll and Geoff Rham. 'We were on the early morning raid on Tokushima. 10/10 cloud hampered the operation and details of any damage inflicted was sketchy. Having returned to the carrier we were approached by the Boss with the news that a Seafire had been seen to go down off the coast at Ise Wan, the large Nagoya Bay, and it would be greatly appreciated if a search could be made of the area. Accompanied by Burn O'Neill and Ian Darby we returned to the coastal area but failed to find anything of significance and we had no option but to commence the return journey. Round trips to the Japanese coast averaged over 3 hours and necessitated the use of overload fuel tanks to complete the trip, so the news that Johnny had noted that a warning light was indicating that all was not well, gave food for thought. In addition Estimated Time of Arrival, as deduced by Geoff's dead-reckoning navigation, failed to agree with the position of the carrier, even the Fleet! This was depressing and Burn and Ian indicated that climbing higher might put us in touch with the radio beacon, a device which in morse code sent out signal letters in many segments of the circle. Eventually contact was made. It was a close call and we had to request a direct approach to land on. Ground crew later expressed their wonder at the frighteningly low content of the fuel tanks. Literally home and dry, with an eggcup of gas.'

There were many rough times when life on a carrier seemed to come cheaply. Did we ever think that any day now 'it could be me!' We were young we suppose and had less sense than we do now, despite the failing grey cells.

July 31st 1945

Indefatigable took on petrol most of the day; tomorrow it was planned to take on oil. There was a developing shortage of Seafires and Corsairs were busy with 'Ramrod' strikes and there always seemed to be the threat of typhoons near us.

August 1st to August 8th 1945

This was a rather dull period; just 'being at sea'. The reasons have been explained very briefly and during this time the Fleet was being replenished in every way. A few CAPs were flown. There were many false alarms and 'promises' that strikes would be staged. First it was the 5th and then 8th/9th.

Croose Parry. 'I remember on one occasion I volunteered to fly a "flyable dud" to an escort carrier in the Fleet Train. The take-off was rather hairy as the engine was not giving its full power and after trundling down the deck, instead of climbing into the sky, the plane sank alarmingly as I left the carrier and just managed to stagger into the air before we "hit the drink". On arriving at the escort carrier I proceeded to make what I thought was a good approach and landing, but I still ended up touching the barrier. It transpired that on catching a wire, the hook broke. Although no other damage was done to the plane, "I still had to render my A25!"

Enemy aircraft were known to be stalking us but the 8th was a very foggy day, "so why", thought Admiral Halsey, "tell them where we are?" '

August 6th, however was a very special day in other respects, though we lived that day, as far as one can remember, in blissful ignorance!

This was the day on which the first atomic bomb was dropped on Hiroshima. The damage caused was frightening and this is not the place to detail its horrors. Strikes had been suspended for a while and we wondered whether it was the threat of typhoons which was the cause. On strikes just before the end of July there had been the casual reference to Hiroshima and areas around, during briefing, to 'stay clear of the area'. It was not until the 7th August that we were informed about 'Little Boy'. The 'Manhattan Project' was at last beginning to show the world and particularly the Japanese what the Allies intended doing to finally bring Japan to its senses, and surrender. Major Cheesman, CO 1770 Firefly Squadron wrote, and was quoted in Stuart Eadon's book, 'Sakashima – and back', 'So many people today condemn the use of the atomic bomb, but had they been out there at the time and been one of those to face the forthcoming carnage which would have resulted among hundreds of thousands of our fighting forces, I am quite convinced they would not be talking as they do today. We who were out there at the time, owe our lives to the use of these two bombs. It was the only answer on this occasion, but let us hope it will never be necessary for anyone to use them again.' Admiral Halsey considered it an unnecessary act to drop the bomb. It was his view that Japan was utterly defeated before the bombs were used. How is it, that such a distinguished leader, failed to understand that hidden away in the forests and hillsides were hundreds of planes? These, allied to the growing force of Japanese maniacs willing to fly them on one final expression of their misguided faith in their Emperor and Sun God, would have meant an awful massacre of our troops and ships. It was a matter of 'them' or 'us' and this war had to be brought to a rapid conclusion.' Our subsequent policing of Japanese airfields after the surrender exposed the potential last-ditch stand of Japan. Where, on airfields we had attacked and filled with cannon shells dummy aircraft or relics propped up on oil drums, there were hundreds and hundreds of planes, with of course the cockpit covers on and the airscrews removed. Major Cheeseman was right. Imagine all those planes each piloted by a 'death-wishing young fanatic' and launched against a series of invasion beach heads. Guadalcanal, Iwo Jima and the likes of such blood baths were what the Americans, who were obviously by now calling all the tunes, wished to avoid. The heat was indeed very hot in President Truman's kitchen, and he, and probably others, had to make one of the most momentous and brave decisions of all time in a conflict between nations. 'But it was a "close-run thing". The American Government wanted to bring the German war to a speedy end and to beat the Germans in the race to harnessing this massive new nuclear power to a destructive weapon. The Germans were forced to surrender before they could advance that knowledge. The Japanese were nowhere near having an atomic bomb but that war still raged; a war which had cost the youth of America very dearly. As we sailed for the Far East the scientific problems at Los Alamos were mounting alarmingly. The conflicts of the morality of such a weapon and the great American conscience were possibly an even greater challenge to the White House, even in the men who led all the way in the Manhattan Project, such as Oppenheimer. General Groves, the driving force of the project was beginning to sense that he had on his hands, "A show that would never open," and it had already cost over two billion dollars! If the U.S. had been forced into relying on invasion of the Japanese mainland they would have been faced with the probability of Russia entering the equation. It was all a matter of intense speed and critical deadlines. It came off . . . and the rest is history. One cannot fail to state again a simplistic scenario. The bomb saved a vast number of Allied lives. The bomb was a diabolical weapon and it cost many Japanese lives, mostly non-combatants. Has it prevented global war for all time? For 50 years, not counting the on-going stupidity of religious sects and zealots of nationalism . . . world conflict has been avoided.'

August 9th 1945

The penultimate day of strikes against Japan; they were to be quite significant in terms of losses to the aircrews of Indefatigable and the other Fleet Carriers. 1772 was involved in two strikes, both against Matsushima airfield. The following is a Strike Report now stored at the Public Records Office. It bore no signature and some ambiguity about visibility probably exists in it.

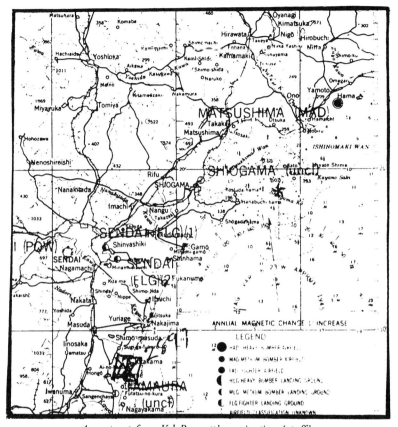

An extract from Val Bennett's navigation 'stuff'.

Strike Report 9.8.45. Firefly 270 (which of the two raids is not made clear.)

Initial view	Airfield seen very clearly
Approach height	5,000 feet
Weather	Visibility poor. Thick haze. Wind light and westerly
Angle of dive	20/30 degrees
Open and cease fire	1,500 to 150 yards
Speed over target	280/300 knots
Rounds fired	400 per gun
Damage inflicted	Flak positions silenced and aircraft hit on ground
Getaway	SE over sea and then NE

Flak	Medium. Intense and accurate. Heavy. Nil
Report	There was no surprise element. Evasive action was weaving. Fireflies were detached by leader and went ahead to strafe airfield. Two flights of four aircraft used. Hellcats were attacking on arrival. Avengers arrived late because of visibility which was poor. No signature.

Chris Maclaren and Wally Pritchard were on both raids and Wally was to add in his log book at the end of his story of the day, 'What a day!' The following is a joint account of their day.

They were in Firefly 274, an aircraft which was to terminate its life that day, being pushed overboard, designated, 'beyond repair'. Over Matsushima they were struck by about 5 shells simultaneously, causing a hole in the starboard wing tip: the port long-range tank and ammunition caught fire. There was a hole in the port flap and the pilot's hood was blown off. One shell burst just aft of Wally's rear cockpit and blew away the aerial. So, badly damaged and with no radio to assist the return to the carrier, they were more than grateful to have Peter Kingston and Val Bennett alongside, to guide them back. Wally said that Chris made a perfect landing though the tail wheel collapsed, because it had failed to unlock. Firefly 274 was then pushed overboard. Wally said that another Observer had taken a photo of 274 with tank ablaze. Where is that photograph? A picture of the sad end of 274 exists in the Yeovilton Museum. On the second raid in Firefly 275, their engine cut at 6,000 feet over the target as they crossed the coastline. Chris managed to get the engine restarted at about 1,000 feet and they made it back to the carrier safely. Their first raid had been launched at 0520 and the second at 1120 hours. There is no record of what they got up to between the two strikes! On the second raid they came back alone with no VHF or W/T. Wally says that the relevant page in this log book is entitled, 'Twitch page'. Glyn Roberts was also hit hard by flak. Both pilots finished the war with a DSC.

Why is it that Observers such as Wally Pritchard and Glen McBride failed to gain awards? Their courage was immense too.

There was the usual daily collapse of a Seafire undercarriage. Lt. Cdr. Jimmy Crossman CO of 894 failed to return from a mission but happily returned to us in Tokyo Bay with Ian Darby and Burn O'Neill.

*Fireflies astern
of the Seafires
ready for take-
off . . .*

**Matsushima
Strike
Sequence**

*1772 cleared for
'Go' . . .*

*Rolling on to centre line . . .
Youngman flaps down*

Take-off . . .

*en route to the Mainland
of Japan . . .*

*Bramhall
and Coles
land on . . .
. . . in one
piece
shipshape
and 1772
fashion.*

(Photos by Val Bennett, Johnny Coles, Sammy Samuelson and Geoff Rham)

Note that 274 going to its watery grave, is the foremost Firefly in Val Bennett's cover-page painting.

By permission of Imperial War Museum.

Chris Maclaren and Wally Pritchard.
Evidently they were not pretty enough to have a crew photograph taken of themselves in 1944/45. This picture of two seventy-year-old gents redresses the balance. Chris was the youngest member of the squadron, followed by Sammy Samuelson and Alan Rowlinson.

(Wally Pritchard)

Matsushima Airfield.
Photograph taken by Val Bennett on the Raid on Matsushima.

Bombardments of the coast continued with the British and Americans joining forces. Targets had been transferred to Northern Honshu; the policy one discovered much later was to stay clear of the next atomic bomb target. There were 407 offensive, CAP and reconnaissance sorties on the day and successes included destroyers, old and new, being sunk, as well as other smaller vessels. Implacable losses included a Seafire hit by flak over Matsushima; he ditched close to shore. Later a Seafire had to ditch near the first one. Two other Seafires who remained to guard the two ditched pilots stayed until low on fuel. They lost their way back to the carrier and baled out. Tragically they were not picked up. The two ditched pilots were picked up by a U.S. Dumbo aircraft. Victorious suffered the loss of two aircraft; the air-gunner of the Avenger

Approaching target – Matsushima airfield.
Also taken by Val Bennett on the Matsushima Raid.

was picked by a nearby Tomcat destroyer. Formidable's loss was the Canadian, Hammy Gray, whose Corsair was shot down after sinking a destroyer. His VC was the second ever awarded to a Fleet Air Arm flyer in WW2. One other Corsair pilot on Formidable was killed when landing-on; he hit the rounddown. Aircrew losses were the heaviest of any period in the Pacific operations. Perhaps the most tragic and ironic was the Implacable loss of four Seafires when the two ditched pilots survived but the two who watched over them died. As John Winton in his book, 'The Forgotten Fleet' said, ' – the two would-be Samaritans were lost whilst their good neighbours who fell among thieves were saved'.

A Typical Task Force 37 Flying Day

August 9th 1945

Time	Mission	Ship	took off	Number on target
0410	Ramrod 1A	Formidable	12 Corsairs	10 Shiogama A/F
	Ramrod 1B	Implacable	10 Seafires	9 Matsushima A/F
	Ramrod 1C	Victorious	10 Corsairs	9 Shipping
0510	Strike 2	Combined	20 Avengers	20 Matsushima A/F
	Escort	Implacable	8 Fireflies	8 do.

	Escort	Implacable	10 Seafires	9 do.
	Ramrod 2C	Victorious	11 Corsairs	11 Shipping
	Ramrod 2D	Indefatigable	9 Seafires	8 Shipping & Hachinoe A/F
0810	Strike 3	Combined	20 Avengers	20 Matsushima A/F
	Escort	Indefatigable	8 Fireflies	8 do.
	Escort	Indefatigable	12 Seafires	10 do.
	Ramrod 3A	Formidable	8 Corsairs	8 Onagawa Wan & Shipping
	Ramrod 3B	Implacable	11 Seafires	10 Shipping
1110	Strike 4	Combined	19 Avengers	19 Kesennuma shipping
	Escort	Implacable	6 Fireflies	19 do.
	Escort	Implacable	12 Seafires	12 do.
	Escort	Formidable	4 Corsairs	4 do.
	Ramrod 4C	Victorious	15 Corsairs	15 Koriyama A/F
1410	Strike 5	Combined	21 Avengers	20 Okotsu & Onagawa Wan
	Escort	Indefatigable	7 Fireflies	7 do.
	Escort	Indefatigable	9 Seafires	9 do.
	Escort	Victorious	4 Corsairs	4 do.
1410	Ramrod 5A	Formidable	11 Corsairs	11 Onagawa Wan & Koriyama A/F
	Ramrod 5B	Implacable	7 Seafires	7 Matsushima A/F & shipping
Various	Photo-Recce			
		Formidable	4 Hellcats	4 Post-strike assessment
Various	CAP			
		Indefat. & Implac.	90 Seafires	88 Defensive Fighter Patrols
		Vic & Formid	50 Corsairs	49 do.

7 aircraft were lost.

The second more powerful atomic bomb was dropped on the city of Nagasaki. 'Fat Man' wiped out the industrial area and killed and injured a very large number of people.

There were two types of radar points which safeguarded the Fleet from intruders and gave allied planes some protection from being shot down by one's own guns. The 'Tomcats' were sort of 'pylons' for these returning aircraft. 'Watchdogs' were usually advanced radar picket groups. At any one time there were usually two 'Tomcats' and one

'Watchdog' and they could be submarines or destroyers. On three consecutive days at the height of the BPF's action 'Tomcatting' handled 1,964 aircraft.

It is a test of the memory, to recall the broad canvas of events shown in the typical BPF flying day on 9th August 1945. The Pacific Fleet, often referred to as The Third Fleet was composed of the American Task Force 38 and the British Task Force 37, 4 large groups of carriers surrounded by the usual protective ring of other Naval vessels. The four separate entities were in the line abreast, the BPF on the right and the most northerly, on a 45 mile front. It was an amazing concept, commented on by several 1772 aircrew in this text; a magnificent finale to an incredible and long battle fought largely by the Americans, against an evil foe, which reached its zenith in the Timor Sea, its turning point in bloody Guadalcanal and its nemesis in the final destruction of the Japanese dream in August 1945. It was Japan's first defeat for 2,600 years!

1772's task was a small part of the role of one carrier; the Indefatigable was but a part of Task Force 37's role. We individuals never came anywhere near in our minds to grasping the 'whole'. The imagination then, was not capable of becoming cognisant of such a gathering of armed might. We lived in our small cocooned world, enjoying it and hating it, and as we look back we are amazed that we knew so little of the total scene.

The major concepts of tactics and strategy, the vast and detailed planning, the problems of victualling, the maintenance of the well-being of men, their health and their safety, as far as it was possible in war and the work of the Fleet Train, 'a motley group of merchantmen and warships', among many laborious tasks was the problem of delivering the mail . . . but with no guaranteed delivery times. Theirs was not a glamorous task for it was a mammoth job and we enjoyed those flying 'off-duty' days when we could promenade the deck, in the spaces not occupied by the ever-busy maintenance guys putting our aircraft into working order, and watch those Fleet Train men hauling the huge 'umbilical cords' across the alarmingly limited space between supplier and supplied. The hangars would be a hub of activity too, sometimes working through all the watches. Dawn would be imminent and the first day CAPs, the overhead watchdogs looking for 'Bogies', would be ranged on deck. In our case these were the Seafires. Then the Ramrods and various strikes in their complex sequence, would make their appearance. It was a veritable theatrical performance of timing and placement and the deck handling parties in their many colours would dance about the deck among rolling aircraft, whirling propellers and incredible din. The Fleet or even an individual carrier would swing into wind and its bobbing attendant destroyers would move into their positions, for carrier protection or air-sea rescue if a take-off went wrong. Set on this given course for as limited a time as possible, the carrier could be at its most vulnerable. There were periods when enemy activity was quite intense around the Fleet and it was then that our Seafires and the Corsairs and Hellcats from other carriers would set about applying their infinite and glamorous skills. The enemy often attempted to locate the Fleet by dropping mysterious little black boxes full of directional equipment: they were very often shot down. The Fireflies of 1772 had established their true role of ground attack and flak suppressor before reverting to the role of stern escort. We would go in first, as fast as possible in an open formation blasting at anything that looked worthwhile, in front of us. The implicit instruction had always been, 'Once only and no second run'. The Avengers would come in above and behind us, each aircraft with a crew of three, bombed-up for their dangerous work because they were, most vulnerable. The fighters would sometimes add their bit to the ground attack. All would go well, we hoped, but there were to be the bad moments when one of us would be hit. Some of the strikes would be quite big affairs. That 45 mile long Fleet would send out its shafts of multiple aircraft, the shafts sometimes joining up into combined raids. There would be smaller attacks aimed at some special target which photographic evidence had brought to light. On the day more photographs would be taken by Observers or by a lone Seafire photo-reconnaissance plane. Before the attack, a mass of aircraft would have formed up, radar units of the Navy in position at specific points to alert the Fleet about enemy aircraft. Air-sea rescue would be in place, submarines or patrolling aircraft capable of putting down on the sea.

'The flying kit, even in the tropics seems to be excessive and inhibiting. You cross the reassuringly solid steel flight deck of the Indefatigable; not the perfect flatness defined by the term "flat-top" for it is covered with knobs and protuberances, but above all the arrester wires . . . a tripping surface! The Fireflies are astern and you weave your way through the Seafires, herringboned in lines and echelons. You climb to the cockpit, chat to the maintenance guy if he happens to be there before you. You settle down on your life-saving pack of rubber and silk, Mae West and parachute respectively. Sort out the tubes and wire and get yourself connected, first to your parachute and then the aircraft. You are tight in both; it is like a tight shoe, but comfortable if you forget the heat and the turmoil going on all round you on the noisy flight deck. With flying clothing, webbing straps, buckles, helmet, goggles and mask, it is a crowded little place. The latitude of the carrier approximates to a position equivalent to North Africa. The temperature in the cockpit is over 100°F and soon the cockpit canopy will turn it into a little hothouse. You sweat and sweat from heat and apprehension. This is just another performance on this huge "revolving stage" and the butterflies abound. You begin to check everything and pilot and observer chat away . . . seriously. The pilot wiggles his moving surfaces, the flying controls. There are many knobs, dials and pieces in the cockpit and you've seen them so many times, but cannot afford to be complacent. The observer in his even less generous space has even more problems within his cluttered world of paper notes, maps, photographs and the pilot can hear him testing his radio. START ENGINES. The timing is crucial and critical for "Wings" and his deck-control teams knowing that Seafires and Fireflies with their liquid cooled engines could overheat if they idle too long. Switches off, compression achieved, switch on and fire the Koffman cartridge which explodes the Griffon into life. Around you, are the hunched figures in their cockpits and they are momentarily obscured by the clouds of steam, gas and fumes, as they'll all start up. Now you check the magnetoes and the Youngman flaps which are so important to get you airborne and even more important to get you back on the deck – three hours later. The Seafires have roared off; they make light work of it. The Fireflies and the Avengers will follow. Your eyes are on the deck handler, flaps in take-off position. He "paddles" you forward to the centre line; there is not far to taxi on a flight deck ranging! You are part of a supreme piece of Royal Naval organisation, not on a Burscough runway where flying control once had the front seats! Now a large mass of gold braid is watching your every action. Brakes on. You are "wound up" by the handler, to maximum revs. The engine is in fine pitch . . . and so are you. The plane ahead has gone and reached the end of the flight deck; he momentarily sinks . . . and then reappears. You hope that you will "fly off" the end and not trundle. You know that you will have to turn to port as soon as you have the airspeed; not create too much slipstream for your pal behind you and also to avoid the one ahead which locks you into an uncanny sensation when you are just about staying in the air and not too far off the stalling state.

This is the point when the thrill and the excitement take over; you are on your own – just for a moment. Blurred figures flash by; the ship's island superstructure has gone by in a flash. You are airborne and into that exhilarating climbing turn. That moment, when it was you and your God . . . or Madam Luck. Mention of her however is an insult to the groundcrew who have sweated in grease and heat to make sure that this machine is in the best possible shape. Years of acquired skill and devotion in the several trades have got you into the air and God willing will get you back. The 'wing and the prayer' part has gone but your 'courage is still in the sticking place'. The Griffon has 'busted its gut' and as soon as possible you coarsen the pitch and adjust everything to economic cruising. The Firefly is trimmed to make it easy to fly as you form up with your section leader. "Christ! I've forgotten to retract the undercart!" No you haven't because 'you have done all those things you ought to have done'. You hope! The gap between aircraft leaving the Indefatigable had been as little as 12 seconds. You are still climbing and you are in position on the Avengers. The Seafires are in that big space above and around us where the Jap 'bogeys' will be. We fly on . . . and wonder!' (Based upon an aircrew's diary notes.)

The strike crews would settle down to their tasks of flying in formation and following the leaders but careful to maintain knowledge of their position should enemy action or cloud and weather scatter the formation. That carrier was such a little object in a vast ocean and it had to be found again, soon, we hoped. Our thoughts no doubt were full of apprehension, but the mind was focused on the briefing details. The attack remains a blur of detail after so many years, but a lot of detail has remained, clear and well-focused. There was the day of the Japanese carrier Kaiyo which was probably the only carrier sunk by British Naval aircraft in the Pacific war. She broke in two and was claimed by all of our four carriers. The Americans staked their claim too. If there wasn't a little piece of personal glory in all of this it seemed a trifle wasteful of one's efforts, but claiming sole responsibility for any one destructive action was a special talent!

Sometimes the weather was foul and the large thermals of the typhoon season were horrendous, dark places and very wet too. The sea could be at one time, placid, beautiful and blue, at other times, a seething, white-crested greyness. Sometimes a colleague 'bought it'. Often it was just another plane, from another squadron, from another carrier . . . and quite anonymous. The flak rose, often in multi-colours; there was wasted effort on dummy targets, even a wasted life and with good luck, the rising smoke and fire from a worthwhile target. The Japanese were finished but at the time, the danger was real and 'we were never really certain that the enemy was spent'. There had been few airborne enemy aircraft; the Kamikazes were always a threat and the flak was always deadly. The rendezvous beckoned and then the journey 'home', mostly in the reassuring company of one's section or the strike leader. It could even be – alone. One could become detached in the filthy black, wet clouds. There had been the panic of holding close formation in awful turbulence. One could try to be so close that the

134

rivets of the leading craft were etched on one's memory! Not every pilot had become conditioned to flying on instruments for long periods. Roger McCahey's description of such an occasion is well told in Stuart Eadon's 'Kamikaze'. His story of the return to the carrier on his own in a Seafire, tells of panic, skill, common sense and the value of deep-rooted drills of what to do in such situations. And a good slice of luck!

The Fleet or the carrier alone, is spotted; the cockpit had been your world for over 3 hours. One could feel the sweat and the prickly heat in delicate areas. The most challenging part of naval flying awaited . . . landing on! The carrier had looked so small. The disciplined curved approach for better vision all the way on to the deck! BB (David Bryce-Buchanan) takes you over with his white paddles or bats; for a few flashing seconds you are again centre stage and every one, simply everyone, has you focused. The carrier a few yards away and the stern end of the flight deck with its round rump – the rounddown, threatens. CUT. BB crosses the bats in front of him. Back comes the throttle and you drop, gently you hope, and wait for the reassuring tug of the arrester wire. There are no thoughts of the safety barrier . . . until you've hit it! – or caught JC – the very last arrester wire . . .' Jesus Christ!

The safety harness is tight; thank God you remembered. Taxi forward, the deck party has you mesmerised until they signal to 'switch off engine'. It is not always like that. Those of us who flew in daylight marvelled at the guys who did it in the dark, landing between two narrow rows of little lights. Only birds and fools fly . . . and birds seldom fly at night! There could be a desperate American in an even more desperate hurry to get his wheels down on any flat-top; the one that first came into sight was the best one. Unfortunately American and British landing control signals were quite the opposite of each other. This could and did cause a special scene of mayhem, even tragedy and all-round disaster and loss of valuable aircraft. Sometimes even the ample deck of a Fleet carrier could tilt from side to side and a relatively fragile oleo leg on one side of the aircraft could suffer too much from the stress of landing. The aircraft in such circumstance could finish on its belly and end up an expendable piece of metal. The Seafires suffered most with their ridiculous, knock-kneed little landing gear. Only in the air was it a thing of great beauty in naval flying. There could be ditchings, some rank stupidity and a little tragedy . . . and 'a seat in the goofers was worth' . . . a nightmare, or two!

Other ships in the Fleet would now and again speed off to positions about two miles off the coast and pump more chaos into the wretched Japanese. Others stayed in close escort to the carriers, screening under the waves and above them for the menacing 'bodies'. Their lives were all naval routine and discipline and maybe it could have been boring for a good deal of the time, but now and again, just for a change, HMS King George V Battleship and destroyers would enjoy letting off their guns. Several of our warships would join such a bombardment or take over air-sea rescue work.

The work of the aircrew finished, having been debriefed, they would shower and view their gentian violet or brown armpits and genitalia with some amusement and discomfort. A gin no doubt was the next order of the day. However the squadron ground crews and the ship's company slogged on with the work of putting all to rights and in ship-shape order. There was the next sortie and early next morning at dawn the planes would be ranged before 4.00 a.m. It was always busy somewhere on the Indefatigable and tomorrow was the 10th August . . . a bad day for 1772!

August 10th 1945

The last full day of operations and the second of two days; two very hectic days, when it was claimed that the enemy lost over 700 planes to the carrier fleets and the Fleet Air Arm lost 13 aircraft and 9 crews. The U.S. Fleet had moved north of Honshu, those in high command obviously aware of the second atomic bomb.

Targets included Masuda, Matsushima and Koriyama airfields and shipping at Hokkaichi and Onagawa Wan. Japanese flak was still very accurate especially over Koriyama airfield. We lost one Corsair, one Avenger and two Fireflies, all in the strike on Koriyama. The two Fireflies belonged to 1772. Glyn Roberts with Glen McBride in the observer cockpit did not survive. Wally Pritchard says that Glyn and Glen were last seen by them, diving on the target; he believed they were hit and were unable to pull out. Nothing has ever been certain about Glyn and Glen's last minutes. Several versions have been set out which include 'the facts': that they had gone down in flames, that they had gone down into the sea and that an engine corresponding to Glyn's Firefly had been found! Crews who remember being on those strikes that day included, Chris Maclaren/Wally Pritchard, Bob Scott/Rollo Norman, Eric Bramhall/ Johnny Coles, Johnny O'Driscoll/Geoff Rham and Teddy Key/Sammy Samuelson. The following Strike Report was signed by Gordon Davidson.

Strike Report Onagawa Wan and Okachi Wan 10.8.45

Target	Shipping
Weather	5/10 at 9,000 feet. Hazy
Wind	270/10

Glen (Mac)
McBride and
Glyn Roberts.

Burn O'Neill and Ian
Darby . . . a very
successful and
compatible crew.

20.07.45 FIREFLY   DT983 1772 INDEFATIGABLE PARRY AC   S/LT(A) RNVR
HOOK PULLED OUT
24.07.45 FIREFLY   MB396 1772 INDEFATIGABLE HEBDITCH DH S/LT(A) RNVR
BOUNCED. FLOATED OVER WIRES, CRASHED INTO BARRIER
30.07.45 FIREFLY MB398 1772 INDEFATIGABLE PARRY AC   S/LT(A) RNVR
BOUNCED & CARRIED ON INTO BARRIER
12.08.45 FIREFLY MB516 1772 INDEFATIGABLE REDDING VJ S/LT(A) RNVR
STBD U/C COLLAPSED ON LANDING
18.09.45 FIREFLY DK458 1772 INDEFATIGABLE KINGSTON PB S/LT   RNZVR
ON PARKING.FUSELAGE HIT CONCRETE PICKETING BLOCK

The A25 Record of the Squadron whilst on HMS Indefatigable.

Eric Bramhall and Johnny Coles
(Johnny Coles)

Johnny O'Driscoll and Geoff Rham
(Johnny O'Driscoll)

Angle of dive	45 degrees
Open and Cease Fire	2,000 to 500 Yards
Speed over target	300–240 knots
Rounds fired	520 per cannon
Getaway	Weaving
Flak	Meagre. Inaccurate
Comments	As leader of Stern Escort detached with section to strafe shipping. Hit on starboard wing. Another hit on starboard wing after low-level attack. R/T torn off. Aerial hit.

Teddy Key. 'Log book says, "flak fairly thick", but I think maybe we in this section which went down to strafe shipping near Kinkasan Point just north of Koriyama, drew the long straw, because those over the airfield certainly had a very bad time. Burn O'Neill and Ian Darby were struck over the airfield by shells. They climbed and baled out over land. Their story is told later, when their return to the carrier in Tokyo Bay was a most joyous occasion.'

Val Bennett. 'Two strikes I remember especially. The first was on 10th August, a strafing attack on Koriyama airfield. As we climbed away after the attack, we caught up with a Firefly trailing white smoke, which was caused by the escaping coolant fluid. We closed and recognised the aircraft as the one being flown by Burn O'Neill and Ian Darby. There was a hole in the side of the engine cowling. As we watched they were jettisoning the hoods and preparing to bale out. The horror of capture by the Japanese could not be avoided. Burn slowly turned the aircraft over and they fell safely clear, the aircraft's nose dropped and went straight down, down, down, until it disappeared. Then a mushroom of smoke on the ground. Two parachutes opened and we headed for the rendezvous. What fate would befall them? In the same attack we lost Glyn and Mac.'

Norman Hanson in his book, Carrier Pilot, describes an adventurous member of his Corsair Squadron, 1833, on board HMS Illustrious, whose name was 'Winnie' Churchill. Glyn Roberts was something like him, brave and fearless, a law unto himself. They both found that sometimes the rules of the game got in the way of their true nature and their intent. 'Winnie' Churchill flew his Corsair to his death over Ishigaki in the Sakashima 'Iceberg' operation, on April 7th 1945; April 13th was the last day of operational flying for 1833 Squadron! He did the second run and was the target really worth his life? To use the CO, Norman Hanson's words, 'My immediate reaction was to be furiously angry. Why the hell did he have to be the clever bastard and refuse to listen? Why the hell did he think he was invulnerable, where so many other pilots had fallen?'

Ian Darby. 'There was no shortage of adrenalin those days and I have vivid memories of certain events such as flying through immense A.A. fire at very low levels, in particular, against airfields. There was no apparent shortage of shells in Japan. I'm sure that I helped the War effort a lot, by dropping empty gin and whisky bottles down the smoke-float shute. At least I was kept busy.' Good old Ian; never a dull moment with him around.

During August 1945, a copy of 'War Illustrated' reported: 'On July 30th, more than a thousand U.S. and British Carrier planes attacked military targets in the Tokyo-Nagoya areas; their original targets, airfields, were blotted out by fog, so they switched to targets of opportunity. The Japanese estimate for that day was that 1,600 aircraft had attacked the Japanese main islands up to 6 p.m.

At the end of July it was announced that at least 1,230 Japanese ships and 1,257 aircraft had been destroyed or damaged during the preceding 22 days by the Third Fleet. On August 9th and 10th the same

Fleet sent more than a thousand planes on a two-day strike against targets in Northern Honshu.'

August 11th 1945

The weather was very bad. The Admirals Halsey and Rawlings met on board USS Missouri: both the Missouri and King George V were alongside the oiler. We were very short of fuel; the Admirals lunched together and the Japanese had asked for peace terms.

August 12th 1945

As far as we were concerned on Indefatigable, the war was not over. Casualties were light, but they continued. The innermost thought must have been, 'surely we are going to make it now, the war is all but over'. The weather was still bad and we were about 400 miles from Tokyo. We received a signal from Admiral Halsey. It read, 'On the occasion of parting company with some units of Task Force 37, I want all hands in your outfit to know that during this past month, the fine co-operative attitude and fighting spirit of the British force, has made as many friends and admirers as there are officers and men in the American section of the team'. Admiral Rawlings also sent a signal to his Task Force 37. It read; 'while the armistice may still be a few days away, today the 12th August is the end of the British Task Force as we know it. I have no hesitation in saying that it has written a memorable page in the history of the British navy. In the time coming, when many of you will be returning to shore life, but to both those who leave and those who remain in the service, I would say two things. Firstly that you will carry with you throughout life a feeling of pride in what you have done out here. And the second that you will realise that I am profoundly grateful to you all. 120236. From Vice Admiral Rawlings CTF 37.' The decision had been made by our senior officers that a combination of the problems of keeping the Fleet serviced and the imminent cessation of hostilities, dictated a reduction in the size of the British Fleet. Task Force 37 became Task Group 38.5 and comprised the King George V, our carrier. Indefatigable, two Cruisers and 10 Destroyers. We were to come under the direct command of Admiral McCain as another Task Group of his Task Force. Admiral McCain's flag was flown from USS carrier, Shangri La. The British Fleet was at large, not very pleased about the breakup. Just for a few thousand tons of fuel, many would not be in at the finish. Victorious, for example was not in the best shape. Her rudder was defective, ('her behind is in poor condition' according to Indefatigable), her steering gear and centre shaft far from satisfactory. They returned to Sydney not dispirited, for size for size, they had pulled their weight with the American Task Groups.

We received another crew, Vin Redding, with Observer, John Prince. They pranged on arrival, the starboard undercarriage collapsing when landing. They were now one of us, but not for long!

August 13th 1945

We went into action with the U.S. Third Fleet. The total bag was 21 planes shot down, 250 in total, destroyed. 1772 targets were designated as 'targets in the Tokyo plain area and 50 miles north of Tokyo'. Generally the directive was 'targets of opportunity' which meant beating up trains and shipping. The briefest of Strike Reports was signed by Croose Parry. He rarely wasted words; even to this day!

Strike Report 13.8.45. Trains and shipping in Tokyo area

Target	Railway stock. Low-level strafing
Open and cease fire	1,500 to 500 yards
Speed over target	280 knots
Flak	Nil
Comments	3 trains strafed, 2 static, 1 mobile. The mobile train was stopped. Lugger hit.

Bob Scott flew CAP in the morning and Chris Maclaren and Wally Pritchard went strafing around Taira. They claimed a train destroyed. The train was hit many times and left smoking. Pilots Johnny O'Driscoll and Pete Kingston were on these raids over Taira on the Tokyo plain. In the afternoon our Fireflies were supposed to be operating with our 820 Avengers but they didn't show up due to adverse cloud conditions. 1772 seemed to have had some fun, and nobody was hurt.

The day was marred by an awful deck landing accident. Lt. Stretton had landed-on in a Seafire and had been unable to jettison his long-range tank. The resultant fire was quite horrendous. Teddy Key said, 'This was one of those times when the fascination of watching one's colleagues land on became a nightmare. I can still see that tragedy as clearly as if it happened yesterday.'

Halsey was still faced with the uncertainty of the war situation but it seemed that the Japanese were ready to negotiate a surrender. They were in no state to negotiate; the Allies awaited the 'unconditional surrender'.

August 14th 1945

We oiled and a CAP Seafire burst a tyre on a heavy landing and tipped up on its nose. 'Bogies' were fairly frequent but the record of 'kills' was still very good. The enemy was still round and about us and one was aware that something awful could happen at any time.

August 15th 1945

This was the last day of WW2 and the Indefatigable launched what were among the final strikes against Japan. At 0400 6 Avengers, 8 Seafires and 4 Fireflies were launched and they were intercepted by 12 Zekes. 4 were definitely shot down, 4 probably and the remainder damaged. One Avenger got through to its airfield target, another was hit by flak and the observer baled out, somewhat prematurely. The plane flew on, had to ditch and the pilot and air-gunner were rescued. Freddie Hockley was shot down over the Chiba Peninsular. He baled out and was executed. He lies buried in Yokohama. His assassins were later executed as war criminals.

Evidence which has come to light suggests that Freddie Hockley took off with his R/T u/s but in spite of Vic Lowden's hand signals to

Freddie Hockley gets his wings, Kingston, Ontario on 6th June 1943.

(Teddy Key)

KILLING OF R.N.V.R. OFFICER
---**---
THREE JAPANESE CHARGED
From Our Correspondent
30.5.47. HONG KONG May 30

By arrangement with the American authorities, as the alleged crime was committed in Japan, colonel Ramura, Major Hirano, and Captain Fujino have been arraigned before the war crimes court here and charged with being concerned on August 15 1945, in the killing of Fred Hockley, a sub-lieutenant, RNVR, pilot of a Seafire from the Indefatigable, who parachuted down uninjured in Inchinomiya.

He landed at 4.30am and was taken to regimental headquarters. The Emperor's surrender was broadcast at noon. When divisional headquarters were asked for instructions it was stated that he was not wanted, and "should be disposed of". A grave was dug and Tamura is alleged to have ordered subordinates to take Hockley away after dark. At 7.30pm Fujino is stated to have led him away into the hills and to have shot him in the presence of several officers and men. He was also stabbed and then buried.

KISARAZU was the last target of 1772 Squadron.

(Val Bennett)

return, he persisted with the mission. Of course, without radio he never got the warning of being jumped and shot down, with the awfully tragic consequences already mentioned. Teddy Key comments that this was typically Freddie. He had joined up with Freddie, both of them Cambridgeshire fellows, and gone through the whole war together until Freddie 'went' Seafire and Teddy 'went' Hurricane. They were 90+% through their life on Indefatigable before they knew that they were together again. Such was the large and sometimes impersonal state of a huge naval ship. Teddy adds that Freddie was a tough and uncompromising guy. He was brave. Why is Freddie in a story of 1772? He was on our ship at the very end; he was the last recorded loss of aircrew of the Fleet Air Arm in WW2. There was a comradeship between squadrons on board the Indefatigable and of course there had to be an interdependence between squadrons when it came to operation flying. There were

143

times when you needed each other. It is said that the sea is one of the last really free places left on the planet Earth but it was a large and lonely space, on it and above it. We relied on each other very often.

The target on this final operation day was Kizarazu airfield in Tokyo Bay. We had refuelled on the 14th, 300 miles away. The strike of four, 1772 Fireflies, six, 820 Avengers and eight Seafires took off at 0400 hours. They met up with the Zekes and at 0700 hours all strikes were cancelled.

Val Bennett in Stuart Eadon's 'Sakashima – and back' expressed for all of us those feelings of foreboding we felt about flying over the mainland of Japan. There was always that dread that something would go wrong. He told how after the loss of the pilot's canopy they had to return via Tomcat, a radar picket force which acted as a filter for aircraft, friend or foe, before being 'allowed' to approach the main fleet. A single, unfamiliar aircraft to the Americans, limping home, was in all likelihood a suspicious object. Two American Hellcats came up behind them, menacingly. A moment of terror, doing the right things, and they were given clearance to return to the carrier. Val had proclaimed at the time of the strike that, 'our part in the raid was not particularly distinguished and the raid had been a mixture of sadness and joy'. Life in Naval flying was full of such incidents and emotions.

Val Bennett. 'The second strike I remember especially, took place on 15th August. By this time the Atom Bombs had been dropped and peace was only a matter of time. A large part of the BPF had returned to Sydney and the Indefatigable joined up in a smaller fleet with the Americans including USS Wasp. Our Captain, Q. D. Graham, addressed us on the ship, "I shall continue to strike". This time it was Kizarazu, a stone's throw from Tokyo and such an action was sure to stir the Japanese. It was to be the only occasion on which we encountered Jap fighters. It was a small strike of 4 Fireflies and 8 to 12 Avengers together with an escort of Seafires. As usual, the Fireflies were to strafe the defences before the Avengers bombed. After we entered our dive and the speed built up to around 330 knots there was a loud bang as Peter's hood flew off. As we eased out of the dive I could hear on the R/T, excited voices of our Seafires as they warned of Japanese interception. Looking up I could see the flash of wings far above. The Japs were attacking our Avengers and the Seafires were into them. An Avenger was hard hit and a Seafire shot down. Sadly one of my closest 58th Observers Course friends from Trinidad, Johnny Bonass was wounded in the Avenger. He must have baled out for he was never heard of again. Freddie Hockley, the Seafire pilot also baled out and was beheaded, it

The signal, 'Cease hostilities against Japan' is hoisted on HMS Indefatigable, 15th August 1945.

subsequently transpired. On return to the carrier the signal, "Cease Hostilities with Japan" was hoisted.'

Croose Parry. 'During the final strike against the naval airbase at Kizarazu I suppose we were fortunate, in that soon after leaving the main force we were recalled and so missed the Japanese fighter attack on the Avengers. On the other hand it could have been an opportunity for a bit of aerial combat, not that we would have been very effective, because Pete Kingston had lost his hood and the R/T on Roy Hebditch's Firefly had packed up.' Keen to the last to get 'a bit of the action' as Ian Darby was wont to say! But then, at that time, Ian was not-so-comfortably tucked up in a POW camp in Japan! It was also a good example of the long and short straws of luck; it was a chancey business and sometimes you were lucky enough to draw the long one.

At 1115 on the 15th August 1945, a signal was hoisted from the yardarm. It read, 'Cease hostilities with Japan'. At 1120, while the signal was flying, another was hoisted, 'Red Alert'. A Judy was attacking us but an American Corsair was on the Judy's tail. The Japanese plane dropped two bombs which missed us by about 200 yards. Admiral Rawlings was heard to comment, 'one looked like a bloody great grand piano'. The pilot baled out but was obviously dead before he hit the water. He hung on the end of his shrouds, very limply. The largest piece of the Judy fell about 400 yards to port and astern of us.

The last attack . . . on us. A Judy drops two bombs and is shot down, 15th August 1945.

Further attacks occurred until about 1300 but all were beaten off. Two were shot down as Admiral Halsey broadcast to the Fleet. Part of his signal is still recalled as one of the great naval signals of all-time. 'It is likely that Kamikazes will attack the fleet as a final fling. Any ex-enemy aircraft attacking the fleet is to be shot down in a friendly manner.' Marshall O. Lloyd, the pilot of the Corsair eventually became an Honorary member of the Indefatigable Association. He died on 6th November 1992 at the age of 72, having battled for a long time against illness.

There were three 'Splice the Mainbrace' signals. Were things getting out of hand? All three tots were 'administered' but with a suitable spacing. After all, there had been enough enemy activity to suggest that they did not share our euphoria.

Admiral Bruce Fraser prepared to fly to join the Third Fleet: he was to sign the surrender agreement on behalf of the British Commonwealth. Admiral Rawlings, from USS Missouri, also broadcast to the men of the combined fleets. 'I believe that the day when either of us abandon Admiral Halsey's advice "to keep the Naval Sword sharp", will bring us nearer to being attacked by such evil forces as those we have now subdued. I would suggest that each will be able to say to himself, "I fought in the Third Fleet under Halsey", and so saying, face up with greater courage to whatever tomorrow shall bring.'

August 16th to August 21st 1945

The ship's log records, 'At sea'. What did 1772 do? Nothing, is the answer, for we have no records. We no doubt played deck hockey and our sports officer, Alan Rowlinson, covered himself in glory by probably taking us to the first round of a knock-out competition! There was the usual CAP flying in which we worked with the 3 American carriers, Ticonderoga, Randolph and Essex.

August 22nd 1945

We carried out a huge flying exercise; about 1,000 aircraft in the air at the same time. Teddy Key says that his logbook records, 'Practice Flight. 4 A/c. 3.30. hours! Bob Scott recalls the flight too and he wondered what its purpose was. The only memorable detail which emerged was that the Seafires complained about the Firefly's excessive cruising speed of 200 knots! Very gratifying.

August 23rd, 24th and 25th 1945

We were entering a period of anti-climax. We knew that we were going into Tokyo Bay, but when? The weather was very threatening and on the 24th it was very hot. There was a warning that a Typhoon was approaching the Fleet: there were probably two of them! During our spell on HMS Indefatigable, these monstrous things were never very far away; the 'weatherman' kept a plot on the Wardroom notice board, so we were always aware of them. We were permanently fixed on that broad autumnal route of typhoons known as the Kuro Siwo Current, the Japanese equivalent of the Gulf Stream. This time they seemed to be more compelling and Typhoon 'Rose' began to hold us in her spell. She was travelling in a more or less predictable east of northerly course when she did a little kick to the west. She was bigger and faster than us, so the Fleet conceded. Her course is shown on the map;

The Indefatigable tried to keep its distance from the storm; that was always a matter of great significance to the ship's navigator. 'Rose' however had other ideas . . . as the map shows. Our luck and skill in staying clear of these monstrous turbulences ran out . . . and there were

two of them this time. The sky, initially blue, turned reddish purple and the sea became calm with an increased swell. The eye of the storm? Teddy Key remembers that it was early in the morning that he was ranged on deck with a flight of Fireflies. The log books record nothing because as we sat there, strapped in our cockpits, no doubt trembling and wondering, 'why?', the operation was aborted and the aircraft were struck below faster than they had been ranged. It will remain just a memory, a long straw again, but who else remembers that incident? We braced ourselves for the worst; on the edge of the storm the wind picked up, whipping the sea into a mist of spray that reduced visibility to zero. All ships were ordered to reduce speed, turn south into the 'teeth' of the wind force – and everyone for himself. Under such conditions ships do not attempt to keep station; there would have been a huge risk of collision when in close company. There were cliffs of towering power all round us and there was an uncanny shrieking. The forward lift was forced downwards and a firescreen on the hangar deck blew out like a paper bag. In all the slogging work below, where cabins became a wreck of strewn possessions and the hangar deck with aircraft wired down to ringbolts were scenes of frenzied activity. We all helped and we saw some remarkable efforts of NCOs and ratings for many hours. Their effort was quite outstanding: there were many injuries of broken limbs and damaged backs. It was an alarming experience to be standing near a plane while men emptied fuel tanks and hearing a retaining wire pop its ringbolt, with a ringing scream. The Indefatigable lost a lifeboat, some rafts, and took on board a lot of water.

Croose Parry. 'Memories of the typhoon remain, watching the destroyers on our flanks disappearing from sight as they were completely enveloped by the huge seas. Visiting the hangar deck to check that the planes were safely lashed down was a frightening experience.'

Teddy Key. 'Someone suggested that I take a look at the sea from somewhere near the bridge. I did; I saw this mighty ship of ours ploughing through a "rage", took a look at the sea "above" me, dived below where the whole ship seemed to be screaming with rage too and everyone was doing something . . . and maybe I prayed a little.'

When 'Rose' had calmed down, we ventured above decks and astern of us was the mighty carrier of the U.S. Fleet, the USS Wasp. About 30 feet of her forward flight deck had been bent downwards.

The USS Wasp suffered somewhat; her log says 'On 25th August 2 storms, "Able" and "Baker" recurved sharply, the winds averaging about 60 k in the beginning and at the height gusts reached 90 k.'

Detail from the records of USS Wasp's plight, told of the buckling at first of the hangar deck-roller curtains. Heavy seas broke over the Wasp and waves rushed down the flight deck. The forward port section of the flight deck was raised above the horizontal and remained in an elevated position for an interval of time. Then this portion of the flight deck collapsed and shortly afterwards "the entire flight deck, forward of the forward focs'le strength bulkhead, at frame one and one-half buckled and sagged down over the bow". There was "negative" damage to the hull but damage was quite considerable in a number of respects. A report of the damage stated, "This was the third similar failure on this class of ship and it would seem that the design of the forward overhang is faulty." A delightful understatement and no doubt Uncle Sam is as good as John Bull at this sort of thing, when it comes to putting catastrophes on paper. The report went on, 'It is believed that this weakness can be rectified by the installation of knee braces at each "1 beam" one leg of the knee brace to be welded.' Out of context, of course, but one hopes the idea worked!

An apocryphal story remains. The Americans signalled from Wasp asking how we had weathered the typhoon. Q. D. Graham, our Captain, signalled back, 'What typhoon?'

August 26th 1945

Still at Defence Stations. Vigilance is still a high priority. During those last days of August the U.S. and British Fleets flew many missions. The word is a very apt one for now we were to be engaged on errands of mercy and peace. We searched for POW camps and 'policed' airfields. We, the Indefatigable, found Yokkaichi on the Ise Wan, just south of Nagoya. It became 'our camp' and we looked after it. We dropped supplies which the chaps on the mess decks had collected and these were all stitched into large canvas bags then delivered by the Avengers. Let Bill Jones, an Avenger crew member, tell his story:–

'The mission that gave me most satisfaction occurred after the war had ended. By mid-August 1945, the Japs had accepted unconditional surrender terms; the bulk of the British Pacific Fleet was on its way back to Sydney and Indefatigable, along with K.G.V, two Cruisers and a number of Destroyers was accompanying the U.S. Third Fleet to Tokyo Bay for the formal surrender.

Our reconnaissance aircraft, whilst out locating P.O.W. camps had discovered an unplotted camp on the coast at Yokkaichi, south of Nagoya, amid industrial plant, an oil refinery and a shipyard. A request to the ship's company for supplies for the prisoners resulted in enough cigarettes, sweets, tinned fruit, other foodstuffs and personal gifts, along with essential medicines from Sick Bay to fill fifteen large canvas kitbags. These, fitted with parachutes, were loaded into the bomb-bays of a flight of 820 Squadron Avengers, to be dropped on the camp. The flight to our destination on the morning of the day of the drop was shorter than usual. Crews were much more relaxed. There was not the same urgency as we searched the skies. We didn't expect to see any Japs, nor did we.

As we crossed the shoreline, I saw the prison camp below; a compound of wooden huts close to the water's edge. Of one cluster of four huts, three had the letters P.W. painted boldly in white on their roofs. Outside the compound on the sandy shore a group of scantily clad figures stared up at us waving frantically as if they had been expecting us. On the sand, written probably in stones, was 'YANKS 296 BR 25 DU 75' which we understood to be the complement of American, British and Dutch prisoners.

We circled the camp before swinging out to sea to make our run-in on a long level approach. Our cargo dropped, we swept round in a wide arc to watch the parachutes descend. Not all of them found their target. Some fell short into the sea and immediately figures from the beach waded out to retrieve them. Others overshot the mark, drifting over the compound before coming to earth.

All the while, the mass of figures on the beach remained rooted, looking up and waving as if afraid to look away lest we should disappear; so near to freedom and yet still a long way from it. We continued to circle the compound equally spellbound until, inevitably, we had to reform and make our way back to Indefatigable. The excitement generated by our mission lasted for much of the return journey.

The supply drop had included a leaflet with a brief message of encouragement to the prisoners; expressing the hope that the drop would be successful and assuring them that their incarceration would soon be at an end. Some of the ship's company had felt the need to write their own personal messages; among them the Observer of our crew, S/Lt. Johnny Walker. While we were still in Tokyo Bay, Johnny received a response to his letter from a L/Cpl. G. Rochester of the Northumberland Fusiliers. It was a very moving letter and I treasure my copy of it.

Some forty years later, when I read 'Sakishima' by Stuart Eadon, (an account of his wartime experiences set largely against the exploits of Indefatigable in the Pacific), I was moved to send him a copy of the letter explaining its background. To my surprise, when he replied he sent me a copy of a further letter from one of the prisoners. This one, addressed to Indefatigable was from the camp's senior officer, a U.S. Army Major, Donald Thompson. It too had been sent to Stuart as a result of his book and, by a strange coincidence, by the pilot of our crew, S/Lt. Roy Hawkes. On a visit to the ship many months after we had all left, he had come across it pinned to the wardroom noticeboard. Both letters were included in 'Kamikaze', Stuart's second book about the British Pacific Fleet.

Before we left Tokyo Bay to return to Sydney, I learned that whilst we had been making the supply drop on Yokkaichi, the Fleet's aircraft had been involved in a mass fly over Tokyo of some 1,000 aircraft. The disappointment at not being a part of the historic flight was easily

Dear Sir, First of all, I wish to make myself known to you. My name is Donald G.Thompson, Major US army Reserve, and I was the Senior Officer present at Yokkaichi, Japan POW Camp, which your men found first after the Japs quit fighting.

It is beyond my ability as a writer to express the heartfelt thanks which my men and myself felt toward the men aboard your ship. The wonderful spirit which they showed in gathering up all of the many food, clothing and tobacco items from their messes is what makes life really worth while. Especially after having spent three and a half years under the Japs!

There were many tears shed when your 'Avengers' came over our camp and dropped the food gabs – I know when I read your note I dropped a tear or so too, from nothing more than happiness. Everything which you and your men dropped was saved, even those that dropped in the bay – we saved all – the personal items which the men sent were truly wonderful and all of us there were mighty thankful for everything.

I wish too, to thank your medical men especially for getting the sulpha drugs to us – we had an American staff sergeant who had been hit on July 30 with a 50-cal explosive bullet in the legs. Both feet had to be amputated. By the time your men arrived over the camp there was much infection forming on both legs, but thanks to Indefatigable and her men, my American sergeant went aboard the USS Rescue Hospital with no infection at all, and in good physical condition, everything considered!

It is my deepest desire that you will convey to all of your men my heartfelt thanks to them all, for their 'gifts from Heaven'.

Hope to be able to meet you and your men personally some day; until then thanks again.

Yours. (Sgd) Donald G. Thompson. Major, US Army.

Reproduced by permission of Peter Bonney from 'HMS Indefatigable, Fleet Aircraft Carrier'.

outweighed by my part in the supply drop. The memory of that excited group on the beach at Yokkaichi is one that has stayed with me to this day.' (Bill Jones. Avenger Aircrew.)

These POW Missions also incorporated a systematic patrol of airfields checking that aircraft were aligned on the airfield with airscrews off and canopy covers on. Where had all these aircraft been stowed? On strikes of the same airfields, where we had seen phoney aircraft there was this huge air force ready to be crewed by fanatics as and when the invasion arrived from such areas as Dutch Harbour in the Aleutians where the Americans had been building up a huge invasion army and airforce. What would have followed had the Atomic Bombs not been

POWs have broken out of Yokkaichi POW Camp. Photo taken on 30th
August 1945. (Val Bennett)

Two Avengers can be seen doing their work. Newsletters were dropped in
Verey cartridge cases . . . on a little parachute made out of Pusser's
pyjamas. The POW's had written in the sand; Yanks 296, BR 25 DU 75.

(Teddy Key)

153

dropped was one final demonstration of the 'Kamikaze mentality'.

When we ceased to fire our guns in anger at the enemy we turned our attention to the duties of airborne 'policemen' but especially to errands of mercy. The other type of flying, pouring streams of fiery steel into . . . whatever, was the job we had to do, but it will always remain a haunting thought, 'did I ever hit a little child?' Anyway, the discovery of the Yokkaichi POW Camp was attributed to a crew of the Squadron and the Indefatigable aircraft, with the help of all on board, helped to relieve the miseries of those POWs who in some cases had been there for an awful long time.

August 27th to 30th 1945

Four intensive days of flying over Japan. On 27th, we were involved in general reconnaissance. Allied ships entered Tokyo Bay. Johnny O'Driscoll/Geoff Rham reported finding Yokkaichi POW Camp. Eric Bramhall/Johnny Coles located Arimatsu POW Camp. Chris Maclaren/ Wally Pritchard did two sweeps on the 29th and included Kimozu Airfield. On the same day Johnny and Geoff carried out missions over Toyohashi and Okazaki. Teddy Key/Sammy Samuelson covered the Yokkaichi Camp and Airfield. On the 30th Chris and Wally and Teddy and Sammy dropped medical supplies on Yokkaichi Camp. Previously the prisoners, having broken out, had written messages in stones on the sand outside the Camp. It was a good time for all of us who shared in this exercise and one had a chance to look upon the Japanese landscape with a little less trepidation.

It was a pleasant task, all very generous in spirit in what had become a hateful world. Both Teddy and Wally wrote in their log books with joy: 'My last flight in a Firefly for 1772.' On 29th Admiral Nimitz arrived and on 30th the Flag Ship, King George V and a hospital ship entered Tokyo Bay. The Fleet's aircraft had finished their mercy job. As Pete Kingston and Val Bennett observed, 'We had seen the Tony's, Georges, Myrtles, twins and singles spread in peace on their aerodromes. Peter managed to take off in an aircraft that had a duff undercarriage, but they took off again in another aircraft and remember how "the canvas bags were enthusiastically collected by the prisoners. The Japs just stare now".'

Ray Battison remembers the roof of one camp daubed in white paint, 'prisoners of Bataan and Corregidor' How long they must have been incarcerated! He says, 'The roofs and the compound were alive with American prisoners, waving their arms, dancing and going completely mad with relief from an ordeal which they, by then, must have thought

As part of the surveillance orders imposed upon Japan; aircraft are lined up on the runways. Note the Dakota type plane with Red Cross markings.

(Val Bennett)

The Airfield at Meiji showing the large numbers of aircraft which had been hidden away in preparation for the invasion of the mainland. The A Bombs prevented these potentially Kamikaze manned aircraft from carrying out their terrible effect on the invading allied forces.

(Val Bennett)

155

would never end.' There was a story that on a mercy mission carried out by the Americans, one canvas bag had seriously injured a prisoner. I prefer the image of Ian Darby who having found a baseball bat in his hands, went outside, and came back with a wicked smile on his face. The action fits the guy, but was it true?

Croose Parry. '. . . when carrying out a supply drop on Yokkaichi, I was intent on watching the Camp as opposed to looking where I was going and missed a chimney by a few feet. I found a grass-covered airfield and Hank Henderson, my observer, suggested we might pay a visit. We decided that a quick touchdown would be more sensible. Anyway we did spend a few seconds on Japanese soil.' Perhaps then, 1772 Squadron was the first one to land in Japan after the war. The record is not to be found anywhere, other than in this book.

Geoff Rham. 'By now we had been at sea for seven weeks with the possibility of getting ashore still remote. The food, which was not improving, being mostly dehydrated, was becoming less edible. It was however described by the Captain euphemistically as 'good wholesome food but rather dull'. This led to an entertaining reaction. Every night the ship's radio, in addition to broadcasting news from abroad, had a short programme of its own, the IBC. One of these, a Brains Trust, invited questions from the Ship's Company on topical subjects; pay, clothing and victualling being under the control of the Paymaster induced one brave soul, who was obviously not impressed with the efforts of the victualling section, to ask, 'should the Paymaster Commander be tried as a War Criminal? 'Whatever the justification for asking such a question, it was promptly answered by the Captain with 14 days No. 11's.'*

The U.S. Third Fleet and the Indefatigable remained at sea to prevent any treachery on the part of the Japanese at the last minute.

September 1st 1945

'At sea and pumping on oil.' Defence Stations were still in operation. 1772 aircrew were still flying over Yokkaichi Camp. As our planes circled, an American B29 dropped supplies.

---

* The No. 11's punishment varied with individual ships and was regarded as a rough punishment. It included rising each day of the punishment 30 minutes earlier, reporting on the hour every hour, no privileges such as the rum tot, no shore leave(sic), being given all the dirty jobs such as painting ship; in fact reduced to a form of slavery. It meant no spare time at all.

September 2nd 1945

A great day! The Indefatigable was put out of action by a U.S. aeroplane, a Hellcat. Kamikazes tried it, but it took one Yankee Fighter!

Sammy Samuelson. 'I was in the "goofers" when a Hellcat landed on. He missed all the arrester wires and ploughed through our only barrier into some Seafires parked just beyond the barrier. He wrote off three of them. The Hellcat finished up on its nose but the pilot was not hurt and clambered out, looked at the Seafires and said, "Gee. I'm sorry." With no barriers, the Indefatigable was out of action.'

Teddy Key. 'We did not fly after that incident, though Bob Scott had managed to get in a POW run and "recce" on airfields, still taking photos. I sensed that our gratitude knew no bounds. Val Bennett had said in "Sakashima – and back", "I would have been very happy not to have to risk my neck, unnecessarily at this stage". The pilot of the Hellcat, from USS Shangri La, a "dry" ship, was sent "singing" across to his ship from our "wet" ship. He had explained in the wardroom that he "had been in that little 'ole drink before and didn't want to do it again. I just kept my little 'ole head down and came straight on in." On this day General MacArthur signed the Surrender on USS Missouri and the Indefatigable put on a "Victory Menu". Ian Darby says that he

The Hellcat appears little damaged, testifying to the strength of American fighters; yet it had put a Fleet Carrier out of action and destroyed three Seafires. The pilot had, 'kept my lil' 'ole head down and come straight on in.' A euphemism for ignoring the batsman . . . totally!

(Michael Quinn)

watched the signing on the Missouri through binoculars, from HMS Ruler. He had been released with Burn O'Neill to USS Benevolence hospital ship, thence to a U.S. APD and via the Ruler he finished up with us on Indefatigable. The latter event took place a few days later.'

The Instrument of Surrender

'We, acting by command of and on behalf of the Emperor of Japan, the Japanese Government and the Japanese General Headquarters, hereby accept the provisions set forth in the declaration issued by the heads of the Governments of the United States, China and Great Britain on 26th July 1945, at Potsdam, and subsequently adhered to by the Union of Soviet Socialist Republics, which four powers are hereafter referred to as the Allied Powers.

'We hereby proclaim the unconditional surrender to the Allied Powers of the Japanese Imperial General Headquarters and of all Japanese armed forces and all armed forces under Japanese control wherever situated. We hereby command all Japanese forces wherever situated and the Japanese people to cease hostilities forthwith, to preserve and save from damage all ships, aircraft and military and civil property and to comply with the requirements which may be imposed by the Supreme Commander for the Allied Powers or by the agencies of the Japanese Government of his direction.

'We hereby command the Japanese Imperial General Headquarters to issue at once to the Commanders of all Japanese forces and all forces under Japanese control wherever situated to surrender unconditionally themselves and all forces under their control.

'We hereby command all civil, military and navy officials to obey and enforce all proclamations, orders and directives deemed by the Supreme Commander of the Allied Powers to be proper to effectuate this surrender and issued by him or under his authority and we direct all such officials to remain at their posts and to continue to perform their non-combatant duties unless specifically relieved by him or under his authority.

'We hereby undertake for the Emperor, the Japanese Government and their successors to carry out the provisions of the Potsdam Declaration in good faith and to issue whatever orders and take whatever action may be required by the Supreme Commander for the Allied Powers or by any other designated representative of the Allied Powers for the purpose of giving effect to the Declaration.

'We hereby command the Japanese Imperial Government and the Japanese Imperial General Headquarters at once to liberate all allied prisoners of war and civilian internees now under Japanese control and to provide for their protection, care, maintenance and immediate transportation to places as directed.

'The authority of the Emperor and the Japanese Government to rule the state shall be subject to the Supreme Commander for the Allied Powers who will take such steps as he deems proper to effectuate these terms of surrender.'

The Instrument of Surrender was signed at Tokyo on September 2nd at 0904 hours. It was signed on board the battleship, USS Missouri. This, the most costly war in the history of man had lasted 1364 days, 5 hours and 14 minutes.

Those who signed the Instrument of Surrender were;

Japanese
Mamoro Shigamitsu   Foreign Minister. For the Emperor
General Yoshikiro Umezu   For Imperial General HQ

Allied Powers
Douglas MacArthur   Supreme Commander
Chester W. Nimitz   Fleet Admiral For USA
Hsu Yung-Chang   General. China
Sir Bruce Fraser   Admiral. UK
Derevyanko   Lt. General. USSR
Sir Thomas Blamey   General. Australia
Moore Cosgrove   Colonel. Canada
Jacques le Clerc   General. France
C. E. L. Helfrich   Admiral. Netherlands
Isitt   Air Marshall. NZ.
Dated 2nd September 1945.

September 5th 1945

Geoff Rham. 'Being the only British aircraft carrier to represent the British Pacific Fleet in company with dozens of U.S. ships, we dropped anchor in Tokyo Bay. During this period we made exchange visits to some of the American ships. Johnny O'Driscoll and myself spent a very pleasant afternoon and evening on board USS Ticonderoga and returned very impressed with their kindness and hospitality and loaded with chewing gum and packets of Camel cigarettes. All U.S. Ships being officially "dry", I imagine that the return visits to us were also appreciated.' They probably returned, appropriately, 'loaded'! Gordon Macrow remembers watching the British Carrier HMS Speaker leaving Tokyo Bay with the first repatriated prisoners. Don Turner remembers

Special GENERAL MESS Menu arranged to celebrate
The signing of the Surrender
of the
Japanese Empire
to General MacArthur on board
USS Missouri in Tokyo Bay on
Sunday 2nd September 1945.
HMS INDEFATIGABLE

Breakfast. Grapefruit Juice, Cereals, Bacon and Scrambled Egg, Marmalade, Roll and Coffee.
Dinner. Giblet Soup, Poultry, Ham, Stuffing, Browned potatoes, Tinned Peas and Asparagus, MacArthur Pudding & Rum Sauce.
Tea. Elderberry Jelly, Jam, Cake of Victory.
Supper. Pea Soup, Cold Tongue, Sweet Pickles, Tinned Pears & Custard, Cheese and Biscuits.

The back of the menu proclaimed an original Limerick Competition. The prize ... £A1 and the runner-up, A 5/-.

the effect the band playing as we entered the Bay, had on him. He tells of a talk given on board by a reporter who had been at the peace signing. 'The Japanese had come to the USS Missouri in a launch. The Japanese Minister had signed with his own pen after carefully inspecting the other signatures. MacArthur signed with five pens and Bruce Fraser

A sample of the currency issued by the Americans for use on U.S. ships and presumably in Tokyo later.

(Johnny O'Driscoll)

160

*'This is something of an historical photograph which was taken from HMS
Indefatigable, lying at anchor in Tokyo Bay before sailing home on 9th
September'.*

(Val Bennett)

signed with 2 pens. He gave one to Rawlings and one to Vian.
MacArthur demanded them back as property of the U.S. Government.
The Canadian signed on the wrong line and so threw all the other
countries out of order. The Japanese refused to accept it thus, so
MacArthur crossed out "the typed countries" and wrote the relevant
country opposite the signatures. The Japanese then accepted.'

It is a trifle comforting to think that even 'the big guns' could make
a cock-up of things; probably extreme nerves. We on the Indefatigable
had entertained the chaps from USS Ticonderoga. Johnny and Geoff
had lived healthily on chewing gum, coke and ice cream. We on
Indefatigable were leading our American comrades astray. Well, so
claimed Johnny O'Driscoll. True we had let off a few flares and caused
some alarm amidst the anchored fleet in Tokyo Bay. When lined up on
the quarter deck for a summary 'bottle', even the Captain was noticed
'to have swayed down the line of aircrews'. We do not remember what
the reprimand added up to in the end.

Admiral Halsey went ashore and together with other observers and
journalists reported on the utter devastation of the Tokyo-Yokohama
region. 'For miles and miles the destruction by traditional bombing had
been complete; not a building was left standing.'

'A dance band party from the USS Warrior arrived in Warrant

Officer's uniforms in order to conform to Wardroom regulations. It was a great evening and they were dispatched back to their ship with a mini firework display of 2-star red flares. It was as usual a silly thing to do because the whole Fleet in the Harbour was put on alert. Who really knew what a fanatical Japanese idiot would get up to? All officers below the rank of 2½ rings were ordered to assemble before the skipper for a "ticking off".' Ray Battison, who tells the story, and one other, turned up. Apparently the flare display had caused all USA guns to be suddenly trained on HMS Indefatigable. Well, it was a 'Red Alert'.

September 8th 1945

'We weigh anchor and leave Tokyo. It is Saturday, the weekend. There is little for us to do. On a useless Fleet Carrier, pilots and observers have a sense of being on holiday. Only a few days ago we had sailed into Sagami Bay, an offshoot of Tokyo Bay, to the sounds of "Hearts of Oak" played by the ship's band. We were in line astern and the crews of the ships were in their whites. We saw both a snow-clad Fujiyama and a devastated skyline of the city' Anonymous diary entry.

September 9th 1945

'It is Sunday. Am thinking about real days again. The ship is placed on "peace-time" routine. We had tried not to look at Fuji. It is said that if you can see Fuji when you leave, you will return one day. Fuji was in cloud yesterday as we left. So be it. But I won't be back . . . ever'. Anonymous diary entry.

By now we had Burn O'Neill and Ian Darby back with us after their ordeal in a POW Camp and Don Banks had earlier returned to us from his narrow escape, after ditching in the Pacific and being adrift for nearly three days. Their stories unfolded during those relaxing days with no flying duties and years later were related in Stuart Eadon's books. On 30th October 1995, the celebration of VJ Day, they broadcast their stories on Radio Pacific in New Zealand, whose catch-phrase was, 'Speak up and Speak Out.' Good Kiwi doctrine. Their interviewer, was by the sound of her, a sweet young thing, who adopted an incredulous air about her brave interviewees and worked hard to make what was in any case a very dramatic and often funny story even more dramatic and amusing. So it was, that three venerable gents (Don Banks added his bit by telephone) presented their stories to the young lady. What follows is an amalgam of all those sources and includes a transcript of the radio broadcast.

They were asked how keen they had been to join the Fleet Air Arm. Ian replied that he had been desperately keen to 'get into the action' and had been inspired by a chap who had had some flying experience, though Ian, in his usual style, had added that perhaps at the time he had been keener on the chap's sister. At this stage it would be better to stress that Ian's style of coming in at the end of a good line, and then enhancing it with his own inimitable style, always seemed to add strength and pith to what had been said. Ian loved to underline the punch lines. That is still true, Ian was, and is, very good value! Burn, the pilot, came over very differently and again, still the same old Burn of Squadron days; always funny in a dry old way. After Ian would come the question as 'to what he thought'. The slight delay was followed by the careful and so logical reasoning, slowly delivered, in contrast to Ian. They, even now, are very different and they made one of the better flying crews in 1772. Their interview was one of contrasting responses and it all fell into place so well, – despite the exasperating and very frequent commercial breaks. And so, slowly, Burn in putting forward his 'enthusiasm' replied, 'No, I had no particular desire to fly . . . but I did enjoy it. Somehow it just came. I wanted to be in the Navy like my father and as a boy I used to love watching films about the navy.' Ian said that his parents tried to dissuade him from a 'dangerous business'. Burn said his parents were quite co-operative about his joining the Fleet Air Arm as aircrew. Ian left New Zealand on 8th June 1942 and arrived in an air raid in UK on 12th February 1943; Burn followed on the next draft and they followed the familiar Lee-on-Solent and St Vincent route. The interviewer, probing the idea of their extreme youth, received the answer, 'Yes, both about 18 or 19, young lads about to become fighter pilots but too young to have the sense or brains to see it all as very dangerous.' The interviewer 'Raw youngsters then, too silly to be scared'.

Burn. 'At first the emphasis in our training was "sailors first, pilots second". One was in the hands of died-in-the-wool navy types; we were made to learn how to tie knots and do semaphore. It struck me as odd even then that trying to do semaphore whilst flying a plane might be a little difficult.' They were tackled on the question of facing up to death as they started flying school in mid 1943. Ian related that it did occur to him when watching the dreaded Barracuda with its very powerful Napier Sabre engine, being flown by a test pilot. 'He was showing off the paces of the aircraft to a bunch of top brass, you know the types, one thick and two thin stripes at least. He was slow rolling and looping the plane and landed quite safely. This very powerful party was then to be flown back to London in a Walrus, also known in the Navy as the Shagbat. A fault, quite minor seemingly, in the front hatch of the plane, caused the pilot to lose control. He was killed and all the senior officers with him. Ian admitted that at that point he did realise that 'it' could all end in death. Burn had a slightly different slant on what could happen if things went wrong. At Elementary Flying School one day in a Tiger Moth, the instructor and his pupil were flying over the Elmdon area and below them was a nudist camp. At that particular point in time, the instructor and the pupil reached a state of indecision as to who had the controls. The Tiger Moth was, for a moment before it stalled, under no control whatsoever. The plane crashed into a tree at no great speed and therefore there were no injuries except that the pupil, a New Zealander, slightly knocked out or winded, woke up with the arms of a naked girl round him. He thought he was in heaven. 'At that time,' said Burn, 'I realised that it was possible to fall out of the sky . . . and live!'

Ian recalled, that of the plus-one thousand Kiwis in the Fleet Air Arm, over 150 had been killed. Both of them had lost many friends. The interviewer probed for the details of the sinister side of Naval flying namely the beheading of the Palembang Nine. Two of the nine aircrew who had been executed by the Japanese after the cessation of hostilities around about the middle of August in 1995, and their bodies thrown into the sea, had been Kiwis.

The interview swung quickly away from the sad times to what the interviewer referred to as 'the exciting part'. This was of course that day just after the Nagasaki Bomb, when Ian and Burn were shot down. Burn relates: 'We were attacking an airbase, well over the mainland and at that time the carrier, HMS Indefatigable, was about 100 miles off the coast of Japan. It was therefore quite a long range target for us. On our run across the airfield, firing at aircraft on the ground, the usual role of the Firefly and before the Avengers came down dropping their bombs, I felt a great thud. The oil gauge needle 'went off the clock' and there was a great deal of smoke and oil flying around. We always went in very low and at great speed and then pulled up as fast as possible to gain the reassembling position. I now had no engine power and pulled up to gain as much height as possible. Both Ian and I knew we had to bale out and we concentrated our minds on the agreed method of 'ejecting'. Uppermost in our mind and particularly in Ian's in the back seat, was that the Firefly had a bad record regarding escape from the rear cockpit. Cockpit hoods had been jettisoned satisfactorily, (even this operation was known to be dangerous in that the tailplane could be chopped off.) The plan was, at our maximum height, to roll over gently and push the stick forward. We would then pop out like two peas from a pod. It worked . . . we were separated and in free-fall. We had never had any real training in baling out, we just worked it out between us sometime in the past when we became a crew.' Ian concurred with this and lives now with the thought that he was at that time the only Observer to bale out and live. Ian went on, 'Thank God I was alive; I'd missed the tailplane. I was falling and falling. Remember that we had only reached about 4,000 feet.' He added that he remembered seeing a parachute opening above him and that the ground seemed to be approaching at an alarming rate, so he pulled the rip cord and landed in a paddy field, "... you know the sort of thing, a field fertilised with 'the business' and every imaginable sort of kitchen waste and muck." Burn told of how he had landed on a small island in the middle of shallow river. The island was about the size of a small room ... and he didn't even get his feet wet. They were both uninjured except that Ian had cut his hand on the safety equipment knife carried by aircrew. They had no idea how far apart they had landed.

Ian. 'Civilian Japanese approached me from a small hill. I received a few mild 'licks' round the head; nothing serious. I was taken to the head man of the village, a nice man who calmed down the mob. I was then taken to a building which I thought was a school or a church. Burn thought it was a little Christian Church. I must have looked an awful sight having landed where I did. Yes, Burn and I were together at this time. Army people then came and they were the ones who beat us up. We were put on the floor of an old Chevvy truck, our hands tied behind our backs and we were made to kneel on the unyielding steel surface. They hammered our heads on the floor of the truck using their hands. It was at that point that death seemed a certainty. We were taken to Koriyama police station, through a crowd of these grinning apes. Remember that the target we had attacked was Koriyama Airbase, a base from which Kamikaze aircraft were known to be operating. The civilians at this stage were not too bad, it was the army who were getting stuck into us. We were stripped and put into cells. Because I had cut my hand severing the parachute shrouds, a doctor arrived to treat it. This man with a American brogue asked me if I wanted him to treat me. I found it all a little hard to stomach, but I considered it was 'dinkum'. He told me he wanted my watch; my father's watch. He said he'd cut off my hand if I refused. This, a man presumably trained in America who had sworn to the Hippocratic oath!'

Subsequent questioning concluded that Ian, well over six foot tall, flame-haired, slim and strong looking, must have been rather intimidating to the more diminutive Japanese; and on top of this was the encrusting 'warpaint' ... of you-know-what!' Burn, one imagined with his quieter style, must have been far less frightening.

Burn. 'We were treated badly. I thought of the image of a Roman

Holiday, being paraded through the streets on a truck. There were the usual shrieks of 'Banzai'. My watch had been taken from me. In the cells I still had only my underpants. We were in different cells. We were taken to another town in a truck and put in a dungeon underground. We were tied up and prevented from sleeping. Our wrists were tied and another rope passed through our arms and pulled tight. It was very effective for what they intended. We were tied also to a wall ring.

Ian. 'Every time we fell over, they gave us jabs with their bayonets. We could not sleep. It was a long night; no water and no food. Yes, I was about 22 years old at that time. We were put on a train going to Sendai. The Jap in charge of us was quite a nice bloke, again with an American accent. If you wanted a smoke, he gave you a cigarette. Unfortunately that state of affairs did not last too long. At that stage I thought every moment was going to be my last one; they were very touchy by this time.'

Burn. 'I had a feeling I was going to cop it here at Sendai. The interrogation was very vigorous. They ask us questions about the fleet and carriers and so forth.' Ian added, 'They must have thought we were Bruce Fraser types. We were not tortured, we were given an occasional belt over the head. After this we were left alone. Starvation from this point on was the worst. They would throw a ball of rice stuff at us. Boiled rice with a bit of soya bean; they would "bowl" it over the floor at us in our cell. We had very little water. The room was about the size of a telephone kiosk about 4½ feet square. We couldn't sleep – especially with my height. I had plenty of time to think of my girl friend and it helped. Burn thought about the atom bombs. They had dropped them on the big cities and Sendai was quite big; he thought that the USA could well decide to chose Sendai as a target. Burn added that he reckoned quite a few POW's could have lost their lives through being very close to Hiroshima and Nagasaki and indeed other cities, through conventional bombing. Ian added, "I get cheesed off with these limp-wristed people who go on about the A-Bombs, but where would we have been if they had not been dropped. It was well known to all of us that Japanese policy, when the Yanks landed on the mainland, dictated that all POWs would be killed."

One day Ian and Burn and others were let out and the Jap soldiers in attendance started clicking their rifle bolts in a menacing and provocative way. "That sort of thing does little for your health," interjected Ian with his usual pungency. They both felt that their time was up. But it was all a big joke!

The war was over and Ian and Burn were sent by rail to Tokyo and then to a Royal Navy craft, by then anchored in Tokyo Bay. They were both reunited with their squadron mates on HMS Indefatigable.

Asked about their attitude towards forgiveness for their captors, Ian responded that he considered the civilians to have been OK, but that he could in no way forgive the Army. He added, 'They were animals.' They began to round off their interview by saying hello to Pete Kingston. Peter, a fellow Kiwi, had been airborne on the same raid with Ian and Burn and had flown over them when they were shot down. Peter in recent years had had a couple of strokes and broken his back. But as they both added, when they had last met Pete, he still had that wicked twinkle in his eye. Burn's comment, was, 'Hi Peter, how are you mate? Haven't seen you for years. I suppose you are still looking after all those Napier pubs.'

Several years ago Ian had written their story in both Stuart Eadon's excellent books on the Pacific War, 'Sakashima . . . and back' and 'Kamikaze'. It is worthwhile commenting on these written accounts since they do add one or two extra points. Whilst in prison, Ian had met an RNVR pilot by name, Vic Spencer, also shot down on the 10th August. He had flown an Avenger with 828 Squadron, operating from HMS Implacable. Ian and Vic began what was to become a long-lasting friendship. The pair of them exchanged details of their existence by morse code through the walls, by tapping dots and scratching dashes. Ian mentioned in his broadcast with Burn that during the journey from Sendai to Tokyo he was accompanied by quite a friendly Japanese. Ian wrote that this rather superior person who had been his interrogator of the week before, kept harping that 'our countries should now be friends'. They were at that time unaware that the war was over.

On arrival at Tokyo they were transferred to an open lorry and blind-folded. They were driven to Omori POW Camp, about half way between Tokyo and Yokohama, and by careful manipulation of their eyebrows (their hands were tied), they managed to see the enormous damage and desolation. As far as the eye could see there was rubble, with only an occasional concrete building standing. Ian stated that he was at that point sure that the Japs would not win the war.

"Omori camp was built on a small peninsula. On three sides was the harbour, and the fourth was the entry and road. Several large wooden huts were built along the two sides, and at the back was a huge cesspit divided in the middle by a path which ran down to the sea. I suppose the dividing path ran about 100–150 yards on either side of which were these huge cesspools. I can't remember how many 'guests' slept in each hut, but I would estimate about 75 to 100. On each corner of each hut, there was a room set aside for the officers and Burn and I shared one which was 'alive' with bed bugs. We were in a 'Special Prisoners' hut. Being an SP meant that we were aviators who had desecrated the soil of the "sacred islands of the sun" and we didn't exist. No privileges! We were kept separate from the other prisoners until the last week, when we were allowed the privilege of hot baths, Jap style with about twelve men in these huge tubs at a time. During the time that we were at Omori, I lost 2½ stone, most of which occurred as the result of a severe dose of the 'Tokyo Trots'. My record for one day was 27 visits to the toilet. Presumably the reason for this was that our water supply was pumped from a well adjacent to the cesspools allowing for free communication of bugs from one to the other.

"One of the most remarkable and courageous men I have met was Captain James who, I believe, was a member of the Hong Kong Garrison and had been incarcerated since 1941.

"He was the Senior British Officer and he took the brunt of the Japs' fury and I believe he had to stand outside in the snow for a day at a time as punishment for crimes, real or imaginary, committed by his men. He later wrote a book, 'The Rise and Fall of the Japanese Empire', which should be required reading for all. He mentioned me in this book as we were in his room when the Americans started to drop their 44 gallon drums (without parachutes) containing food, medicine and clothing. They bounced every fifty yards or so, demolishing parts of the buildings on their way, so we dived under the table while one or two of these drums hurtled over our heads, through the hut completely and so on down the line of huts. Miraculously, no one was even scratched. By this time we were allowed to mingle with the other prisoners, but following this we, as the latest captives, were asked to keep our eyes open for further 'attacks' by the Americans. When they flew over, I tried to communicate by zig-zag morse, but no one could understand, until the next day, down came the Superiors with their bomb bays open and we ran to the path between the cesspools to guide them on to this path, but they didn't seem to realise that on either side of the path was human excrement from about 1941 into which we didn't want to go! I must say that their bombing was accurate, but we each had to take a dive in the 'pool', hurriedly made an exit when the Yanks had stopped dropping and we both rushed down to the harbour and dived in to remove the mess, without a 'by your leave' from the Japs. Normally we would have been for it, but I suppose even the Japs must have a sense of humour.

"It was tremendous to get these supplies, particularly tinned fruits, vegetables, meat, vitamin pills etc. and clothing of all sorts. My heartiest thanks go to the Americans for their generosity.

"The day before the U.S. Navy came to liberate us, Japs in large numbers made their way to the roadway leading to the Imperial Palace where they proceeded to commit 'Hari Kiri' (suicide), to which none of us objected. Instead of following this example, our guards decided to get drunk on Saki and that evening they went berserk and they particularly wanted to 'get' the Special Prisoners. Burn and I armed ourselves with baseball bats, courtesy of the Yanks, we being the fittest of a bad bunch and prepared for the worst. The door at the end of the building burst open and we were about to swing the bats when a hand reached up and grabbed the sword by the blade, which didn't do much for the hand. The hand belonged to a Prince of the Realm, (Hirohito's clan) and when the guards realised what they had done, they panicked and ran off, never to be seen again. Maybe some of them finished up on the aforesaid road!"

An Extract from Ian Darby's account of POW life.
By permission of Stuart Eadon

September 1945
Burn O'Neill, Stanley Maxted (a Canadian reporter), Ian Darby and Jimmy Crossman return to Indefatigable after their ordeal in Omori POW Camp. Always a slim trio, they look as if they are in pretty good shape, despite the maggoty food, diarrhoea and losing several stones in weight. Tenko rules were harsh beyond the imagination of normal man; it was these terrors that we secretly harboured in our minds during an occasional sleepless night!
By kind permission of Stuart Eadon

Don Banks' Story

Don Banks, the third Kiwi interviewed, had a very different story to tell. Yet another fear! If one came down into the sea how would one ditch a Firefly? One never practised that exercise, except in the head. Who would come to one's rescue – friend or foe? There was the possibility of being afloat with injuries and getting very hungry. And maybe the sharks! Don met them all, in varying degrees.

Extract from log of Submarine USS Sterlet commanded by Lieut. Cdr. Lewis.

26th July (1945)

> 1446 received report of a downed flier in raft about 30 miles from us. Report, sent via 4475 kcs., was from orbiting Privateer.
> 1447 sent ETA 1630. Headed towards, making full power.
> 1633 Picked up Sub. Lieut. D. W. Banks RNZNVR of HMS Indefatigable.
> Position Lat. 32.58N Long. 136.33E. He had been in the water for two and a half days, was slightly bruised and sunburned, but in very good condition. Communications were excellent; the position was extremely accurate and when we reached the position not one but three planes, two Privateers and a B17 were orbiting the downed man.
> 1830 sent Sterlet first to IFO Liaison Officer reporting pickup.
> 1925 sent Sterlet second to COMSUBPAC reporting pickup.

Don's story was unfolded on Radio Pacific during the interviews with Ian Darby and Burnie O'Neill.

Don and Ian Darby were together for 3 years and did all their training together. Don was on a raid on Takamatsu Airfield and having attacked the airfield his pilot Maurice Goodsell was forced to ditch the aircraft. They were then about 160 kilometres short of the carrier. They had been hit over Takamatsu and presumably the long-range tanks had been holed. They ditched at something between 80 and 100 knots. The aircraft sank very quickly; Maurice was unable to escape his cockpit, for reasons not known. Don surfaced in his Mae West and he 'popped' his little one-man dinghy. The aircraft communications were out of action. Teddy Key flying on Rod Steven's wing in the most appalling weather conditions says that he has a memory of hearing either Don or Maurice calling base. They didn't seem to have sufficient height to obtain signals from the ship's homing beacon. Don records that he was in the dinghy for nearly three days. He had food and water, an emergency kit the size of a sardine tin. The food was in the form of tablets. He had 'speed' tablets and pain killers. Plus three condoms! When asked what he was supposed to do with them, he replied that there didn't seem to be any mermaids around. They were in fact to be used to keep watch and compass dry. Sounds like 'very safe sex', the young lady interviewer suggested. He had sharks for company and they rubbed their noses on the bottom of the dinghy. It was a scary thought knowing that the relatively thin rubber skin of the dinghy separated one's bottom from some pretty awesome teeth. He didn't sleep very much. The Pacific waves had a way of tipping the occupant upside down. It was quite an exhausting job getting back into the dinghy. Eventually on the third day the submarine picked him up. The sailors on board told him that in fact the sharks were very friendly in that part of the Pacific! 'Buck' Benny, the Executive Officer pulled Don from the dinghy.

'Hey, Captain, he's a goddamed Limey.'

'Well throw him back,' came a very prompt answer.

'Hey,' said Don, 'I'm a New Zealander'.

'Alright then, he can stay', said the Captain.

The Captain in fact gave his bunk to Don, in order to speed up his recovery. They gave Don a large slug of brandy and Don added, 'Under the shower, I sang most wonderfully'.

The Radio Pacific interviewer asked Don if at any time he had thought of 'giving up'. His answer was to tell how on his return to the Indefatigable, just three weeks after he left, as Maurice Goodsell's Observer, on the Takamatsu raid, he had had interviews with three naval padres . . . 'one of each brand'. The black-bearded one, a hard C of E man, had asked Don, 'Tell me Don, did you ever pray?' 'Only once,' Don had answered, 'I looked up to heaven, shook my fist and shouted, 'look here mate, you got me into this mess, you bloody well get me out of it.'

'Well . . . he did, didn't he,' concluded Don. The Padre's answer is not recorded. What kept Don going? There was no training in this matter, it was just one of those things you picked up. After about 4 hours adrift the official opinion was that 'you'd had it'.

Ray Battison stated in one of Stuart Eadon's books, that Don was fortunate not to be spotted by a Japanese aircraft on one occasion when it passed overhead and on another occasion an enemy destroyer had circled him, but had ignored him. Don had a number of flares with him, and a bit of luck, so he said. There should have been six in the dinghy pack, but he had been Gunnery Officer in the squadron and therefore was in charge of flares. He had therefore stuffed in an extra one. It was that last flare which went off when he signalled the submarine; it was that one which had been effective in attracting attention when he was almost finished and in quite a bad way. It is a quite feasible story but somehow those stories which get tossed around after a time sometimes, just maybe, sound a little better. In flying terms, another form of line-shooting! The embellished story went that, way back in Burscough, a bunch of guys developed an appetite for creating their own brand of rocket. This was done with the help of an old bicycle frame, Koffman Cartridges, which were used to start the Griffon engine and of course flares, – red star type. The story goes on record that when Don came to signal both the Jap aeroplane and the Jap destroyer, they were duds . . . because of these boyish pranks. Well . . . that was real luck. Sorry Don, if all that was just Branch Type invention . . . you know how things get embellished at times?

Don was safe in the skipper's bunk and the skipper slept on a table. The skipper one morning decided to shell the mainland of Japan, the town of Shingu. They set alight some oil tanks, hit a power station and torpedoed their harbour bridge. Quickly they got out of it, away from shallow water. They had no sooner got into reasonable depths of water when they were depth-charged and bombed. 'God' thought Don, 'this is dicier than bloody flying.'

Don was transferred from USS Sterlet to another submarine and taken to Saipan. He was flown to Guam and was there when the A Bomb was exploded. He was flown to Iwo Jima and by bosun's chair was moved from one destroyer to another and finally back to Indefatigable. As Don said, 'All that took about three weeks and not a scar to show for it all.' Don said that he did two more operational trips on his return.

Don had written to Maurice Goodsell's family; Maurice had been the only son of elderly parents and their loss was particularly hard for them. Don had been returned to his old squadron friends. In recounting his ordeal, he said, 'No I wasn't scared . . . just bloody terrified.'

We arrived at Manus on 14th September and departed the following day. Our arrival near Sydney, accompanied a heavy swell and flying off was delayed. 1771 and 1772 Squadrons were disbanded and we were fragmented again. The team had broken up and we settled down in different parts around Sydney before being embarked on the Stratheden and Andes. But we still had to say our fond farewells to Oz. On leaves, at weekends and in those final few days, Sydney had looked after us, 'fair dinkum'.

The Squadron was disbanded in indecent haste. As others have testified in this story, we were but part of that sad dismissal of a great naval force. Admiral Rawlings was at the forefront of this great disappointment and he wrote most feelingly on the matter. His statement was to be quite prophetic, but, at that time his plea fell on deaf ears. The Fleet quietly faded away, a Fleet which was probably the largest assembly of Commonwealth ships in history. John Wilton in his book, 'The Forgotten Fleet' was to add, ' – but like the old ladies locked in the lavatory, nobody knew they were there'. We had to wait until September 1995 for a token of recognition.

"I have not seen the personal signals, or indeed seen all the official signals, but I am in no two minds about one thing; that the 'fading out' of the Task Force and the manner in which this is being done is not only tragic, but is one which I would give much to avoid.

"To me, what is happening to its personnel and its ships seems to ignore their feelings, their sentiments and their pride; in so doing quite a lot is being cast away, for that Fleet accomplished something which matters immensely.

"I am not speaking of such enemy they met, nor of the difficulties they overcame, nor of the long periods at sea; I am speaking of that which was from the start our overriding and heaviest responsibility, the fact that we were in a position which was in most ways unique and was in any case decisive; for we could have lowered the good name of the British Navy in American eyes for ever.

". . . I am not certain that those at home have any idea of what these long operating periods mean, nor of the strain put on those in the ships, so many of whom, both officers and men, are mere children. I have in my Flagship, for instance, Leading Seamen of 19 and Petty Officers of 21. When I look back on that which this untrained youth has managed to accomplish and to stick out, then I have no fear for the future of the Navy, provided, but only provided, that we handle them with vision and understanding, and that we recognise them for what they were and are – people of great courage who would follow one anywhere, and whose keynote was that the word 'impossible' did not exist.

"And so I question the wisdom of dispersing a Fleet in the way in which it is now being done. At the very least there should have been taken home to England a token force somewhat similar to that which was left in the operating area with the American Fleet when the tanker shortage required the withdrawal of the greater part of the Task Force.

"It seems to me that here was a matter which could have been utilised in a dignified and far-reaching manner – the arrival in home waters of ships who had represented the Empire alongside their American allies, and who were present, adding their not ineffective blow, at the annihilation of the Japanese Navy and the defeat of Japan.

"It may well be that the days will come when the Navy will find it hard to get the money it needs. Perhaps then a remembrance of the return and the work of the British Pacific Fleet might have helped to provide a stimulus and an encouragement to wean the public from counter attractions and those more alluringly staged."

Admiral Rawlings.

Like one that on a lonesome road
Doth walk in fear and dread,
And having once turned round, walks on,
And turns no more his head;
Because he knows, a frightful fiend
Doth close behind him . . . tread.

The Rime of the Ancient Mariner
Coleridge.

FAREWELL OZ AND THANKYOU.
...WELCOME HOME TO THE FORGOTTEN FLEET

There is a Tavern in the town and there my true love sits him
*   down,*
Fare thee well for I must leave thee . . .
And remember that the best of friends must part . . .
Adieu, adieu, kind friends, I can no longer stay with you . . .
I'll hang my heart on a weeping willow tree,
And may the world go well with thee.   *Anon*

From the middle of March until we left for the UK in September 1945 all of us had made some sort of contact with Australians. Usually through the Victoria League we had met Australian families and we had been 'adopted' by them. During our time off, during leaves and at the very end when we were 'kicked off' the Indefatigable, our homes were often with these very kind and often very candid people. They were 'Grippos', the naval slang for those kind Australians who entertained servicemen and opened up their homes. Some of the friendships which grew then, still survive today. Let the individual stories do the telling. Alan Rowlinson. 'We were transferred from the ship, "to share digs"! The Squadron wasn't just disbanded, it was allowed to disintegrate. I spent some time before departing on the Andes with Croose and Val together with Phil Rowell, a Seafire pilot and Robin Gray, a ship's officer, in Hobart, Tasmania and there were quite a few parties of farewell. We sailed on the SS Andes, a "dry ship", much to our regret. In my time with 1772, my pilot, Geoff Gill was transferred to 1771, it was great to be back in the UK where in time I became his best man when he married his Delphine.'

Croose Parry. 'I remember continual games of Bridge, calling in at the Yacht Club in Bombay and trying to maintain our secret stock of cans and bottles on this dry ship'.

Johnny Coles. 'I was very sad when the Squadron broke up, but I was so glad that the war was over.'

Chris Maclaren. 'I have nothing but praise and admiration for the

The Friendly Squadron

An extract from
an Australian
local newspaper.

FLEET AIR ARM OFFICERS on leave in Hobart, were hosts at a sherry party at Wrest Pt. Riviera Hotel on Friday night. Members of the RNVR, the officers are in the HMS Indefatigable. L to r (back), Sub-Lt (A) Val Bennett, Betty Atkins, Sub-Lts (A) Philip Rowell, Alan Rowlinson, and Croose Parry; (front), Sub-Lt Robin Guy and Judy Bennett.

way the Aussies in Sydney threw open their homes to the boys of the BPF. Nothing was too much trouble and no expense was spared in order to entertain us. Roger McCahey, a Seafire pilot in 894 Squadron, with whom I had trained and myself were given the address of the Cook family in Rose Bay, Sydney. They had a son who was in the UK with the RAAF at the time. They also had two lovely daughters, but in spite of this, they took us in and treated us as part of the family; they were simply wonderful and I will never forget their kindness.

I remember they invited us to stay with them at a hotel in the Blue Mountains. One morning a crowd of us boys and girls decided to go trekking on horseback for the day; as I had not ridden since I was about 8 years old, I selected a staid and stolid hack as my horse. One of the girls, who fancied her chances, plumped for the biggest horse, a chestnut stallion of magnificent proportions. Unfortunately when we were well into the bush, the stallion suddenly shied and threw its rider, who fell awkwardly on her face and broke her nose. The horse ran off and was nowhere to be seen. Volunteering to ride back for a doctor and transport, I galloped for what seemed a mighty distance until the drive of the hotel came into view. At the end of this drive was a cattle grid, so in true cowboy style I flung myself off the horse with the intention of throwing the reins over the hitching rail. I hadn't reckoned on the devastating effect a few hours in the saddle could have on one's muscles. In consequence, when I leaped from the horse my legs simply buckled and as I was incapable of standing: I had to crawl the rest of the way to the hotel for help. I took some time to convince the staff that the doctor was not for me and they were duly despatched into the bush. I spent the next two days trying to regain the use of my legs.' Not even a romantic ending Chris; no sinking sun in the west and a warm embrace. A story nevertheless full of passion, climax and symbolism. The moral of the tale will be left to the reader. It was not a line; every word in this book is true!

Teddy Key, knowing about this tale of Chris can claim an almost identical piece of Australian hospitality. 'This was my last spell of real time with Steve as a companion before we went north. We decided too to go 'to bush' and stayed at a hotel in the wilds, at a place called Bundanoon. There we became children-minders in a hotel full of golf-mad mums and dads. We went buggy riding with the children and did some horse riding too. On the first evening, we could not find our dinner places, eventually finding them set out on the mantlepiece. So we ate our dinner standing up and bluffed our way through the whole affair. Well, I was bluffing because I was rigid, even to the neck! Steve was always made of sterner stuff and riding was "a dolly" for him. But no fair maidens in distress, just a load of tough little Oz kids. Steve, George Trollope and myself had also had the good fortune to meet a lovely family, the Meloccos, a family of naturalised Italians. They had the most beautiful house looking straight out across the Sydney Harbour to the famous "coathanger" bridge. It was indeed a great base for the whole time we were in Australia; such incredible hospitality! As a bonus they had two beautiful daughters, Helen and Jean, who also had a beautiful friend named Greta. All very tidy! We had our own room too in this home. Space forbids the detail of the extent of what this family meant to me. The parents died and the

*The Melocco Family –
beautiful 'Grippos', on
the terrace of their
magnificent home
looking towards Sydney
Harbour and 'the
Bridge'.*

*Jean Melocco with
a Sydney Tan.*

*And we all had a bush picnic . . . or
a beach party at some time.*

Photos Teddy Key

178

young ones married and now they remain just a great memory.'

Wally Pritchard. 'Through the Victoria League Bob Scott and I met the Edgells at Bathurst. They owned just about the biggest canning factory in Australia. The Edgells and their daughter Sally entertained us royally. We played tennis, went shooting at kangaroos and rabbits. Sally taught me to drive a car so well that for 51 years I didn't have an accident. That friendship has prospered through many returned visits back in Oz and here in the UK. We were with them in Sydney on VJ Day and holidayed in Katoomba. Bob, Sally and I met up again in June 1996 in Australia. Sally is still very beautiful.'

Bob Scott and Wally
Pritchard have kept in
touch with Sally (1996).
(Wally Pritchard)

Bob Scott. 'I suppose we all have stories of fun we had on leaves. Dare you print Forêt Millar's story? I was fortunate to find a billet at the home of one of the girls in the "university crowd". I have a hazy memory of swimming, beach parties, night clubs. A great deal of fun, but not high on culture. We still had the ability to find duty-free drinks and these helped open doors at the Roosevelt Club. Then, with sad farewells, on to the SS Andes and home before Christmas, playing bridge with "Madame Arcati" and listening to "Don't fence me in".'

Alan Rowlinson. 'A charming young lady at the Victoria League asked us what we wanted in the way of hospitality. Our list included, a father who enjoyed a drink, a mother with a spare car, two daughters, a tennis court and a yacht. We discovered Dr and Mrs Cutler. Virtually all our desires were satisfied! It is slightly ironic that although 1772 were

179

quite proud of their Rugger team it was a soccer fanatic in our midst, Eric Bramhall, who let drop the news that he had fixed us up with a match against Drummoyne, the Harlequins of Sydney at that time. It was likely that such a fixture would be too much for us, so we conscripted a few players outside the Squadron and we were billed as, "The Royal Navy Combined Sydney XV". We played on a rock-hard pitch and we were quite pleased to have lost by only 11 points to 8.' It should not be lost on the reader that this man, Alan Rowlinson, who currently bears the title of "Reluctant Chairman" of 1772 Squadron was once our outward going sports officer... to a fairly unfit outfit!

Sammy Samuelson. 'In Collary, I had the pleasure of meeting a very kind, pleasant widow, Mrs MacMaster, about the same age as my mother. She had two sons, the elder one was in the Army in New Guinea and the younger one was a navigator on Lancasters in the RAAF and had been shot down over Germany and taken POW. All the RAAF and RNZAF POW's on release from POW camps were sent to the Grand and Metropole Hotels in Brighton, only 13 miles from my father's farm. So I wrote to Mum and she got in touch with the appropriate authorities and "Bo" was able to stay with Mum and Dad for a while. Small world! After we got back from Japan, Bo was back in Sydney and I met him and we got on very well. Tragically when I got back to England I had a letter from Mrs MacMaster to say that Bo had bought a motorbike, had crashed into a bus and was killed. This, after surviving everything else.'

Johnny O'Driscoll. 'I have very pleasant memories of the Imperial Services Club in Sydney; Royal Naval officers had been made Honorary Members. The bar seemed to be open very long hours and there was a snooker room. It was an up-market club and exclusive. "Christies", "Princes" and "Romanos" were the premier night clubs of Sydney and we enjoyed them to the full. "Romanos" had a bust of Napoleon on the entrance stairs. We invented "the Drool", a slow-moving, rotating shuffle for up to twenty chaps. Lunar Park provided fair-ground entertainment after a few beers. Unfortunately, late-night travel was problematical and I can recall sharing a telephone box with Ray Battison for an hour in an endeavour to obtain a taxi. A beer in the "local" was represented in Sydney by a scrum in a bar. Opening hours were 6 p.m. to 7 p.m. and bodies lined the bar about 6 deep, the object being to obtain two or three rounds in one order, as a return to the bar was out of the question.'

If there was a tavern in the town which remotely compared with the English Pub, then we never found it. The beer was thirst-quenching but always ice-cold and ultimately dyspeptic.

Gordon Macrow. 'Petty Officer Stanworth, Petty Officer Ferris and myself spent a leave in Adelaide and stayed in Glenelg where the first

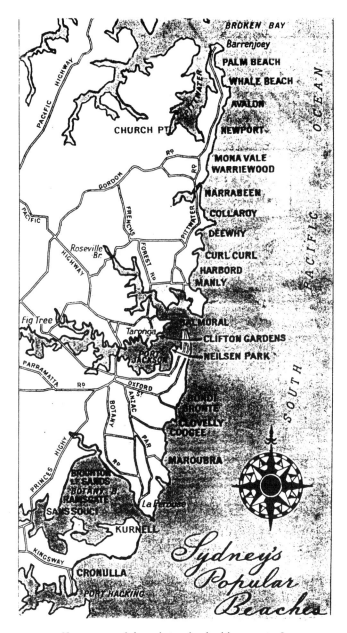

How many of these bring back old memories?

settlers in South Australia landed. We had two extra days because the RTO was unable to book us on a train back to Sydney, via Melbourne.'

Sammy Samuelson, the adventurer and Bon Viveur. 'Sydney was fabulous, with Christies, Romanos and Princes nightclubs. Johnny Walker Whiskey was 4 shillings a bottle and there were steaks, oysters and bananas, theatres and cosy Italian restaurants: trying to drive the girlfriend's Standard 8 and getting out of the tramlines after getting stuck. One family I met was the Robinsons. Dr Robinson owned two racehorses and Randwick Races was a venue to meet "real Aussies". The Robinsons lived in a beautiful house in Rose Bay. During the last days in Sydney I got digs in Kings Cross. I was innocent of its Soho similarity. There was a murder in the house opposite and I couldn't wait to get home.'

But . . . nothing was the equal of coming home, saying 'Goodbye' to Oz was sad, but it is so long ago now. We were however still young, brash and above all, resilient and full of the desire to get stuck into the 'real world'. This was easy for some, difficult for others and if you got this far in our story you will know all about these guys – their madness and then their mildness.

Here and now we formally apologise for our indiscretions to anybody 'wounded' by us. We did apologise to the Imperial Services Club in Sydney because they had been most hospitable to us. One evening dining there, a small bunch of us watched as a few old Aussies recalled 'Hill 60' of WW1, by means of salt and pepper pots etc. Not to be outdone, in a neighbouring room which had a large polished table we easily associated this shiny 'flat top' with a carrier. An individual, arm outspread, was propelled round the room together with all the jargon of landing on, and 'spilled' just before the rounddown – and sent sliding in search of a wire, but more spectacularly, finding a barrier; usually another prone 'subby'. All very good fun; who has not used a bed as a trampoline or other furniture for an activity for which it was not designed? The crunch? The buttons on our officer jackets were not compatible with a polished surface. Sorry! Sorry! Sorry! Have we created a story, desirably in a lighter vein, which has turned out to be varicose or as a critic once wrote of a play, 'This play gives failure a bad name?'

We were to a man, grateful for the hospitality of the Australians. Truly they were magnificent, even when we did not behave ourselves. 'May the world go well with thee,' if you are still on this mortal coil. The journey home was for most of us, an anticlimax. There was fun and adventure to be had in Fremantle and Bombay but the ships, Stratheden and Andes, belted through the waves in almost indecent haste. We dreamed over the ship's rails, talked and wondered about the future. The flying fishes and porpoise swarm alongside us and the weather was for the most part very tranquil. The ships did their best to entertain us with ship's concerts. Johnny O'Driscoll recalls another fine Club we were allowed to join, the Yacht Club in Bombay. One show on Andes he remembers was, 'So long Diggers'.

What were our thoughts then and years later?

Don Randle. 'Sadly I lost touch with Forêt Millar, my "looker", in Sydney. I think now that we drank too much but we had a phenomenal

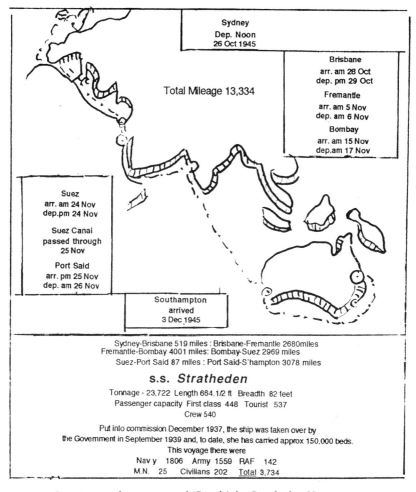

Sydney
Dep. Noon
26 Oct 1945

Brisbane
arr. am 28 Oct
dep. pm 29 Oct

Fremantle
arr. am 5 Nov
dep. am 6 Nov

Bombay
arr. am 15 Nov
dep. am 17 Nov

Total Mileage 13,334

Suez
arr. am 24 Nov
dep. pm 24 Nov

Suez Canal
passed through
25 Nov

Port Said
arr. pm 25 Nov
dep. am 26 Nov

Southampton
arrived
3 Dec 1945

Sydney-Brisbane 519 miles : Brisbane-Fremantle 2680miles
Fremantle-Bombay 4001 miles: Bombay-Suez 2969 miles
Suez-Port Said 87 miles : Port Said-S'hampton 3078 miles

s.s. Stratheden

Tonnage - 23,722 Length 664.1/2 ft Breadth 82 feet
Passenger capacity First class 448 Tourist 537
Crew 540

Put into commission December 1937, the ship was taken over by
the Government in September 1939 and, to date, she has carried approx 150,000 beds.
This voyage there were
Navy 1806 Army 1559 RAF 142
M.N. 25 Civilians 202 Total 3,734

A route map from a copy of 'Struth' the Stratheden Newspaper.

183

British Fleet's Air Arm's Farewell To Sydney

FLYING IN FORMATION over the Harbor Bridge, these Fleet Air Arm aircraft dived in salute and farewell to Sydney today. Lower left are flights of Fireflies, famous British fighters; next come Vought Corsair carrier-borne fighter aircraft, and finally h . . . . . Avengers, naval fighter-bombers (the largest . . . . . in the ser. . . .
[SOME CAPTIONS DETAIL LOST].

degree of recovery. Were we adequately trained to fight in the Pacific War?'

Alan Rowlinson. 'We began the war with a poor collection of carriers and aircraft, but were part of an incredible Fleet at the end of WW2. As an aircrew Observer on several raids in which 1,000 plus aircraft took part, it was not possible either to see the whole fleet at once, because it was spread over such a huge area of sea, or to comprehend that I was part of such a huge naval force. The carrier had become a most potent force. I have the abiding memory of the role I was privileged to be a part of and it will always be one of my pleasures to have been there and great sadness that some of us who are not here cannot share that feeling of pride.'

Burn O'Neill. 'If I were to be born again, I would say, "Let me be a pilot in 1772 back in 1944". Where is that photo of Glyn Robert's aeroplane smashed up on the flight deck? Do you remember Glyn's statement, "I've done dozens and dozens of ADDL's and only bounced once." But what a bounce. "Whatever happened to the Squadron line book? It is all in there." ' (Sadly, Burn, it was whipped, pinched, purloined, hoisted . . . or whatever).

Johnny Coles. 'We must have been a very expensive squadron to maintain and perhaps the least cost-effective squadron in naval history. We did our best and in retrospect, it was one of the finest educations any young man could wish for.'

Wally Pritchard. 'Hindsight is a wonderful thing and one would find it difficult to live without afterthoughts. I would say that it was all very worthwhile, but with what I know now I would not volunteer for the FAA today. The achievements of the FAA although great, were very costly in terms of human and material resources. The experience of our wartime careers has produced a profound comradeship and fellowship which could not be surpassed.'

Ray Battison. 'One has such vivid memories and though the whole war was a colossal catastrophe, it is ironic that for so many, certainly for me, it was also a period of the most precious times of my life. There were wonderful friendships, a tremendous sense of camaraderie, never more so than in the Fleet Air Arm, which we all referred to as "The Branch". To quote the opening lines of "A Tale of Two Cities" by Dickens – "It was the best of times, it was the worst of times". One's memories of the best times seem to wipe out the worst times.'

John Price. 'A thought comes to mind immediately; won't it be nice to get back home and sit in front of a coal fire knowing that it is cold outside. This thought comes to mind in a hot ship and on the way home. A lasting memory was on the way out to Australia when I saw an Albatross for the first time. What do I remember about the Indefatigable? The 4 best liquids were, soup, cocoa, limejuice and rum.'

The slightly more bizarre happenings after the war, were that Johnny O'Driscoll and Croose Parry became Flying Instructors. Alan Rowlinson obtained a driving licence in Australia and passed his test on a 10 ton vehicle. Sammy Samuelson, Teddy Key's observer, passed his solo flying test at Dale and for a brief time became an instructor. Not a lot of people know these facts.

Whatever the memory, the fact is plain to see; the grey cells have suffered. We became small pieces of that 'thing' called the 'Forgotten Fleet'. We didn't really care; we were home and we wanted to settle down and it may be something of a pun, but a very down-to-earth lot we are. Like Peter Ustinov we hope to outlive the date on our passports. As he says, 'to do otherwise would be an awful waste.'

One of the more useful things we have done since 1945 has been 'to keep in touch'. Our reunions began with 'stag' affairs. Who eventually suggested that we include our ladies is not really certain, but for a long time we have enjoyed their company.

Alan Rowlinson. '1772 reunions started somewhat erratically, mainly because of the general need to establish a future and of course they were mainly attended by those who lived within a reasonable distance from London. One in particular, in 1950, happened to be on December 2nd and I don't believe Ann, my wife of one year, could quite understand me when I said that I hoped she wouldn't mind if I went to "see the boys" . . . on our first wedding anniversary! The situation was not improved a lot when a year later the reunion was scheduled for 13th May and again I hoped she wouldn't mind if I went. Unfortunately on her birthday! One can only assume that Alan kept his marriage together by suggesting that we asked the ladies to come along the following year.

Ian Darby, of course, had to keep contact with us all from a very long way away. For him the first time he met us all was 1979 at St Stephen's Tavern. He and Ngaire came over for the big celebration in 1995. Many of those, he chooses to call 'Poms', have been to New Zealand over the 50 plus years. They included Les and Dorothy Wort, Ray and Edith Battison, George and Joyce Trollope, Harry Russell, Gordon and Brenda Macrow, Alan Rowlinson, Bob and Anne Scott and of course Burn O'Neill; Don Banks and Pete Kingston have always kept in touch. Ian has always been the contact boy and has served us well in the UK in keeping the others in touch too. He always likes to point out that the term 'Pom' is applied in a friendly way; it is in Australia that 'Pom' is a term of denigration. That should make some enemies!

The success of the reunions was largely due to Johnny O'Driscoll and Johnny Palmer who put in so much effort to keep us together. The venues included, St Stephen's Tavern, opposite the Houses of Parliament, the Four Feathers just off Fleet Street, the Coal Hole in the Strand, the Savoy Tavern in Savoy Street, the Hurlingham Club and the United Services Club just off Edgware Road, near Marble Arch. In 1989 we had our first HMS Indefatigable reunion at the New Cobden in Birmingham. After these reunions, which were held again in 1991 and 1993 a very few of the chaps who maintained our aircraft joined us. Since then Gordon Macrow, Harry Russell and John Price have been with us at our reunions, which are now organised by a small group of us who meet bi-monthly at the Duke of Wellington Tavern in East Horsley, Surrey.

We celebrated the Anniversary of the forming up of the Squadron with a gathering of nearly 50 people at Sherborne and Yeovilton, in

An early reunion . . . where? But it was STAG.

(Johnny O'Driscoll)

The picture above shows a very shy figure just coming into view. This man later became our 'Reluctant Chairman', having developed somewhat, in self confidence. 'Lock up your wives . . .'

. . . but later, the ladies joined us.

(Johnny O'Driscoll)

May 1994. We repeated the exercise in September 1995 at the same venues to celebrate our version of the 50th Anniversary of VJ Day. A few members attended the big affair at Lee-on-Solent as part of the 'Forgotten Fleet'. On this occasion, Ian Darby and Ngaire had travelled from New Zealand to be with us and we were delighted to welcome Dorothy Wort, Les's widow and their two daughters, Sue and Jenny. Joan Wright, Glyn Roberts' sister, Joan Gillingham, Glen MacBride's

50 YEARS ON
RNAS Yeovilton 1995.

188

● SAFETY CHECK: A member of the Historic Flight ensures war veteran Donald Randle is strapped in the aircraft cockpit before the accident.

Seamen injured as plane crashes into van

A REUNION flight at RNAS Yeovilton was grounded when the historic aircraft taking part hit a vehicle as it was attempting to take off.

War veteran Donald Randle, aged 70, had travelled to the Fleet Air Arm museum from his Gloucestershire home to meet other former members of 1772 Naval Air Squadron.

He won the flight in a Fairey Firefly in a raffle at the reunion and took the back seat in the plane – the same type his squadron used against Japan in 1945.

But as the aircraft, piloted by Lt Cdr Don Sigournay, started up the runway, it struck a maintenance vehicle containing two Royal Naval seamen.

Neither the pilot nor Mr Randle were injured but the two men in the van were cut by glass and had to be taken to Yeovil hospital for a check-up.

"There will be an investigation carried out to determine why the Firefly and vehicle happened to be close together," said Yeovilton's community relations officer, Vic Sirett.

The engine and propellor of the Firefly, part of the Royal Navy's Historic Flight, was damaged. But, as it is the only flying model of the plane, the specialist engineers at the base will begin work straight away to repair it.

Alan Rowlinson presents a cheque to Lt. Cdr. Deuxberry CO of the Royal Navy Historic Flight.

widow, who also travelled from New Zealand and Alan Gittins, Glyn's nephew were also with us on this great occasion. We raffled the rear seat of the Historic Flight Firefly Mark V, a very generous gesture by the CO, Hugh Deuxberry. The event was to be overshadowed by a minor disaster and a disappointment to the winner Don Randle. The reader will have guessed that the accident was a taxiing accident . . .

A pleasant ending resulted in Alan Rowlinson presenting Hugh Deuxberry with a cheque for £350, for RN Historic Flight Funds. The amount was supplemented by a biggish profit on the previous night's beer kitty. Now that is a sign of the advancing years of 1772!

Ray Battison. 'When Les died in the mid 80's, Dorothy Wort suggested donations to the Fleet Air Arm Museum instead of flowers. I therefore wrote to old 1772 members asking for donations towards some specific memento in the museum. A painting was commissioned, to be painted by Brian Witham, of that raid on Takamatsu Airfield, with the Avenger bombs falling all around. The legend on that painting, now in the Museum, reads, "In memory of 'the Boss' Lt. Cdr. Les Wort DSC, RNVR, from the officers of 1772 Squadron."

We have returned to the old haunts such as Yeovilton, Burscough,

A painting by Val Bennett, was presented to the FAA Museum in 1995 to commemorate the 50th Anniversary of the Squadron. The painting depicts 4 Fireflies approaching the Indefatigable prior to landing on. The picture is shown on the front cover of the book.

A recce to the 'Bull and Dog' just to reassure ourselves that it was still there, September 1996.

(Ormskirk Advertiser)

Lee-on-Solent, Australia and Pensacola and perhaps nothing can ever be quite the same. It is however still good to 'walk backwards'. Anne and Bob Scott recently wrote from Australia, for they have returned, permanently, 'Funny business, isn't it, going back to places from the past?' Ian Darby, from New Zealand has written to say that there was some contemplation of returning to the Omori POW Camp in Japan. 'Ian, from an honest old Pom, the old place won't seem quite the same.' That restlessness and a wee tinge of adventure still lingers in the blood, but . . .

> Oh to be in England
> Now that April's there,
> And whoever wakes in England
> Sees, some morning, unaware,
> That the lowest boughs and the brushwood sheaf
> Round the elm tree bole, are in leaf,
> While the chaffinch sings on the orchard bough
> In England . . . now.
>
> Robert Browning

DRAMATIS PERSONAE – THE PLAYERS SPEAK THEIR PIECE

'History is the essence of innumerable biographies.'
Thomas Carlyle

If you wish in this world to advance,
Your merits you're bound to enhance.
You must stir it and stump it
And blow your own trumpet,
Or trust me, you havn't a chance.   *W. S. Gilbert. Ruddigore*

The characters in this 'play' were trained in various ways. From May 1944 to September 1945 we grew up together, had fun together, lived dangerously together, miss those who lived too dangerously and those who ran out of luck. We have remained in touch as each one of us, from 1945, went our way in terms of family and careers – retired and now – are creaking a little more. Most of us have been pleased to contribute our stories, not because we want to tell the world about ourselves because in truth we were very ordinary men whose contribution in WW2 was but a small one. It was however an honourable one and these are the stories, brief to long, according to modesty, memory and energy. They complete our diary, of a significant fellowship which will one day merely pass down to our grandchildren, who will at first think that '1772' is an historical date!

The squadron was in no way a regular team, for pilots and observers came and went. Between the two dates of May '44 and September '45 approximately 50 aircrew belonged to 1772. Some were with us so briefly that we remember little about them.

Some of the stories are written by relatives who have since VJ Day become firm friends of the Squadron and now rank as 'honorary members' and join us at our reunions. Many characters are unfolded on the following pages and it was inevitable that repetition would occur. Every attempt has been made to keep repetition to a minimum.

For the most part the ranks of the aircrew have been omitted. Many started as Midshipman(A) and became Sub-Lieutenant(A). Several acquired the second wavy ring; some are not certain what they became, so in the cause of uniformity, plain 'mister' it must be.

Pride of place in the order of the following potted biographies goes to 'The Boss', Les Wort to whom the book is dedicated. The book is also a testament to the sacrifice made by those who gave their lives in action and training, and to those who have died since 1945. The Boss would have had it no other way, if he were still with us.

LES WORT
CO 1772 Squadron
Lt. Cdr(A) RNVR, DSC.
Pilot

Peter Sellers tells the story of the smug pianist who claimed he could play any tune on request. He was asked to play, 'That's what you are' and of course the pianist, 'was lost'. He asked the punter to sing the words. Out came, 'Unforgettable, that's what you are.' Teddy Key says that he can remember two particular occasions when he had reason to recall the Boss. Once at college just after the war he felt obliged to add his piece to a debate which seemed to be in a cynical mood and was for the most part 'knocking' the qualities of leadership which had prevailed during the war. He remembers stating quite firmly what he thought of some of the leaders he had met and The Boss was number one on that list of men he considered had been more than exceptional in those qualities which were needed to bring men together and produce, 'the right stuff'. The other occasion was many years later when he was asked to give a talk to a group of quite elderly men. Teddy says that he needed to emphasise again those qualities of leadership which had meant a great deal to him. The audience, now a sympathetic one, which understood to a man what he was saying, rose to his evaluation of a guy they never knew. Teddy Key in Stuart Eadon's book "Kamikaze", wrote, 'On the morning of my first operational flight over Japan, I sat next to the Boss in the Wardroom trying hard to eat my breakfast. He looked at me and said quietly, "Nervous?" "Yes," I answered, "Very." "So am I," this man who had won a DSC, replied. The answer was typical of the pragmatic, tolerant, uncompromising, competent and efficient but very human fellow he was. He was a most able yet friendly leader and Les Wort had made us into a very respectable, hard-working unit. Goodness knows how good or bad we really were as a squadron, we will leave that for others to decide and judge. He was uncompromising when it came to the standards he required of us and the standards he expected of himself as a commanding officer. He was in fact a thoroughly nice, caring man and I for one am grateful for his life and the privilege of serving under him. Looking back over nearly 40 years of teaching I pay him a high tribute in believing that he would have made the sort of Headmaster that is badly needed now. Les Wort was a great guy and he restored our respectability and confidence, for when he took command of 1772, morale must have been at its lowest and things were not going well at all.'

Johnny Coles. 'The Boss joined us in November 1944 and I remember meeting him in the bar on the evening of his arrival. It was of course dark outside and he asked what was all that flying going on. The answer came, "That's your squadron, night flying." A short pause and then, "I'll put a stop to that, it's too bloody dangerous." Night flying for 1772 Squadron ceased forthwith!'

Ray Battison, who was his Observer until the end of the war and remained one of his staunchest friends until the Boss died in the mid 80's. 'A happy squadron it most certainly was; as to our efficiency, we must leave that judgement to others. I am certain that not a man in either aircrew or ground crew would have failed to follow Les to the end of the earth, if that was what he wanted. There was no "pulling of rank", just simple honesty and sincerity. As a pilot he was perfection for me. Deck take-off and landing is not exactly the safest pastime in the world and the Squadron had a fair share of mishaps. During our flying time together we had only one prang, when landing on the Indefatigable. Les was given a "Wave-off" by the batsman just before touchdown, but unfortunately our hook had already caught an arrester wire. The engine was pulling us skywards at full throttle and the wire was dragging us down on to the deck. The inevitable happened, when at bridge height we dropped like a stone, hitting the bridge superstructure with our starboard wing. The aircraft was a write-off but neither of us suffered so much as a scratch. The sequel to this happened just a few years ago when Les sadly died. Dorothy, his wife, gave me our aircraft clock, beautifully mounted on a piece of the aircraft's wooden propeller. Members of the ground crew had obviously done this for their CO and it still sits on my desk.'

Johnny Palmer knew a Dick Allen who was with Les, flying Wildcats when they shot down an FW Condor, operating from HMS Fencer.

Through Johnny we are grateful to Dick Allen for providing some information about Les. 'Les was on Course 26 at HMS St Vincent and he was in the first group to be trained at Pensacola in Florida. This was in late 1941 to early 1942. He went to Dekheila in Egypt with 884 Squadron and returned to the UK about mid-1943. In July 1943 he was posted to 1832 Squadron under the command of "Tommy" Harrington and they were based at Eglinton and Speke where they "worked up" for fighter flight attachments to TBR squadrons on convoy escort carriers. From November 1943 to October 1944 he was Fighter Flight CO flying Wildcats and attached to 843 Swordfish TBR Squadron on HMS Fencer. It was here that he was awarded his DSC for the shooting down of the Condor and no doubt his all-round qualities came into this award. Within a month he became our CO.

Les became a leading light in the British Pensacola Veterans Association and was one of a party of ten who visited Pensacola in 1975 at the invitation of the U.S. Naval Attache in London. This was a precursor to a number of subsequent organised visits by BPV members and their wives, one of which in November 1982 was attended by Les and Dorothy. Les was a keen Rifle Club member at Woking and he had shot at Bisley in a number of events. In retirement Les and Dorothy were involved in local civil defence at the time, the 'Cold War' put an emphasis on Local Government Authorities to raise the awareness of nuclear warfare.'

Les and Dorothy.

One night at Schofields in New South Wales, a very balmy night one remembers, instead of being in our woodshack-style Wardroom, we had lit a bonfire outside and we roasted potatoes. All good clean fun and just the stuff to get the lads in a relaxed and happy frame of mind.

Unfortunately things got out of control and the bonfire sort of took control of the dry, bush type growth around us. The fire brigade had to be sent for and there was trouble, trouble, trouble. The CO was asked to provide a list of all those officers responsible for the 'forest fire'. This he did but his name was at the top of the list.

One of his characteristic 'stances' in the crew room, which in Australia was usually out in the open, was to sit back in his chair in the most laid back manner (he could well have invented that modern phrase), feet up on his desk. As a birthday gift we gave him a pair of stirrups, 'to prevent his feet from slipping off the desk and causing him some grief! He joined in all our good humour, his style being quite droll and dry. He knew how to mix with us but at any crunch point, The Boss was the boss.

Lt. Cdr. Les Wort, DSC, RNVR

Les Wort joined the fleet Air Arm from local government in Stockbridge and Romsey in 1941 and was on the first fighter pilot's course to arrive at Pensacola, Florida in July of that year before the U.S.A. entered World War Two. After service in North Africa and the Mediterranean in late 1943, he took command of 842 Squadron's Martlet (Wildcat) Flight in protection duties and particularly on Russian convoys. He was awarded the D.S.C. for his part, with Dick Fleishman-Allen, in shooting down a Focke Wulf Condor.

In November 1944, he assumed command of 1772 Firefly 1 Squadron and in July and August 1945, in H.M.S. Indefatigable, took part in operations in the Pacific against the Japanese, being present in Tokyo Bay when they surrendered in early September.

After the war he returned to civilian life and was the Deputy Clerk at Hartley Wintney. During this period he read Law in his spare time, and qualified as a solicitor. He was appointed Clerk to the Midhurst Rural District Council in 1949 and, ten years later, Clerk at Bullingdon in Oxfordshire from where he retired to Midhurst in 1974. Les, who in 1944 was the present Museum Director's C.O. in 842 Squadron fighter flight, became a close friend and helper, particularly with the historical research side of the Museum in recent years. He was a founder member of the Society of Friends.

He died very suddenly and unexpectedly, aged 68, on 28th March 1983. His funeral near Midhurst, West Sussex was attended by many friends from the Fleet Air Arm and civilian life where his interests included rifle-shooting, the Royal Observer Corps and Scouting. All were greatly saddened by the sudden loss of such an outstanding patriot and a very great English gentleman. We offer our condolences to his widow, Dorothy, to his two daughters Susan and Jenny, and to all his family.

At their suggestion, his friends have very generously donated to the Museum a considerable sum of money which is being used to purchase, in his memory, a water colour by Roy Perry, R.I. 'Towards Stanley from Two Sisters', which will be part of the Museum's permanent Falkland Islands Exhibition.

DCBW

The above obituary, written by Denis White was published in 'Jabberwock', the journal of the Society of Friends of the Fleet Air Arm Museum. We are grateful to Frank Ott, DSC, for permission to print The Boss's obituary.

ROD (STEVE) STEVENS
Lieutenant(A) RNCVR
Senior Pilot
Killed in action over Japan
on 28th July 1945

This is a story of Steve, written by Agnes, his widow, now living in Montreal, Canada, in the Stevens' family home. It is a wartime love story, written as she says, 'in tears and laughter'.

The young Charles Peter Rodger Stevens weighed in at 12 lbs in Kingston, Jamaica, the son of G. R. Stevens and Mrs Z. L. R. Stevens. Mr Stevens at the time was Trade Commissioner of Canada to Jamaica.

Steve made his first sea journey at 10 weeks old and arrived at the family home in Montreal West, where I still live. By the age of 5 Steve had lived in 6 countries where he was educated by either a governess or in a private school. He finished High School in Montreal and after graduation he and his pal Jim Carter were accepted by the Royal Military Academy in Kingston, Ontario. In 1941 he transferred to a Royal Navy Pilot Training Scheme. If he failed that, he would return to the Canadian Military with a commissioned rank.

In 1940 I joined the WRNS and was first posted to HMS Condor at Arbroath. I arrived during deck landing exercises which a German aircraft tried to join. He was shot down and I saw my first German . . . a dead one! At my next posting in Rosyth, one day, a Canadian destroyer received the signal, '100 tits have to be fumigated' The corpus of naval signals has for ages provided an amusing record of the deliberate and accidental prose. That Canadian crew had planned a 'pantie raid' on our Wrennery led by none other than Lieut. Jim Carter. Late into the 60's, Jim, living in Halifax, Nova Scotia, still possessed that key to our quarters . . . as a paper-weight. Steve was at the time doing flying training at Lyme (Sic) where one day his idea of getting 'a line' to home was to pick up three of them, wrapped round his Harvard tailplane!

Steve got his wings and commission whilst I was at Donibristle. He was then at Errol, between Perth and Dundee. Steve and I met at a dance and via a merry round of dancing dates we continued our association. He was then posted to the Doni-B (the familiar abbreviation of naval men) Ferry Pool. One day Steve walked into my office, an hour before that posting to Errol. It was during the 'dog watch' and we arranged to meet after my duty and go to the camp dance. That was the night I became an 'item'. Our friends included, Forêt Millar, Croose Parry, Jackie Ramsden and Glyn Roberts, who were all to join 1772 later, on 1st May 1944. We shared our off-duty hours between the 'Star and Garter' and the 'Woodside'. Forêt, the 1772 pianist, would always end an evening with 'Paper Doll'.

Steve and I got engaged at a New Year Dance at Doni-B and the wedding date was set for 11th April. The family in Canada were delighted; Steve's father at that time was a war correspondent and a PR Director with the Indian Army. My dress would arrive in a Diplomatic Bag and things for the wedding flown over by Ferry Command. Canadian neighbours arranged 'showers' for us and again 'things' were flown over. Word got about and one day the wardroom was festooned with Canadian nighties, underwear, nylons and so forth. Plans were to be thwarted. On 8th April we were summoned to the Admiral's Office and told that all leave was cancelled and secrecy was number one priority. Messages were sent conveying a spurious story and Steve arranged the wedding for the 11th. This called for new banns and several changes of plans. Wren Connie Tough became my bridesmaid and Jackie Ramsden became Best Man. The 'stage' was at the 'Star' and the reception at the 'Woodside'. We were given 10 days leave; the train would be stopped at Doni-B. Our travelling companions were to be 700 members of the ATS and we remained sitting upright on our wedding night!

Steve and Agnes marry. Jackie Ramsden is Best Man and . . . a bad weather approach!

We returned to find that Steve had been posted to Burscough to join 1772. The 'boys' went south and I went north.

1772 settled down quickly and on 3rd May, the third day of the Squadron, they had a 21st birthday party. In the first month the CO, Gough, froze the wardroom bar bills. The 'Bull and Dog' and the 'Red Lion', became worthy substitutes, though unfortunately the landlords only understood the word 'cash'. I joined Steve at Ormskirk and we worked at my discharge and ultimate transportation to Canada. We rented a 3-bedroomed house at 95, Southport Road where Teddy Key was a frequent visitor and in no time, 'he had his feet under the kitchen table'. This has to be a doubtful claim since that table was a 4 × 8 board which hinged back to the kitchen wall. You were then into the bath tub and going out of the back door, down the garden path, through the coal shed. Under each bed was a 'thunder mug'.

Life was soon to become dramatic. Steve's comrade, Andy Andrews 'bought it' and the mid-air collision, costing the lives of Jim Sloan and Monty Baker, occurred. In August we had 2 weeks leave which we spent in Scotland with Gordon Davidson and the other Scots in 1772. We returned for the Admiral's Ball. We were greeted by that first lady wearing an evening gown patterned with red cabbage roses and a wide green sash. We recognised it, having done some trousseau shopping, as a dressing gown from Etams. Steve became very protective of me and wouldn't let me dance with the other guys. I was pregnant.

1772 was not knitting together as a team and 'the boys' were becoming very depressed. Letters from Steve were beginning to unfold the dissatisfaction with Gough. Gough and the Senior Pilot were on the move. My child was due in early 1945 and I moved north. Des and Betty Mullins moved into No. 95.

1st November. Farewell party for Gough at the 'Bull and Dog'.
4th November. A party for new CO, Les Wort, at the 'Red Lion'.
20th November. Squadron knitting together. Canadians and others are knitting for the baby! The doctor in Scotland tells me, 'it is to be twins'. Glyn Roberts arranged a duty rosta of 'uncles' to make sure the sprogs were looked after. George Trollope had married his Joyce and she was also expecting. Steve and I took family planning classes.
21st November. Burnie, Croose, Pete and Steve were up before the Captain for buzzing Southport. Was this a celebratory fly-past to mark the departure of Gough?
23rd November. 3 weeks leave.
18th December. Mike La Grange's party at 'Bull and Dog'.

23rd December. Steve flew to Doni-B for a compass swing. Because of snow Steve was able to make it 'home' for Christmas Day. He and Forêt flew back to Burscough on Boxing Day.

5th January 1945. Steve hears from Shiner Wright that he is on a Hellcat Course, 'A pre-twitch course for anyone with a record of many prangs'.

8th January. Glyn Roberts throws a 'Bull and Dog' party to celebrate his engagement to a Wren named Sylvia.

10th January. Pete Kingston was in the station cinema projection room with his girl friend when she skipped a reel, put on the next, upside down, then put on the missing reel. I guess the title, 'Candlelight in Algeria' was having some romantic effect on him!

17th. Our daughter, Merlin Louise is born. It took a long time before Steve got the news. Every other member of the Squadron seemed to know before he did, judging by the telegrams which began to arrive. There was much celebration apparently, and even the RAF joined in. I owed much to Roy Melville on that day. Something happened to Steve that day. From then on all his letters were signed 'Rodger'. I will never know but Teddy says that he went AWOL.

19th January. Steve sent a telegram from Belfast saying, 'Arriving 1956 hrs. Can I see you?' He was able to be with me for 45 minutes. The next day he bought a pram and made two more visits. Perhaps Steve did break a few rules . . . ever so slightly, but it was worth every minute. Mail was by then being censored.

26th January. The Squadron was suffering severe rationing of spirits and beer but you would be allowed one sherry extra on Sundays!

7th February. Steve had devised a simple code system so that I would know where he was. He had tried to contact Midge, an old Wren friend of mine. He was in Egypt.

16th February. You were back at sea and Les Wort was the proud father of Susan.

19th February. Today you donned 'tropicals'.

7th March. You were all at a place where Jerry Morgan had 'bought it'. You were at Colombo.

16th March. A beautiful bridge. It had to be Sydney.

3rd April. Movietone were at Schofields and filmed some of your deck landing practice. Steve and Glyn seemed to have had some fun. Mike LaGrange was making a name for himself as a rugby football hero and was getting all the headlines.

7 April. Steve received 19 letters and he applied for his priority for release. Steve wished to be discharged from duty, asap. The strange thing is that this form is missing from his personal files.

10th April. George Trollope did it again. Whilst showing a Commodore the basics of ADDL's he selected 'UP' for his undercarriage . . . whilst still on the ground!

11th April. Our first anniversary. Steve arranged a small dinner and dance at 'Princes' for the three Melocco sisters and George and Teddy. The six of them got into a small Austin and off they went. Helen decided that they should compose a note to me so with the help of Jean and Greta I received their joint good wishes. Teddy reminded me in that note that I still owed him a breakfast of pancakes and maple syrup. I finally fulfilled this promise at an Indefatigable Reunion in Birmingham . . . 48 years later! Having seen the girls home to Vaucluse, they caught the Parramatta train back to base. Two years running Steve had spent the 11th April on a train . . . this time with two men!

15th April. George, Croose and Glyn with 5 others joined 1770. Steve and Teddy went to Kaola Park for boomerang target practice.

17th April. Steve's birthday. The New Zealander's leave is extended from 40 to 80 days.

24th April. You go to Queensland for Commando or survival training. You are not overjoyed about the whole business and Steve was not enamoured of the Aussie kit issued to him.

2nd May. Steve says that there is a lot of work involved. You are all trying to keep clean and healthy. You suffer 'early to bed' and drink milk! There was laundering and Johnny Coles boiled his trousers with his watch in the pocket. It still worked.

8th May. Back at Schofields and VICTORY IN EUROPE. Australia went 'dry' overnight and you had free beer at camp.

9th May. 10 day leave and Steve, Teddy & George went into the bush to a golfing fanatics hotel at Bundanoon. You babysat about 16 children. A friendly rivalry exists between Les and Steve regarding the physical growth of Susan and Merlin.

23rd May. Steve again bypassed for early release of Canadian 'Hostilities Only Personnel'. Steve's mother preparing the nursery for our arrival in Canada and a neighbour is holding the sale of her house for Steve and I to purchase when we return.

27th May. Steve and Teddy both have colds and are restricted to low flying. I'm worried about Steve, he seems to be depressed and not sleeping too well. Glen (Mac) McBride married Linda on leave. Most of the New Zealanders had returned to the Squadron and letters from Steve seemed to have given him the impression that I was in Canada with Merlin.

2nd June. Steve said that he was beginning to feel 'scruffy'. I sent out his 'blues'.

5th June. Steve received 3 letters which I had written in the nursing home in January. Steve was telling me that I was a bad letter writer. It was only now that Steve had found out Merlin's full name. The Squadron is complete again.

8th June. The Meloccos throw a big party for the Squadron or as many as could make it. Steve wrote about the frequent good wishes from the guys in the squadron.

28th June. Steve again applied for leave. The CO said that he would have to apply through the Canadian Navy and the Admiralty. At that time he seemed to have no idea where I was.

On that day I received a wire from him. I had not been too well and wired back immediately, that I was well again and still in Scotland. There were no sailings since priority was being given to troops returning from Europe. My wire arrived at Schofields and was signed for and opened by Maurice Goodsell. Everybody knew where I was. So off to sea you went.

12th July. Steve said he would try again for leave after the current trip.

27th July. His last letter, which said that he would not be writing for a few days.

14th August. I received the telegram with 'the news'. I contacted Steve's Father who was later able to deploy a Regiment of Ghurkas to search Honshu Island. He was misinformed and nothing turned up. In the meantime we kept our fingers crossed and Teddy and I were in touch. Mrs Robinson was very good and held the house off the market until May 1946.

Teddy Key. . . 'During the ensuing years I kept in touch with Agnes: My daughter Rosalyn paid her a visit in Montreal. In 1972 the Stevens family gave a cocktail party at the Royal Court Hotel in London: the Keys were there as well as Eric Lathom and family. Eric had named his son, 'Rodger' after Steve. I often tried to persuade Agnes to come to one of our reunions. At that time they were the larger variety; reunions of the whole Indefatigable company. She finally managed to fit in a visit to Birmingham and found that the bond she had established at Donibristle and Burscough was as strong as ever. It was good to have her back with us again after all those years, after Steve's death. After that reunion in Birmingham, on her way to her beloved Scotland, she began to read "Kamikaze" by Stuart Eadon. In it she read about certain theories that Steve's and Mike's deaths were other than what some of us knew. The old Green section was with Steve on that fateful day. What we saw suggested that there was no way that aeroplane could have survived anything other than total destruction. It was a great shame that comments which were based only on hearsay evidence should have found their way into that excellent book. Nevertheless they did and it caused a great deal of hurt and anguish to the Stevens Family. Merlin had never known her father and in her mind he was none other than a hero. With customary thoroughness and courage, very noted in the Stevens family, they set about eradicating the rumour and falsity of the statements in the book. They wrote to Prime Ministers, a Minister of Defence and to all of us who could have had a bearing on the incident. All was resolved, eventually and time has healed. But the scars will remain.

'Agnes's story is a love story. In some way or another it must have been repeated many times during the war. There were the frustrations of letters which never arrived or arrived hopelessly out of sequence. The problems of censorship, transportation, or just simply, finding enough time to be together. There were love stories and love stories in 1772, but Agnes's and Steve's story is a particularly poignant one personally because I witnessed a great many of the heartaches involved. Her story has evolved as a form of diary which over the years she has based on Steve's letters. The writing of the 1772 story prompted her to go over it all again. In a letter to me she said, 'It has taken me much longer than I thought as it was very hard at times and funny at others. There were two whole years of Steve's letters, and you know what a letter writer he was!' She wrote this story for the "Friendly Squadron" in tears and laughter.'

Rod 'Steve' Stevens was our Canadian Senior Pilot after the transfer of Shiner Wright to a Hellcat course and I was in his Section, Green Section, together with pilots George Trollope and Harry Garbutt, in the early days of the squadron. I remember many things about Steve because we had struck up a very strong bond of friendship. One particular incident was the situation mentioned in Agnes's story when at any cost he had to see his newborn child. We were in that difficult situation of transferring the whole squadron, literally, lock-stock-and-barrel from Burscough to the Clyde to embark for the Far East. Censorship was very strict, communications were very difficult even between our squadron and the ship. Just when would the ship sail? Steve took an enormous chance and travelled across Scotland. Agnes tells how he succeeded and how much she valued that small amount of time they had together. She tells how much that very limited time the three of them were together was to mean to her, all her life. She tells too of the impact that Les Wort, so ably supported by Steve, was to have on the morale of the squadron. Steve's father was a distinguished military historian among many other things. Steve did not bear outwardly the characteristics of such a background, for, not to mince one's words, he could be a scruffy individual. Relaxed he was and seemingly very casual. I feel that perhaps, he knew himself very well, and that perhaps the Fleet Air Arm would be more his type of scene than a Canadian Military Academy. But these outward characteristics did not portray the true characteristics of leadership which he undoubtedly possessed. He was very easy to work with but if you erred in terms of accurate and sensible, safe flying, he could be as hard as nails. He was supremely confident, competent as a Naval Officer and as a pilot. He was so eminently dependable and trustworthy. I suppose that in many ways he was a complex character, but he was fun to be with for he had a wry sense of humour and was capable of enormous kindness and selflessness. Behind that rugged 'outback' style was a gentle, retiring, family man. He was in every way the epitome of the 'Hostilities-Only' officer material. As pilot and section leader he was in my opinion quite outstanding; I would even at this stage like to put it on record that 1772 had many really outstanding flyers. I remember Steve once telling me over a quiet beer how much he rated the aircrew of his squadron. Before Gough was replaced it angered him considerably that the full potential of the Squadron was not being developed. He was angered by the way that we seemed to be always associated with incompetence rather than

Merlin Stevens ... the little girl Steve was to see for but a short time after her birth in Scotland in mid January 1945.

205

skill. In the air, Steve was skilled but not foolhardy and he found it hard to suffer fools gladly. He was a courageous and fearless man and on 28th July Steve died in action with Mike LaGrange attacking the Harima Shipyards.

Relating to that day again, Admiral Halsey was to signal to the Fleet, 'they paid the price with their courage, their blood and their lives'.

Well, that was Steve. Perhaps we did not know Mike as well. But to me Steve was a brilliant pilot, a very close friend. I remember with everlasting gratitude how the day before he died he got Sammy and me back to the carrier on sheer flying skills and that remarkable tough style of his. We were on the edge of one of those typhoons which lurked around the Fleet with alarming regularity. Those towering masses of clouds filled with amazing turbulence demanded all one's instrument flying skills. Not one of the skills I rated very high in my armoury. Something was a little wrong in my cockpit; there was one nasty little red light which ought not to have been there. My homing beacon was far from satisfactory. I could not afford to lose touch with Steve's wingtip. At one point I changed station completely, such was the turbulence. With cockpit hood back a little, the driving rain rendering visibility through the perspex hood impossible, we arrived back dead over the carrier in clearing weather; I was given a priority landing. Thanks to Steve alone we made it. On that day Maurice Goodsell did not. He failed to read his beacon because of lack of altitude, (we could hear all this over the R/T). Maurice was killed in the ditching; Don Banks survived. But, that is another 1772 story.

ROBIN (HANK) HENDERSON
Lieutenant RN
Senior Observer

Robin, it is believed, got his name from Steve Stevens and as 'Hank' he was always known to us. Since he was in the Royal Navy . . . proper, he remained in the service until his retirement as a Commander. He settled in Australia with his wife Mary and it was in the Summer of 1995, the year of much Fleet Air Arm celebration, that the pair of them came over to UK and on one lovely summer evening a small group of us celebrated a mini 'Forgotten Fleet' reunion at the 'Inn by the Lake' near Godalming to reminisce.

Now back in Australia he writes to say that his memory is like the Bellman's Map, 'a perfect and absolute blank.' When asked to comment on a number of things, he wrote 'Golly, really, was I there?' Today he is a full-time grandparent and travels vast distances, such as Sydney to Adelaide and back, to see the 'Darlings'. He claims to have just missed a kangaroo on the road, at 100 kph and to have enjoyed his visits to Cook's replica of the Endeavour. He ends his letter to the Squadron by saying that when trying to find St Merryn near Padstow when he was over here he was unable even to find the Dockyard at Portsmouth, or the barracks and he wondered about his navigational skills. We have no record from our pilots! As Ian Darby might have said, 'Hank was a good bloke', but he might have added, 'considering he was one of those "regular" fellows, he was a bloody good bloke.'

After September 1945 Hank (or Robin) finally made it back to the UK like the rest of us at the end of 1945. He was told that he had 'volunteered to start a pilot's course in January, as the first of a band of 'F' officers'. He says that he never knew what the 'F' stood for. With half a dozen other Observers he went into the pipeline of Tiger, Moth, Harvard, Firefly instructors, deck landings included, and he finally emerged into a front-line 812 Squadron equipped with Firefly Mark 5's. 812 was part of the 14th Carrier Air Group destined for HMS Ocean, a Light Fleet Carrier. He worked-up off Portsmouth and then went to the Mediterranean. On arrival at Malta they disembarked to Halfar and stayed rather longer than planned as the ship lost an argument between her screws and a large buoy and had to retire to dry dock. After about 18 months with 812 he was given command of 796 Squadron at St Merryn, which was an Observer Training Squadron equipped with Barracudas and Firefly 1's. He was married to Mary after a year and was then drafted to 827 Squadron as CO, with Firebrands; not a great aircraft, very clumsy and the hydraulics tended to fall into bits in the air. 'We went to Malta via Marseilles, two "dropped out" en route, one with the dreaded hydraulics. We joined HMS Eagle. I was promoted Commander and became Commander Air of HMS Triumph which was the Deck Landing Training Carrier.' That was most enjoyable and he then went to the Admiralty in the Directorate of Air Organisation. Two years was more than enough for Robin and he was posted to Yeovilton on the staff of Flag Officer Flying Training, responsible for front-line squadrons and arranging the annual inspections of the Air Stations. This he considered to be

Robin and Mary Henderson at a mini-reunion held on their behalf in the summer of 1995.

'great fun'. He then joined the staff of C-in-C Home Fleet. In this role he had a NATO hat. He had an office in Northwood as Staff Officer Plans to go with his seagoing job as Fleet Aviation Officer. He was 18 months in this hybrid existence and became Assistant Commander (Navy) at the School of Air/Land Warfare at Old Sarum. This was very interesting, working with NATO students on a 3-week basis. The courses were very flexible, regarding rank and army service. After 2 years he became Services Adviser to the High Commissioner in Colombo. He implies that life was very comfortable as regards work-load and he and Mary enjoyed the diplomatic life and they enjoyed the company of the Sri Lankan people. He returned to Portsmouth and the Staff of C-in-C Portsmouth. Domestic decisions, such as schooling for the four children who were by that time at High School level had to be made. The decision was therefore to resign from the Royal Navy. They flew to Australia in November 1966. Mary went into teaching. Eventually Robin became a Director of Learned Activities in the Institute of Engineers, Australia, with responsibility for publishing Members' technical papers and organising technical conferences each year running a lot of committees. His office moved to Canberra in 1976 and the family stayed there until 1991, when they returned to Sydney. Family ties meant a great deal of travel between Canberra and Sydney, but in the end the ultimate base became Manly, Sydney.

DON BANKS
Observer
RNZNVR
Don died on 13th June 1996

Don was by New Zealand standards, a quieter more retiring sort of fellow than other Kiwis. This is in no way offensive to that average Kiwi style of 'down-under' candour. We POMS grew to enjoy it, in a way, but Don was a quiet fellow and the years between 1945 and 1996, when he died, proved to be difficult times to prise news from him. Like many he was happy to settle down to a private and quieter family life with his Ailsa and family. Don was a strong character, very courageous

'Mac' McBride and Don Banks – Kiwi 'Lookers'

and resilient, as his ditching in the Pacific was to prove. We remember his sunny countenance, warm nature and friendly manner with much affection and a sense of real joy.

Don died in 1996 from a heart attack after years of loyal nursing of his wife Ailsa during her long illness. Much of Don's story is told elsewhere, for he had a good story to tell about his long sojourn with the Pacific sharks as his only company, when his aircraft ran out of fuel and he survived, though his pilot Maurice Goodsell did not. Don in his civilian life, before retirement was Secretary to Air New Zealand.

It is a characteristic of our family squadron that we have kept in touch with the families of those who have died. Graham Banks, Don's son, joined us at one of our Duke of Wellington meetings early in January 1997.

RAY BATTISON
Observer

I was born on 9th November 1922 in Millwall on the Isle of Dogs . . . within the sound of Bow Bells. So, as a genuine cockney, I am writing with fond recollections of my war-time 'China Plates'. Our family moved to Wellington in Kent when I was six months old and at the age of eleven, won a scholarship to Erith County School. I worked for a Provision Merchant near London Bridge from the age of sixteen where I met a smashing girl! Edith and I were 'just good friends' until after the war when we married in 1946. Present at the wedding were Les and Dorothy Wort and Johnny and Madge O'Driscoll. When the war broke out I very much wanted to fly, but also to follow in my father's footsteps, he having been a Leading Torpedoman in the First World War, the battle of Jutland amongst others. There was only one answer to that, namely, the Fleet Air Arm.

I volunteered at the age of eighteen as a would-be pilot and eventually joined 32nd Pilots Course at Lee-on-Solent, then HMS St Vincent. Whilst at Lee we were given two very interesting talks. The first was a very fascinating account by Lt. Cdr. Esmonde about his pre-war career as a pilot with BOAC. Four months later he lost his life leading the Swordfish attack on the Scharnhorst and Gneisenau in the English Channel for which he received a posthumous VC. The other was from a certain Lieutenant(A) Ralph Richardson. He demonstrated by moving his pipe backwards and forwards whilst pronouncing, 'you move the stick back and the nose goes up; you move the stick forward and the nose goes down.' I think we must have known at least as much about the theory of flight as he did, but he was after another Oscar!

After St Vincent I went to Elementary Flying School at Sealand in Cheshire. During the whole of January and February of 1942 the weather was so bad that after two months, I had managed just about 9 hours of dual instruction with an RAF Spitfire pilot, taking a rest from operations. He was a lovely chap. He was also a bloody awful instructor. I met him again by pure chance after the war. Before de-mob we were both attending a course on Current Affairs. He recognised me and came up to me. He described his ability as an instructor in exactly the same words. After failing a Chief Flying Instructor's test I returned to St Vincent to join 55th Observer's Course.

I am sure we all remember so many stories about St Vincent, mostly involving Chief Petty Officer Willmott, but the one thing I remember best was being marched into church by a Petty Officer Drill Instructor after Sunday Divisions. One of our course forgot to remove his cap on entering church, which brought forth a loud command from the Petty Officer. 'Take yer bleedin' 'at orf in the 'ouse of Gawd.'

I next moved to Eastleigh to do a Signals Course and then to Trinidad for Flying Training. After passing out I returned to the UK to pick up a naval commission and two weeks 'knife and fork' course at Greenwich Naval College . . . in order to learn how to be an officer and a gentleman. This brings to mind the definitions of RN, the RNR and the RNVR. 'The RN are gentlemen trying to be sailors. The RNR are sailors trying to be gentlemen and the RNVR are neither, trying to be both.'

After Greenwich, a posting to the USA to join 852 Avenger Squadron, forming up a U.S. Naval Air Base, just outside Boston. The CO was Bobby Bradshaw. After a three-week working-up period we flew across the States to join HMS Nabob in San Francisco Bay. The ground crew went across by train and arrived several days before us, but we did enjoy ourselves, on the way. Nabob was a 'Woolworth' carrier built in Portland, Oregon and the ship's company were Canadians. We came back to the UK via Panama and the Norfolk Navy Yard. We then acted as escort to what was the longest Atlantic convoy of the war. We were in thick fog most of the way. There were no casualties.

We subsequently operated out of Scapa Flow as part of the Home Fleet, off the Norwegian coast, our main duties being mine-laying in the Norwegian Fjords and bombing German shipping and airfields. We then became involved in what was at that time the largest Fleet Air Arm operation ever planned. It was called 'Operation Goodwood', the objective being to sink the Tirpitz in Alten Fjord. Our task and that of 846 Avengers from Trumpeter could only be described as suicidal. The Tirpitz was at anchor against the side of a 2,000 ft cliff with torpedo nets around her. The 'plan' was for our 24 Avengers to fly at 0 feet over the top of the cliff and drop an assortment of magnetic and acoustic mines between the side of the cliffs and the Tirpitz. Some of these were intended to rise to the surface of the water, blowing the bottom out of the ship.

We were roused at 0330 on the morning of August 22nd 1944 for a breakfast and final briefing. A Seafire had been flown off to carry out a reconnaissance of Alten Fjord and reported thick fog over the target. Our take-off was therefore put on hold and we stayed at action stations in the ready-room. The fog remained over the target and eventually by late afternoon action stations were secured and the aircrews thankfully retreated to their cabins for a 'zizz'. We had hardly got our heads down when at 1716 hours, a huge explosion rocked the Nabob. We had been hit on the starboard side by an acoustic torpedo from U-Boat 354. All electric power immediately failed and the engines stopped. Another torpedo was fired at us and because our propellor had stopped, the acoustic torpedo went past the Nabob and hit the destroyer 'HMS Bickerton' (subsequently sunk after taking off survivors). We all rushed up on to the Flight-deck, by which time we were 38 feet down at the stern end and had a very heavy list to starboard. The Captain (H. N. Hay) gave the order to 'prepare to abandon ship'. The Damage Control Party went into action, as it was never expected we would be able to fly off again, it was decided that squadron personnel should be taken off and on to HMS Kempthorne. Before all the squadron had been taken off the Engineering Department had managed to get the propellor turning again, albeit very slowly and further transfers were stopped.

Early the following morning we received a report that a U-boat was closing in on us rapidly from astern. With Nabob unable to do more than 9 knots it was decided to catapult two Avengers, the CO Bobby Bradshaw and Don Jupp and their crews in order to at least make the U-Boat submerge. This they did and eventually managed to land back aboard the listing ship, though Bobby Bradshaw went into the barrier. Both pilots were awarded the DSC. Nabob eventually completed the 1,000 mile journey back to Scapa, although it took 7 days. Twenty one lives had been lost but she was the only escort carrier in the war to survive a torpedo attack. On return to Scapa she was found to have been holed below the waterline, a hole approximately 50 feet in diameter. After going on 'survivors' leave' the squadron was recalled and we carried out several more operations off Norway, some aboard HMS Fencer or HMS Trumpeter. Later that year the squadron was disbanded and over Christmas I was aboard the troopship Durban Castle bound for Ceylon.

After twiddling my thumbs for a while at RNAS Katakarunda a signal arrived asking for a replacement Observer for 1772 Squadron aboard the escort carrier HMS Ruler in Colombo Harbour. I applied and eventually went aboard when I not only met up with a good friend from 'Fencer', Les Wort and then CO of 1772, but also Steve, the Senior Pilot from my 32nd Pilots' Course and Mike LaGrange from 55th Observers' Course. Unfortunately neither was to survive the war.

My memories of 1772 are dealt with elsewhere in this book. One other recollection was that after the war, I began to study for accountancy and to qualify as an accountant. I wanted to find a more appropriate job than with my then present company. Johnny O'Driscoll was working in the city just the other side of London Bridge and once a month we would meet up for a lunchtime chat over a beer or two and a sandwich. One day he told me that Watney's, the brewers, had a vacancy that might suit me. I applied and was taken on. The 'beer and sandwich' shaped the future for Edith and for me. I eventually retired as Group Financial Director of Watney, Mann and Truman Brewers . . . Good old Johnny!

VAL BENNETT
Observer

I was born in 1923 in London but I remember Buckinghamshire more clearly. After boarding school I went to Winchester College: I was always homesick. My early interests were aeroplanes, warships, model making and collecting moths and butterflies and breeding them. Playing cricket I could be easily distracted by a beautiful butterfly. Drawing, painting, shooting and fishing were early passions. In 1939 with a year to go at Winchester, I remember a visit to Eastleigh and seeing the sleek Spitfires rolling off the production line. I could often see the old FAA biplanes and Fulmars flying overhead, which were based at Worthy Down. I had decided to become a designer of aircraft and in 1940 I joined the de Haviland Aeronautical Technical School at Hatfield. I started in the junior drawing office at the time the factory was producing the Airspeed Oxford trainers and the Dragon Rapide. They were repairing Hurricanes and there was talk of the hush-hush new Mosquito.

Air raids were part of life and one day a JU 88 had dropped its bombs on the factory doing much damage. The Junkers was shot down. I cycled to work in the wind, rain and snow and I graduated to a 98 cc autocycle: I had had visions of something grander. These were great years and I worked on the Mosquito, now in production. There were parties and pubs and those terrifying things . . . GIRLS. The urge to get some real action was strong in all of us and I decided to join the FAA rather than the RAF. In my case, classic misinformation controlled my decision and destiny. I had been led to believe that the medical was less tough in the FAA than the RAF, for flying duties. My interview board in London convinced me that because 'they had too many pilots, I would be better suited to the role of observer, 'the real decision makers.' At the end of 1942 I was on the 58th Observer Course. Life was one of some discomfort and new adjustments to naval life such as Nissen Huts, iron-frame beds, a low-efficiency central stove, using chairs for fuel. Being tall, short blankets offered a choice every night – cold feet or cold shoulders. The 'wakey-wakey' Tannoy at 6.30 a.m. was a shattering experience, even when playing 'Ave Maria'. For the first time in my life, I had to do my own washing, ironing and darning and the sailor's uniform was such a challenge, especially getting in and out of the tunic after a series of 'medical jabs'. Dismantling a Lewis Gun on a freezing day, liberty boats and other Royal Navy rituals contributed to an austere but not unfriendly atmosphere.

The St Vincent Barracks at Gosport, once used to house French prisoners in the Napoleonic Wars, followed Lee-on-Solent. Here we came into contact with Chief Petty Officer Willmott, (later awarded the MBE) and cockroaches. 'Chief' Willmott was a character known to every impressionable FAA lad; short on stature, loud of bark and one huge forceful presence. HE had to be obeyed, but I found him to be civil and helpful. They say he had a kind heart and was intensely proud of his charges! The main congregation of cockroaches was to be found in the kitchen. The currants in the 'plum duff' sometimes turned out to be these creatures which had skidded on a greasy patch on the ceiling and plopped into the vast copper cauldron which was the source of the 'plum duff'.

The training included morse code, basic gunnery and seamanship. We fire-watched and slept in murky passages and we square-bashed. We went 'ashore' to Portsmouth to get a decent meal at the YMCA or see a film.

My next posting was an 8-week radio course at Eastleigh and we learned about radios the likes of which we would never see again, especially in the Firefly. We learned semaphore, I became a Leading

Naval Airman and wore my 'killick' on my sleeve. I then completed a 2-week gunnery course at Devonport. More drill, more nasty verbal exhortations from a 'chief' who had little regard for airmen. The Royal Navy to him was ships and ships alone and the new air branch was an intrusion in his life, made up of these new RNVR people. After some leave I at last reached the flying part of my training. I had a choice of Arbroath or Piarco in Trinidad and I chose the latter. This Observer Flying Training School included 5 a.m. parades and Sunday Divisions but there was now less 'bull'. Training included navigation, radio skills, air gunnery, ship recognition, spotting for guns and bomb-aiming. It was hot and we worked a tropical routine with a siesta in the middle of the day. We flew every day on a variety of exercises. On one you were expected to press a stop-watch and drop a smoke-flare down the shoot. One of my peers managed to get the sequence reversed. To reach the bomb-sight in an Albacore you had to hang your head down through the 'bomb aperture'. One character did this, shouted 'Bomb' to his pilot and his false teeth went too. We flew in Stinson Reliants, twin-engined Grumman Geese and Percival Proctors, as well as the Albacores. The old Walrus also figured in our training. In a brief moment one could enjoy the Carribean sunrise and the cloudscapes. The days were delightfully full. Sometimes a routine exercise would end with some illicit low flying.

We had some very good friends who lived near Port of Spain, the Rapseys. They had a huge home, a lovely garden, a seaside pavilion and boats . . . and 3 daughters with whom we had many happy times on picnics and beach parties.

Slowly we improved in all our subjects and eventually all but a few passed out successfully and returned to UK. I was retained at Piarco, commissioned on the spot and enjoyed the enhancement to officer status and the facilities of a Wardroom, complete with swimming pool. The next six months passed agreeably enough and it was satisfying to see one's pupils progressing until it was their turn to pass out as fully-fledged 'O's. I returned to the UK, first in a U.S. Navy Mariner flying boat, island-hopping through the Caribbean, then a crack U.S. train, the Silver Meteor, to New York, 2 to 3 weeks in the Barbizan Plaza Hotel and then a crowded journey back with 20,000 American servicemen on the Queen Elizabeth. I reached Scotland on 6th June 1944 to the news that the invasion of Europe had begun. As we sailed past Ailsa Craig an aircraft not familiar to me flew over us, waggling its wings in greetings. That omen proved to be a Fairey Firefly.

A course of 'Naval manners' followed at that splendid Royal Naval College at Greenwich. The enjoyment which should have ensued from this posting was marred by the too-frequent interruptions of air raids. From the fire-watching post I remember watching in horror the rumbling passage of a V1 as it made its destructive way to the heart of London. In October of that year I reported to Burscough to join 1772, where as a newcomer I was received in a very friendly manner. It was evident that the Squadron was deeply split between its CO. and Senior Pilot and the remainder of the Squadron, including our large NZ membership, who did not take kindly to 'bull'. The situation had not been helped when the CO. and Senior Pilot collided during formation manoeuvres and both observers were killed.

I was lucky to have Pete Kingston, from Napier, NZ, as my pilot, in whom I always had every confidence, and I found most of the flying exciting and exhilarating. There was much competition between sections to see who could fly in the tightest formation. I thought our Blue Section was the best but sometimes with wings seeming to overlap it was a trifle scary. Low level flying was fun, though once, over Cumberland, Pete managed to bring back some vegetation; flying 50 feet above the Irish Sea was very exciting. I did not enjoy night flying and on a wet night the rear cockpit was a confusion of observer's gear and poor vision with rain water spreading over the canopy. Off duty, the beer-drinking activities were considerable – to say the least!

On a murky day in Autumn, that single event, when 3 aircraft pranged in what was supposed to be a 'carrier deck ranging exercise' occurred. All three aircraft were needlessly written off. This was the final straw for their Lordships and the CO. and Senior Pilot were replaced. Les Wort, an RNVR man, became the CO. and the appointment of 'Steve', our popular RCNVR pilot as Senior 'P', transformed the atmosphere and from there on it was much happier. Under their new leadership training continued and new aircraft were delivered to us in December.

I embarked on HMS Activity for transit to the Far East and I entered the Naval world of 'Officer of the Watch'. Duties occurred in the rough seas of Biscay and idyllic nights in the Med. and Indian Ocean. There were the ports of call in which we spent a good deal of time in exchange for those 'watch' duties.

We renewed training at the newly hutted camp at Schofields, 40 miles out of Sydney. We lost aircraft on ADDLs exercises as well as on deck landings on the Ruler. Stu Jobbings was lucky to survive a stall on the stern of the ship when he fell back into the sea. The New Zealanders went on leave and with a real aircraft shortage problem, 4 crews were posted to 1770. I was allocated to Glyn Roberts as pilot since Pete Kingston had gone to Napier on leave. With this extrovert Welshman, I joined HMS Indefatigable in Leyte.

(Val's description of our crews' part in Operation 'Iceberg' is the only first-person story we have.)

The Indefat. had been hit by a Kamikaze shortly before, on April 1st., and had suffered several casualties. She was one of four carriers forming the core of the British Pacific Fleet, then engaged in neutralising the Sakashima Islands, where 3 airfields acted as staging posts between Japan and Formosa, which the Americans were attacking at that time.

The carrier was very short of accommodation and all that I could be offered was a camp bed in a passage, but this was not for long. While the carrier was still at Leyte, replenishing and making ready for the next phase, some Avengers with wings folded were parked at the stern. A mechanic working in the cockpit accidentally fired the .5 calibre gun in one which was fitted in the folded wing. The aircraft was parked in the extreme stern and behind the armoured deck and so the stream of bullets went down through deck after deck killing one of 1770's observers in his bunk. And so it was that I was given his bunk and was left to look at the gaping holes in the deckhead just above me. (It is a coincidence that Sammy Samuelson, a little while later, was given this same bunk, on the final assault on Japan.)

The neutralising of the airfields on the Sakashimas had been going on for a month during operation 'Iceberg' and the Japs knew the routine very well. They were adept at deception and placed dummy aircraft to attract our fire and concentrated their anti-aircraft guns accordingly. They had plenty of shooting practice and during 'Iceberg 1' there had been a steady attrition of our aircraft, for very little visible return, except a few more holes in the runways which were soon repaired.

For these reasons therefore, it was not surprising that at the briefing for our first strike orders were given to make 'one pass only, fast and low and towards the sea', so that if we were hit we would ditch in the sea and stand an excellent chance of rescue, rather than on the land, where an unenviable fate could await us.

For me, this first strike was also the first time I had flown off a carrier; an amazing experience, which soon became routine. As we gathered speed past the ship's island, in the dawn, many faces watched us. Would we see them again? Concentration on the navigation kept such thoughts at bay and very soon the islands of Myako and Ishigaki came into sight. We formed part of a combined strike with Avengers, who would do the bombing, with Corsairs as escort.

Soon, our Fireflies drew ahead and our noses went down. The speed built up rapidly as the target airfield grew rapidly clear. Soon the thumping of the 4 cannons told me that Glyn was firing at his target, which I could not see. We fled, weaving and unscathed and to my surprise Glyn went into a turn and so in spite of my protestations, he went round and made another straffing run. Again we were mercifully unscathed. We found the others at the rendezvous and returned to Indefatigable in formation. My first deck-landing was the next experience. Luckily, although undisciplined, Glyn was a good enough pilot and he set us down safely on this occasion and all others. Indefatigable's large and steady deck made it a lot easier than the small deck of the Ruler had been.

Life on the Indefatigable with 1770 was different. Led by 'Cheese' Cheesman, a flying marine officer, it had established a distinguished record aboard Indefatigable, taking part in raids on the Tirpitz, Norwegian targets and a leading part in the successful Palembang oil refinery raids. Having discovered that I could paint, the Major set me to the task of illustrating the Squadron's history and activities, so my time was busy when not flying, making 12 paintings which were subsequently purchased by Faireys and used to illustrate a booklet on the squadron. Although they flew as an efficient team, this did not extend to off-duty relationship and there were some seriously incompatible situations. Among their number was a Plymouth Brother to whom alcohol was forbidden. One or two others who liked their drink, having used up their Wardroom alcohol allowance for the month, (£3 for a Sub. Lt. and £5 for a Lieutenant) began to book drinks to his Mess Bill. This naturally caused an explosion. At this time a generous gin measure cost 2d and a whiskey 3d so a Subby could drink 150 gins or 100 whiskeys in a month. For a Lieutenant the numbers were 250 and 160. Beer was in short supply and cost 6d, so if you were offered a drink you were very unpopular if you asked for a beer.

Operation 'Iceberg 2' continued for 4 to 5 weeks during which we each took part in about a dozen operations along much the same lines although sometimes the targets could be small shipping, radar or radio stations, which were attacked with rockets.

During this time several attacks were made on us by Kamikazes and all the carriers suffered hits, Formidable twice! In most cases damage was slight, but Formidable had a deck full of aircraft when attacked and although the Kamikaze did not penetrate the armoured deck, burning petrol did cause a damaging fire in the hangar and she lost a lot of aircraft. The routine was to operate for 2 days and then meet the supporting fleet-train ships for 2 days, refuelling and replenishing. A U.S. Navy Task Force alternated with us to maintain constant pressure on the enemy. After over 2 months at sea the British Fleet was in need of a return to Sydney for repairs and preparation for the assault on Japan. We sailed into Sydney Harbour, magnificently, early in June.

1770 now left Indefatigable and was replaced by 1772 and we four crews returned to our original squadron. For me it was a relief to find myself flying with Pete Kingston again. After a short leave which Croose Parry and I spent as guests of an Australian sheep farming family, riding, shooting and enjoying the hospitality, we rejoined the Squadron.

Refitted, re-armed and with the squadrons all at full strength again, the Fleet left Sydney for the assault on Japan on 28th June. Indefatigable however was in dry dock, still with problems being remedied. We hastened north at great speed behind the main fleet. We did some exercises to sort out procedures with the ship. We recognised that this operation would be no picnic and it was with a degree of dread that I thought about the prospects, albeit with a feeling that we were going to deal some blows at the enemy in his own homeland at last.

Details of operations which I regarded as special are recorded in the chapter dealing with our overall performance. After the cessation of hostilities it was the unbelievable relief to know that accidents apart, one had survived and no dreadful fate at the hands of the Japs lay ahead. We counted our grievous losses which amounted to 4 crews in the last two weeks of operations, a quarter of our strength. If the war had gone on even another month, our chances of survival had to be minimal. We blessed the A-Bomb!

Now began a truly happy period. We were briefed to locate and supply POW Camps and to monitor some of the armistice agreements by checking out Japanese airfields. It was an emotional experience to fly over the POW Camps and to see the wild excitement of their occupants and it was very satisfying to drop supplies to them and see them running to gather them. It was good to fly in safety over Japan.

On pilots in general, 'an Observer needs a good pilot and in training, particularly at Piarco in Trinidad, observers flew with a wide variety of them. No doubt, from a pilot's point of view, the job was boring; he was little more than a taxi driver. In some cases a pilot's posting to an Observers' Training School was something of a punishment for some transgression. For a navigation exercise they had to fly conscientiously and accurately and generally, they did, unless they were 'hung over' from the previous night's excesses. Having completed the dull part, some of them would indulge in something a little more 'exuberant'. On occasions I flew with a Petty Officer pilot who would endeavour to reach the speed of sound by putting the aged Proctor into a terminal velocity dive. It was alarming to hurtle earthwards in the frail looking old machine, vibrating and shrieking until one felt sure it would fall into pieces. The pull-out came at the last possible moment. Sadly one of the first aircrew funerals I attended was this pilot and his two pupils who died because of his stupidity. On another occasion I was with another pilot in an Albacore on a gunnery exercise. It seemed simple enough but the drogue bore little evidence of the hundreds of rounds I had fired. This pilot's fun was to scream at nought feet across the Trinidad countryside. Anything was fair game and after a high (sic) old time, frightening fat old ladies on bicycles and donkey carts, we came to a field of sugar cane. Cahill, the said pilot, found that flying through the cane was very exhilarating. There were questions to be answered when he taxied in at Piarco with streamers of sugar cane around the undercarriage!

Having completed the training I was thrilled to be posted to 1772 Squadron in October 1944. What could have been better than being in a squadron, flying the fastest and most modern aircraft available to an observer. I was teamed up with Pete Kingston and as far as I was concerned this was a great stroke of good fortune. I can honestly say that I never had any doubts that my life was in the safe hands of Pete. I think he was a naturally gifted pilot and in all the hours I flew with him and the deck landings, we did nothing too dangerous. Nothing untoward ever happened, although we did fly through some small trees on a low-level cross-country exercise somewhere near Lancaster one day. I enjoyed it as much as Pete . . . and it was an authorised low-flying exercise. Some of our longer exercises took us over Ireland and 9 miles north of Dublin, my godmother lived in a castle, Malahide Castle. She had been most helpful to me and helped a lot in my upbringing. I visited her every year before the war. Bending the rules a little this time we deviated from our course, cooked the log a trifle and at low level flew along the estuary and made a couple of passes while I dropped messages down the flare shute. We escaped as fast as we could to evade the Irish Air Force. I found afterwards that my godmother and her husband were away from the castle and only the butler witnessed our show. The messages were never found.

Indefatigable later joined a smaller combined U.S. and British Fleet in Tokyo Bay. We took the opportunity to socialise with our American friends and as U.S. warships were 'dry', we had lots of visits and great parties with these visiting Americans, who showered us with presents from their 'PX'. After leave in Sydney I came home in our old friend, the 'Ruler'. Home for Christmas; my two older brothers and a sister had survived the war too and it was indeed a time for rejoicing.

There was little use for aircrew once the war was over and so by April 1946 I was out of the Navy and resumed my course at de Haviland. I remember being staggered by the performance of the new jet Vampires which were then in production. I found it hard, after 4 years in the Navy and having got used to Wardroom life, to return to life as a student.

There were quite a few others like myself and I found that life as a designer had lost its appeal and I became more orientated towards PR and Sales. On completing the course I joined the Sales department of de Haviland Propellers but after a year or so was offered a job as a sales engineer for a company making specialised aircraft equipment, based in London, but with the factory in Wales, where in due course, I moved.

I spent 25 years or so, becoming Sales Director with that Company until with re-organisations of the industry and the bankruptcy of Rolls Royce, our principal customer in the early 50's, the business was taken over by a competitor and I was out on a limb.

At this stage I turned my art hobby into a business and began the commercial production of a range of bronze wildfowl miniatures. They found a ready market and I attended exhibitions with them in the USA, France and Holland as well as the UK. My home had outbuildings which readily converted to a workshop/studio and so I was able to live and work at home in the Brecon Beacons National Park. In 1957 I married Mary Ann Menzies, a daughter of Duncan Menzies, a Fairey Test Pilot and cousin of Duncan Simpson, chief Test Pilot of Hawkers. Aviation is much in the family. We have 3 children, a son and 2 daughters and at the time of writing, 2 grandchildren.

JOHNNY COLES
Observer

A Windsorian born and bred, at 18 I volunteered for the Fleet Air Arm which I saw as an attractive combination of naval and flying service.

I joined 53rd Observer Course at St. Vincent in March 1942 and from August until March 1943 flying training took me to Trinidad.

In April 1943, following the customary 'knife and fork' course at Greenwich I was posted as Temp. Midshipman (A) to Capetown, joining 789 Squadron at RNAS Wingfield in June and 799 Squadron in September. Both flew Albacores. Following this I joined 1772 at its birth on 1 May 1944. The rest, as they say, is history.

My excellent pilot throughout was Eric Bramhall, who hailed from Manchester, a mere 20 miles from Burscough. Many were the happy visits, aerial and otherwise, to the family home. Eric emigrated to Canada fairly soon after the war where he sadly died some years later.

In 1946 I returned to Barclays Bank but in 1948 I joined the National Institute for Research in Dairying at the University of Reading. In 1979 I moved to the then Agricultural Research Council from which I retired in 1983.

Marion and I were married in 1955. We have a son and a daughter and four grandsons who keep us well occupied. Retirement has been very active working in the Voluntary Housing Movement. When time allows gardening and gardens are a busy leisure activity, not to mention regular visits to the local gym!

IAN DARBY
RNZNVR
Observer

I was born on 28th January 1923 at Lower Hutt New Zealand, attended school and college between 1929 and 1941 and my naval career stretched from 1st January 1942 to 1st January 1946.

An early passion was to fly and 'get into the action'; the quickest way I was told was to volunteer for the Fleet Air Arm. We would then be sent straight to the UK. Ours was the last draft to go to the UK in civilian clothes. 'It didn't interfere with the neutrality of the USA'. Glen McBride's draft was the first New Zealand draft in uniform.

I started out as a pilot trainee on 38th Pilot Course at St Vincent, thence to the USA to Grosse Ile for initial flying training. I achieved 50 hours flying before being remustered as an Observer trainee. I passed this course and was commissioned on 23rd December 1943. I then went to the Royal Naval College at Greenwich to become a temporary gentleman!! I was on leave until posted to 776 Squadron at Speke, near Liverpool. On the 1st May 1944 I was posted to 1772 at Burscough; a founder member! Burn and Don the other Kiwis in 1772 can speak for themselves but Glen McBride can't. Glen was scared out of his mind and his pilot didn't help at all. I admire Glen's courage; he could have asked for a transfer I suppose or seen the CO and sorted something out. He was older than most of us, an extremely good tennis player and I was delighted to become his best man when he married Linda in 1945.

We were delighted to have Linda accompany us to the reunions at Portsmouth, Lee-on-Solent and Yeovilton in September 1995. We have kept in touch with each other since and she is coping very well. She has said how wonderful it was to meet all the squadron and for Ray Battison and Edith to offer us all hospitality at their home at Ferndown. Ngaire and I were grateful to all those in the Squadron who gave us hospitality. George and Joyce, Joe (Bob) and Anne, Val and Mary Ann and Alan and Ann. It was a pity we didn't have more time to stay with all of you. Most of my thoughts re my involvement in the war were largely positive. I can't understand why we were not used earlier, even in Europe. We seemed to be endlessly flogging around instead of participating in a shooting war, but so much of war means wastage and inefficiency. I thought that we could have been a much better squadron with better leadership initially: apparently we got a poor reputation by association with Gough. That of course altered when Les Wort took over and we became blooded in action. So in the end we were very pleased with ourselves.

It is most displeasing to me to see how well the Japs have done with American Aid help. Britain, Australia and New Zealand on the other hand have had a long hard grind to achieve results with much pain for their people.

Our destiny I am sure, lies with the Pacific rim countries and our markets are opening up for two-way trade.

There will always be great contact however between the UK and NZ as most of our people originated from there: New Zealanders have a reputation for travel in large numbers.

When we were in Auckland for our New Zealand-wide broadcast to talk about out POW experiences (50 years on!), Burnie and Mary and Ngaire and I went to see Don Banks and his wife Ailsa. Sadly Ailsa was afflicted with Altzheimers and she was not really understanding everything we had to chat about. During the radio broadcast Don was telephoned to recount his experiences about being downed in the Pacific and spending three lonely days in a dinghy on his own. It was again something for us to look back on.

Teddy Key, 'Ian's potted autobiography is short. His exploits as a POW on the mainland have been recorded at length elsewhere in this story of 1772. But Ian is not SHORT. He is not short in any way. Ian is a large, kindly man with a big heart, huge courage and a massive commitment to everything he ever does or has done. His candour is monumental and his zest for living and his brio during our squadron days were legendary. Ian has always spoken his mind. I enjoy it; it's a way of really knowing a person. His phrases such as 'shooting war' come through as typical of him, but having known him, I automatically translate those words into true Darby dialect. His angst against the Japs is understandable.

Ian had a colourful style and used the word 'pom' affectionately, we are certain! Once, when he entered the luxurious home of the devoutly 'Roman' Meloccos, his first enthusiastic comment was 'Jesus Christ!' John Darby, after a visit to the Rowlinsons, told his mother that Ann Rowlinson always cut a cross at the base of Brussels Sprouts. 'Must be very religious,' said father Ian. Most definitely he was a man of faith . . . and very strong views.

Ian was and is a great talker: he loves it. When asked to contribute to this book he was requested to lace his contribution with 'sugar and spice'. If he once mentioned the word 'POM' it would be cut out. Not one 'POM' was there. But I could hear it as I read his story. Ian cares for people and he has a great charm. I remember my wife, Mary's, judgement of him. It had something to do with cuddly bears, so I ignored her, on this occasion.

But he and Glen formed such a strong bond between them and he felt extremely deeply about Glen's death. His feeling about Glen's pilot, Glyn, is maybe still very strong in him: such was the conflict of war for him. Glen was the stuff of easy-going charm and Glyn, the stuff of carefree dare-devils. Glyn should have been strapped in a Seafire. He could have won a VC. He was not the type of pilot for Glen.

Ian finally arrived in Auckland on 27th September 1945 and was 'fed and watered' and then flown to Wellington, his home town. There he was met by his family and his wife-to-be, Ngaire. He found it extraordinarily hard to settle into peace time routine and had a succession of jobs, none of which suited, 'until I was talked into studying radiography which I pursued, both in diagnostic therapy and private practice in hospitals until my retirement, with the odd digression, here and there'. This means that Ian possessed a small holding which he farmed. In his own inimitable way he 'shifted around a fair bit, chasing opportunities'. He says that he became increasingly cynical about politicians especially in relation to the Japanese. 'As a family group we are very happy, 2 fine sons and 3 fine grandsons, a nice home and 4½ acres which I am trying to sell because the body is getting a bit tired of hard work'. After his and Burn's return to the Royal Navy in September 1945, they were summoned to Admiral Vian's office. They were sent away, 'to put some beef on their bones'. Well, Ian at least obeyed that last order and now he has the bulk of a Jonah Lomu and the good looks to go with it. Burn we would suspect is still much like Cassius, lean and hungry.

GEOFF GILL
Pilot
Died 8th December 1977, aged 54.

(Delphine Gill)

Delphine, better known to 1772 as Dell, Geoff's widow, has provided us with the following information, with the help of Alan Rowlinson.

'Many very close associations were established during the 1772 phase of our lives and these, almost without exception, have lasted over the years.' Geoff was Yorkshire born, (a twin), Leicester-based and as Alan remarks, 'For his sins he was linked with Geoff as his "looker", in July 1944.' A great friendship began which was shattered in the autumn, when Geoff was posted to 1771 Squadron on HMS Implacable. It was one of those situations when they had a need for a pilot and not a crew. In the hard world of logistics and men, those who made such decisions paid scant regard for the bonding which had begun in this crew: war is no place for sentiment. These bondings were very important and in 1772 crews in many cases did stay together the whole time. In a few cases the crewing did not work; there was the choice of asking for a change, by mutual arrangement, or one just put up with it and did one's duty. Geoff in 1771, although the youngest in 1772, taking over that dubious role from Sammy Samuelson, was to be in action before any of us. That has to be a testimony to his skill as a pilot. With the Implacable he was destined for service over Norway and of course involved in the Tirpitz attacks.

He then headed for the Far East and the British Pacific Fleet. Geoff and Alan met again in Sydney when both the Implacable and the Indefatigable had returned from Japan after VJ Day.

After the war Geoff married Dell in December 1945 with Alan as best man. The honours were reversed when Alan married Ann four years later. Dell could not be present for the latter affair because of the imminent arrival of Philip and Christopher.

Geoff Gill was born on 19th July 1923 and ended the first part of his education at Oundle School. This part of his life stretched from 1936 to 1941. Regarded as, 'not academically brilliant', he gained his colours at Rugby, Rowing and Fives. When he received letters of congratulations on receiving his colours, the letters were usually addressed . . . 'Dear Blondie'. He was apprenticed to Ruston-Hornsby in Peterborough before joining the Fleet Air Arm and progressed via one of the familiar routes, Elmdon, Ontario, and Henstridge, before arriving at Burscough to join 1772.

After the war he joined the family firm, Midland Dynamo, in Leicester and as Dell relates, had to work very hard to make up for his 'flippant' years in the Fleet Air Arm. He not only became Managing Director in due course but was involved with Boys' Clubs, Boy Scouts, Samaritans, Freemasons, the Leicestershire Golf Club and for good measure was a Justice of the Peace on the local Bench.

Geoff and Dell attended some of the 1772 reunions but very regrettably Geoff died of a heart attack on December 8th 1977 at the early age of 54.

Geoff was a very warm person. He was an equable man, not prone to moodiness: he was in fact great company. He was a 'Branch Type' and his activities after the war reflect that selflessness which was essentially his character. He was a most refreshing and charming extrovert and those of us of 1772 who remain, remember him with great affection.

MAURICE GOODSELL
Pilot
Lost at sea on 24th July 1945

Maurice at once became the Squadron Secretary, or one remembers in more Naval correctitude, 'Executive'. It was a task which fitted him admirably for he was correct and meticulous. Had Maurice survived the war he would have become a very talented 'Personal Secretary'; a neat and tidy straight-down-the-line man and if one attempted to place him as a Branch flyer, one would be tempted to say, 'Well, if you knew Glyn Roberts – just about the opposite.' Who can remember Maurice at a Squadron 'session'? One of his passions was, 'the movies'. As Johnny O'Driscoll comments, 'He was quite a film buff, his talent and knowledge in this area being quite exceptional, not only on the films and the stars but on producers, directors and even the studios. Maurice was rarely defeated on any small detail. Maybe Barry Norman would be unemployed today if Maurice had survived that ditching in the Pacific.' Both Maurice and Don Banks, his Observer have died and in the later years Don was never forthcoming on such details as flying with Maurice, for a very long time. Maurice never had a supreme confidence as a pilot, but he ditched that Firefly with enough skill to permit Don to escape his rear cockpit even though he did not escape from the pilot's seat.

A. H. GOUGH
Lt. Commander. RN
CO 1772 1st May to November 1944
Lt. Cdr. Gough was Commanding
Officer of 825 Squadron, once
commanded by Lt. Cdr. E. Esmonde VC,
from 29th February 1944 to April 1944

He was appointed CO of 1772, which began its forming up period on 1st May. He was replaced by Lt. Cdr. Les Wort DSC. RNVR. in November 1944. With hindsight, it is possible to conclude that the particular chemistry of 1772 needed an RNVR CO from the very beginning. As Croose Parry says, 'By the time 1772 was formed, the Fleet Air Arm was very much an RNVR organisation and I don't think that the fact that Gough was RN, helped.' No doubt there were faults all round. Pure and simple, in those first few months, the squadron just did not come to terms with itself and there were far too many silly mistakes and just a trifle too much pilot error. Don Randle thought 'that he did not know how to treat RNVR types.' Don was one of the three pilots, the other two were Geoff Gill and Gordon Davidson, who were involved in that ultimate and unnecessary taxiing accident on 25th October when three aircraft were written off in the fog, and perhaps an accident which could have resulted in tragedy. As a result Lt. Cdr. Gough was relieved of his command. Don says that 'it was not wholly Gough's fault but he had to "carry the can".' Don Randle adds, 'he did however throw a farewell party in the Wardroom on 31st October. He was most likely, pleased to be relieved of us!' He had been CO of 825 for 65 days and our CO for 154 days. A more serious event had occurred earlier, on 29th July, when two of our Fireflies collided in mid-air, killing Lt. Jimmy Sloan and Lt. Monty Baker. The CO and Shiner Wright the Senior Pilot baled out. Lt. Wright left the Squadron soon afterwards. Croose Parry says, 'I suppose, through bad briefing he (Gough) must be held responsible for the mid-air and runway accidents. After that I think we lost respect for him as our CO.' He adds, 'The last straw as far as I was concerned was the occasion when he ordered night flying exercises on the evening of our return from leave.' These views were shared by Johnny Coles. Johnny wondered why we practised formation night flying and formation take-offs. Neither of these activities were ever relevant to our role as a carrier-based squadron. It did seem to add up to some very inadequate briefing, or maybe we were just not bright enough for him! He was over-ambitious and far 'too keen' for 1772. Ian Darby recalls some dialogue. Ian was the CO's observer on this occasion. Gough said to me one day, 'Darby, we are going to test a new G.C.A. gadget. I want you to fly with me tomorrow at dawn's early light, irrespective of weather and you can guide me back to the airfield.'

'Yessir.'

We couldn't see the end of the runway. A total clampdown but once airborne Gough turned every-whichway, totally confusing me.

'Darby, where is the runway?'

'Right in front of you Sir, if you go lower you should see it.'

'I say Darby, you're spot on, there it is.'

'I didn't know whether it was Burscough or Machrihanish. So the good Lord was looking after us that day. All that was on 4th July 1944. The gadget was called ZZ Homing. I was hoping it was called NZ Homing.'

Teddy Key recalls that on the day of the fatal accident he and Sammy had been part of Gough's folly of trying his experimental type of open formation flying. He recorded in his log book, 'Firefly No. Z2015 Squadron Formation flying. A shaky do!' The old and widely used patrol formation was a tried and proven method of flying in open formation. Why did he not leave well alone? Had he done so of course, he would have interfered with the destiny of 1772!

Lt. Cdr. Gough was known to have retired to New Zealand where he became part of the wine trade. Rumour has it that he did at one time run into Don Banks.

RHYS HEAVEN
Observer

Rhys was one of the aircrew who were transferred to 1771 Firefly Squadron, whilst finishing our training in Australia. Rhys's pilot was Stu Jobbings, but somehow they have always been 1772 and over the years they have both been frequent attenders of our reunions. It wasn't their fault that we lost them!

Stu and Rhys were not without their own brand of adventure, for whilst they were in active service with 1771 on HMS Implacable and frequently flying on strikes with 1772 over the Japanese mainland, they had on one occasion been forced to ditch their aircraft. Rhys reports, 'Despite the Youngman flaps dangling and the aircraft fuel leaking, (they had been hit fairly comprehensively by flak,) they managed to reach 'the outpost flotilla' (Tomcat). This was essential for identification purposes in approaching the fleet. I think it was then, but it might have been on reaching the fleet, that the 'fan' stopped! Thanks to Jobber's skill and I think, phlegmatic temperament, we ditched safely and were picked up shortly after by the destroyer, HMS Termagent.' He added, 'after beating off hundreds of sharks with my bare hands.' Well, he wouldn't lie, being a Welshman, even to the point of misjudging the degree to which the Welsh XV have counted all their rebirths! Rhys records that a few days after their return to Implacable they were interviewed for at least 30 seconds by Commander Flying. He made them take to the air as soon as possible; Rhys adds, 'I think he was cross because we had mislaid one of his aeroplanes.'

'Obviously he had not heard of stress, counselling, compensation or other such flim-flam we are given these days but I honestly do not think that neither of us felt a thing.' Rhys wondered if Stu's version of the little incident was in any way different from his. 'Mine is vulnerable to geriatric amnesia.'

Stu and Rhys also partook in the operation of dropping supplies on POW Camps. He recalls, 'One day we slipped a packet or two down the flare shoot, not condoms as they would have to be today. At the same time a Flying Fortress flew over, opened its bomb bays and dropped tons and tons of good things. Sort of put the UK/US into perspective.'

For Rhys too there are the crazy memories. Sitting on the latrine bucket in what was presumably the only 'heads' at Schofields (Australia) alongside him one day, was the station commander, on a similar receptacle. 'I was certainly the more embarrassed but at least he was there before me, so I did not have to stand up and salute him.'

Rhys modestly refers to his education as being bog-standard Welsh grammar school and then after a bit of this and a bit of that he qualified as a professional company secretary ending his career as a secretary of a £250m take-over of a PLC in electronics, headquartered in the Welsh Valleys. He was also a director of several group companies. The company which occupied most of his professional life was one of the three biggest companies in Wales, 'but was small beer by national standards'. He adds, 'Since I retired the company has declined, though there is no connection with my retirement and it was taken over by an English company.'

'My one approach to distinction lies in having been married to the same person, Joyce, for 48 years. I think that others in the Squadron can beat that, but these days it warrants a mention for 'quaintness'. We have a daughter and son but no grandchildren.

I regret that I cannot say that I played rugger for Wales or with a little less regret cricket for Glamorgan. I am only a social member of the golf club. Idle as well as unenterprising!'

Rhys's distinctive welshness became evident to Teddy Key one day when playing rugger for Richmond against Llanelli at Stradey Park. In a silent moment, Teddy tells that an unmistakable voice was heard from the stands, 'Get your bloody feet off the ground, Key.' The 1772 affection lives in Wales too!

TEDDY KEY
Pilot

'Average'. All aircrew kept a flying log book. I have two of them, fading greens, weathered, much used in the last months and much treasured, reminding me of my good luck and a great adventure over a modest 600 hours of war-time flying. These books were signed monthly by a commanding officer and these gentlemen were to smudge, ever-so slightly, my considerable enthusiasm, by assessing me as . . . AVERAGE. Those books are then, a record of average attainment, but a great deal of excitement, panic and good fortune. That mediocre skill and above average luck . . . got me home! But unknowingly, those senior officers came close to the judgement I have of a Jack-of several trades but master of few.

This book displays many examples of the short and long straws of life. In one respect I drew the longest straw possible. It is a schoolmaster's cliché when despairing of an occasional child that 'the most important thing that a child ever does in his life is to choose his parents well.' Cynical, maybe, but in my case, I was so lucky. That luck extended through a sister and brother, and later my own family, with Mary my wife and daughter, Rosalyn. That good fortune now extends, (the luck of a wonderful wife having been extinguished with Mary's death,) to Rosalyn's family, husband Brian, and two wonderful little monsters, Amy and Emily.

I had the good fortune to be born and live a great boyhood on the Grantchester fringes of Cambridge. Here I legged it to school across college playing fields and later I would run touch-lines for a bob or two, scrounge cricket teas after a half-a-crown's worth of scoring or bowling at undergraduates in cricket nets. It was a great life for an aspiring Tom Sawyer and across the Grantchester meadows, the clock no longer stands at 'ten to three'.

The running and joyous life produced a very average school career despite the nut-brown colouring and strong wind and limb. Schooldays did however produce one significant influence, a mentor known to us as 'Uncle' Boyle. He taught me mathematics and geography and though the war years dulled my mathematical skills I was to take his enthusiasm for geography into my working life as a schoolmaster; I did return to him for teacher training after Oxford. I still know that I owed him a great deal. In the academic sense however, my studies produced a very 'average' response.

Before I was 18 years old, I volunteered for flying in the Royal Navy. I 'ducked out' of school, in retrospect, a bad judgement, and tried my hand in the world of banking; good judgement, and luck, because it convinced me that on return to civvy street I would have to think again! The familiar pattern of flying training began in 1942; Royal Arthur at Skegness, St Vincent, occasional shortish postings to Lee-on-Solent, Tiger Moth training at Elmdon and then Canada and gaining one's 'Wings' and commission, first as a Midshipman and then Sub Lieutenant(A) RNVR. Fighter School at Yeovilton followed, even now the 'spiritual' home of all 'Branch Types'. An operational squadron followed a brief spell of 'stooging' and it all came to a dramatic end on HMS Indefatigable and at Tokyo Bay. Throughout all that time I travelled with an old Cambridge friend, Dickie Reynolds, who was to become a distinguished flyer, compared with my average state . . . damn him! We still communicate. I met another friend on the way to Royal Arthur on Peterborough station, Freddie Hockley, the last Fleet Air Arm pilot to die in WW2. He was on the Indefatigable with Dickie flying Seafires and he was shot down almost at the same time that the cease-fire signal was hoisted on the ship's mast. He was executed by the Japanese and his murderers were subsequently put to death.

Royal Arthur was a rude awakening to the true facts after the gentle ways of family life with Mum and Dad. On the very first morning, having acquired our sailors' rig, one was awakened by the cruel banging on the chalet door. 'Hands off cocks, on socks.' Vincent was even harsher, and slimming. The food was disgusting and the physical regime tough. I grew to six feet and began to feel, 'tough'. Flying was fun, simply that; it was a sport . . . and free! My RAF instructor in Tiger Moths was named Dick Whittington, his real name, and for me, he was good; another piece of good luck for one often heard of other chaps who had less good fortune. We seemed to take our time because there always seemed to be a built-in fog at Elmdon. Here one survived the first solo spin and we spun at other venues to the sound of 'Jealousy' and 'In the Mood'. Kingston, Ontario, was in the grip of a familiar Canadian winter; the snow landscapes were tremendous and I still had the company of Dickie and Freddie. We learned to fly the Harvard under a section of Australian RAF instructors and here perhaps I was not so lucky with my mentor. I was approaching the 'below average' state and with the feeling that I would never get my wings the CO took me up for a test flight. On landing he looked me in the eye and said, 'There's nothing wrong with you my lad, you're doing fine'. The cause, maybe, had been a prang when on landing my Harvard I had careered all over the runway from one huge snowdrift to the one on the other side. This antic, I reproduced several times causing much damage to the plane. I still believe that my instructor did not know that it was not me who got the blame, but Flying Control. At the very time I was beginning my landing, in an aircraft not renowned for its fore-and-aft stability, a line squall had occurred and I had landed in a considerable cross-wind. Such luck, but it was a moment of panic.

The three of us were still together when resplendent in our officers' uniforms, we went solo on Hurricanes at Errol in Scotland. We lost contact with Dickie who went to a Seafire Course. Freddie and I were posted to what was to become the last Hurricane course at Yeovilton. It was in a way a significant part of my destiny in that Freddie did progress to a Seafire Squadron whereas, after a spell of stooging with 771 Squadron, RNAS Twatt in the Orkney, doing all sorts of exercises with the fleet in Scapa Flow, I was posted to 1772. I was sad that I had not gone on to fly the glamorous 'Spit' but in the Orkney I had the opportunity of flying many types of aircraft, not the least the once glamorous Gladiator. Now that was real flying! A feeling of genuine good fortune has overcome me over the years because I have returned to Yeovilton almost every year, a sort of pilgrimage. I have looked across that airfield to just about the spot where the Royal Navy Historic Flight exists today and where our little section under the control of Stuart Jewars was based in its wooden huts. Freddie died tragically, Derek Steele was killed a few days after I had pranged him by driving my Hurricane up his tail and nearly chopping him in half. I got away with that one too because it was proved that in the pitch black of night flying, whilst taxi-ing, he had switched off his navigation lights! Ian Hatton, having survived his time in action in the Pacific, was on his way home via the 'show-the-flag' cruise of the Indefatigable, to New Zealand and South Africa, and was killed in a flying accident landing on. I still wonder what happened to Dusty Miller. Where are you?

In the final show, we went to Australia; the laboured working up of the Squadron has already been mentioned. The Burscough birth of 1772 was a most significant affair for all of us. Through the problems of changing COs and some silly accidents we gained a poor reputation. There were good times and bad times and our reunions testify to the multitude of memories we can still recall . . . and improve upon! Above all it was to be the beginning of a comradeship which was to last and prove its capacity to be a truly 'friendly squadron'. There were tragedies, the loss of Steve was especially sad for me. We lost Monty, Ken, Jim and Harry at Burscough and later in action, besides Steve, we lost Glyn, Mac, Mike and Maurice. We were to grow fearful of the base nature of the enemy and probably four of them were to suffer those abominations. There were the experiences of the strength of the sea in a Typhoon, the sheer terror of the first strike over the mainland of the enemy. There were the sublime pleasures of finding and sustaining POWs and the magnificent joy of watching an American Hellcat putting the Indefat. out of action. The Kamikaze failed to do that and in any case I'd had enough and wanted to go home and become a schoolmaster.

Flying for me had finished and my average skills had seen me through; war had in the end seemed such an awful business and from then onwards I wished to be creative. The luck had held, not the least in the hazardous business of landing an aircraft on to the deck of a carrier. My first deck landing had been carried out in a Hurricane on that old war-horse, the 'Argus'. Here I had a brief conversation with Commander Flying, who suggested rather sarcastically, I thought, that it does help the batsman, if on your approach, you do not disappear from his sight below the rounddown. More luck, but perhaps just a little judgement . . . average, I would say!

There were girls of course and I can honestly say that even in this precarious area of male experience I had some remarkably good luck. Before becoming a sailor and after schooldays I skirted the fringe of passion with a young lass who was to become a principal singer in the D'Oyly Carte Opera Company. Through her I was to meet the great Jack Hobbs who had been a junior post office messenger boy with her father. Tea, cucumber sandwiches and Jack Hobbs on a number of occasions did not add to our passion, but she was my first 'real' love. My Ringtail love was truncated after 1772 left the UK. It was not to be forgotten . . . for a long time. There were other flirtations of course but in any case I reached my ultimate marital bed, 98.5% intacta; a genuine virgin sailor and you'd better believe it! Years later when Ian Darby came to England with his wife Ngaire, Mary and I were entertained to dinner by George Trollope and his wife Joyce. Ian with his usual candour remarked, 'I always remember Teddy because he always seemed to be in love with someone'.

The entry into Jesus College Oxford was bordered by more good fortune. I had the good luck through the family, of meeting Jimmy Steers, a distinguished Cambridge Geographer who introduced me to a most understanding opposite number at Oxford, Johnny Baker. He took a chance on me and no doubt found me to be 'hard work' during tutorials. But both men were strong influences on my destiny. During most of my teaching years and retirement I counted as a special friend, Gus Caesar, Senior Tutor of St Catharine's College, Cambridge. Until his death recently he was a great inspiration and encouragement to me in an academic life which I did not always find easy. I went to Oxford before being demobbed for I was a part of a 'forgotten fleet' and nobody seemed to care. Despite the problems of adjustment to an academic life I was more than happy to be in such a distinguished environment and I was on my way back to the classroom! The years of cerebral decay in a life of hedonism in which I had graduated in the '1772 Academy' were not helped by the fact that I would not give up my love for sport. I was in the varsity rugby squad during my whole time at Oxford, having reached county level in rugby football. I did not get a coveted 'blue' but I mixed with some remarkable talent. This was my rugger education which took me, well trained, into school coaching. I rowed at college and enjoyed two Ladies Plates at Henley. At one brief moment in my life I stood next to Grace Kelly and said 'hello'!

I had the enormous luck to join the staff of Tiffin School in Kingston upon Thames in the summer of 1949. Here I had the good fortune to join a great Headmaster, Brigadier, J. J. Harper, the 'Brigadier' or 'JJ' to all of us. I joined him and I helped him, with a superb teaching staff which he gathered round him as ex-service men returned, to turn a good grammar school into a superlative state school which over many years defied the occasional Labour government's plans to destroy – excellence. I became his Deputy Headmaster and this time I question the role of luck: he chose me! I spent almost forty years at the same school and besides teaching Geography I coached Rugby Football, and Cricket, a game I had to relearn after the war. They were great and fulfilling years; I had made the right decision and luck was on my side, all the way.

Life had been good and apart from a few minor brushes with the NHS and in a rugger scrum, I have enjoyed good health.

I met Mary in my last year at Oxford, we married in Bedford and I had a marvellous honeymoon year studying the imprecise skills of teaching at Cambridge. I had returned home . . . again, where the family Key still lives. Mary died in 1993 and the good luck ran out, but I still have my family, Rosalyn, Brian, Amy and Emily. Retirement has been more than full and Mary and I enjoyed 10 of those years, caravanning, walking the cliffs of the South West, sailing, gardening. I had a great deal of pleasure from my own hobbies of painting and sculpting in which pursuits I went 'back to school', even to being taught sculpting by one of my former school rugger boys.

One learns that nothing lasts forever, and life, as the cliché goes, must go on, treasuring one's family and some very supportive friends. One learns too that gratitude for what one has had, is important. I have seemed to emphasise 'luck'. We may have some control over our destiny but in that part of one's life which covered a war, there had to be some luck. I have had some 'above average' luck; I survived that war and now a fair old chunk of peace, with a large number of good friends, many of them, 1772.

There is one final point regarding "only average achievement". I receive occasional mail addressed to Sub. Lieutenant(A) E. A. H. Key, RNVR. Now that is very average promotion after over 50 years!

MIKE LA GRANGE
SANF(V)
Observer
Killed over Japan 28th July 1945

Mike was born on 18th December 1923. He was born to Mrs I. B. La Grange at Albertinia, Cape in South Africa. His name is also written as La Gronji and it was in his Afrikaans tongue that one remembers his maddest moments, because Mike was in every way, 'one of the boys'. He had some of his own drinking songs. One seemed to have much to do with a 'Sugarbush Tree' and ended in what must have been quite a rude way, because there was the instruction, 'to do vith your poupon, vot you vill'. Mike came to us with a great Rugby reputation as a Springbok. In his native South Africa he was in the forefront as a near-international full-back, though with us, at our level of rugger, a very good stand-off. It has been difficult to verify information about him.

Some of our facts have come from the South African Naval Museum in Simonstown. Don Randle flew with Mike for some time as did George Trollope. On his last operation with Steve, Steve's observer had been grounded. Mike took over as Steve's observer. Short straw? Ill-luck? Destiny? Who will ever know? Mike being a South African in the Fleet Air Arm was something of a rare breed and Don recalls that he had to press hard to get into the Branch. Mike's father was strongly anti-British; the family of La Granges having fought against the British in the Boer War. Mike had been a late child and the family took his loss very badly. Don Randle visited South Africa quite a good deal in the 70's, he was in the tobacco business before he retired, and still has contacts with that country. One day on a visit he glanced through the internal telephone directory of his company when he was visiting Stellenbosch, he noticed the name 'La Grange' and rang the number. It turned out to be one of Mike's brothers, an ex-security employee. They met and it proved that Don was the only contact the family had had with the Fleet Air Arm. Mike's mother was at that time still alive in Capetown. With some photos that the brother brought with him Don was able to fill in some of the gaps in their knowledge of Mike's life in the British Navy. Unfortunately Don lost contact with the brother. Mike was a great extrovert and was a fine companion to have around. Never more so than when we played representative rugger in Sydney. Mike got all the newspaper billing on the sports page. 'Springbok Mike to play Oz in Sydney'.

From South Africa snatches of information of Mike's life emerge. A stop-press item is that Mike played rugby for the Buffalo Rugby Club in East London, South Africa. In civilian life he was employed in the Systems Office of S.A. Railways in East London.

A Mr Hardwick, through Major Bisset of the South Africa Naval Museum, wrote, 'Mike played for the Buffalo 1st Team at centre and sometimes fly-half, at a young age prior to the war. As I played wing, I was a good pal of his and remember some very fine left-footed 'drops' by him. None of us remaining in East London remember where he went to school.'

Mr Hardwick, now 78 lives in East London, South Africa. He played against Sam Walker's British Lions in 1938.

CHRIS MACLAREN
Pilot
Won the DSC serving with 1772
on HMS Indefatigable

'I was born on the 10th May 1925 at Richmond, Surrey, but moved to the Midlands when still very young. I attended Grammar School up to the outbreak of World War II. When I was 17, I went to the local RAF recruiting centre. I was always keen on aircraft and wanted to fly. There I was told I was too young, but, 'come back in 12 months time'. I was bitterly disappointed as I walked out of the door and looked up to see a large hoarding saying, '17¾ years old, Fly with the Navy.' It so happened that the Naval recruiting centre was next door to the RAF one, so I did a U-turn, advanced my age to 17¾ and walked in. Here I was received with open arms, passed the appropriate tests and medical and was presented with the King's shilling.

From then on, it was the usual square-bashing at Lee-on-Solent, then on to St Vincent. After a short leave, I was posted to Kirby for transportation to Canada to begin my EFTS at a new station at St Eugene, near Montreal. From there I went to SFTS at Kingston, Ontario. Having gained my 'Wings' I then returned to the UK and was posted to the Advanced Flying Unit (AFU) at Errol in Scotland. Here I flew Miles Masters. From Errol I went to a commission board who asked, 'why did you join the Navy?' Being very young and naive I told the truth. After a lot of 'Tut-tuts' and 'Hums', I was told that perhaps I should remain a Petty Officer a little longer. I was then posted to RNAS Henstridge where I flew Spitfires and Seafires. After an Air-firing course at St Merryn I completed my initial deck-landings aboard HMS Ravager. After some more leave I was posted to 1770 Squadron to fly Fireflies and then to 1772 Squadron.

After the war I joined a family concern as representative, progressing up the ladder to become Sales Manager. I married Sheila and have a son and a daughter, but to date, no grandchildren. I live in hope.'

Chris Maclaren was gazetted on 20th November 1945, 'For services in the Far East in July and August 1945.' Wally Pritchard adds, 'This seems to be the only direct 1772 honour.'

BUCKINGHAM PALACE

I greatly regret that I am
unable to give you personally the
award which you have so well earned.
I now send it to you with
my congratulations and my best
wishes for your future happiness.

George R.I.

Lieutenant (A) C.D. MacLaren, D.S.C., R.N.V.R.

27 November 1945.

Sir,

I am commanded by My Lords Commissioners
of the Admiralty to inform you that they have
learned with great pleasure that, on the advice
of the First Lord, the King has been graciously
pleased to award you the Distinguished Service
Cross for courage, skill and determination in
air attacks against the Japanese during July
and August 1945.

This Award was published in the London
Gazette Supplement of 20th November 1945.

I am, Sir,
Your obedient Servant,

Temporary Acting Sub-Lieutenant (A) Christopher David
MacLaren, D.S.C., R.N.V.R.

240

GORDON MACROW
Petty Officer/Radio

I was born in 1923 at Walthamstow and educated at Sir George Monoux Grammar School and I joined the Royal Navy in June 1942. A school visit to the Portsmouth Dockyard sowed the seed of interest in the Navy and having sorted out my left foot from the right one, I was selected for training as radio mechanic and via HMS Shrapnell and HMS Ariel I passed out as a Leading Radio Mechanic. My first draft took me to Seafire Maintenance Party 2 (SMP 2) which was a team of five specialists, one from each trade. Our commission was to advise on installation and maintenance of equipment of the many squadrons under formation in the UK. Though attached to HMS Daedalus we travelled the country. These travels included St Merryn, Belfast, the RAF at Speke and in Northern Ireland as well as Burscough. In April 1944 I was drafted to HMS Ringtail to join 1772 Squadron. Earlier I had been rated Petty Officer.

The radio team of 1772 comprised 6 mechanics. The senior Petty Officer was Fred Stanworth; others were George King and Alan Sharp, with whom I have lost touch. Tom Alcorn and Nick Turner have been contacted on squadron matters and we hope 1997 will see them at our reunion.

With new aircraft came new problems and the beginnings of friendships which have lasted for many years. Some friendships crossed to other trades and our liaison with aircrew established the early stages of the 'Friendly Squadron'. With the aircrew, the station at Burscough was ideal for many off-duty happy hours playing them in 'friendly' competition at badminton and table tennis.

During the journey to Australia I was on HMS Activity, a carrier jammed with people, aeroplanes and equipment. We weathered the storms of the Atlantic, where as senior NCO I had plenty of work to control, in seeing that aircraft were tied down; the storm in the Mediterranean, whilst damaging other ships in the convoy, did not damage us. Our stops took in Aden, Colombo and on the way we picked up survivors from USS Sylvester. We crossed the line on 22 February 1945 and homage was duly paid to 'King Neptune'.

We berthed ahead of the main convoy at Woolloomooloo, early in March. The MONAB workshops at Schofields became our home though some of it was in tents-still. The conditions and atmosphere were very different from Burscough especially in terms of off-duty facilities. Leave was spent in Adelaide and the hospitality of the Australians was very warm. We enjoyed the beaches of Luna Park, Manly and Bondi. Some ratings even found friends in the 'outback'. But our job eventually was to relieve 1770 Squadron on HMS Indefatigable.

The radio workshop on that huge Fleet Carrier was on the port stern quarter just below the flight deck. I spent much of my time here repairing radios, in particular the 1161 which invariably went out of tune after deck landings. This workshop was also my station during the typhoon looking after all our equipment. I remember interesting breaks in the monotony of routine, because life in this phase of the Squadron, was all work and no play. One interlude was the visit of the C-in-C BPF, Admiral Bruce Fraser, and the other was when the fighting stopped, we visited USS Ticonderoga and gained an insight into the workings of the U.S. Navy. The entry into Tokyo Bay with the Royal Marine Band playing was a very special occasion for all of us. The fly past of Allied aircraft over Tokyo was most exciting and we all took pride when the carrier on one occasion landed 61 aircraft in 59 minutes.

The break-up of the section was inevitable, as was that of the Squadron as a whole. We left Indefatigable and I was drafted to HMS

The radio unit of the 'Friendly Squadron.'
Top L to R: Gordon Macrow, Stanworth, Sharp, Turner. Sitting: King and Alcorn. Centre back and front are Ray Battison and Wally Pritchard, the aircrew radio officers.

Golden Hind for demobilisation. Via USS Winchester Victory I was discharged from the Royal Navy at HMS Daedalus III on 18th May 1946.

I returned to Henley Cables to continue training and I moved from there to Spillers with the role of Assistant Pensions Manager. With the qualification of Company Secretary I became a specialist in Pensions Management. I had become a Founder Associate of the Pensions Management Institute in July 1976 and retired from Dalgety (formerly Spillers) in 1994 when I was made a Life Member.

I was married to Brenda in July 1953 and I have two sons and a daughter, and now six grandchildren.

My service with the Royal Navy led me to joining the Royal Naval Association and I was made a Life Member in 1988. I was a founder member of the Indefatigable Association and I am now a Life Member.

THOMAS 'GLEN' MCBRIDE
RNZVR
Observer
Lost over Japan 16th August 1945

Glen McBride, 'Mac' to his service mates, was born in Petone, Wellington, in November 1917 and graduated from Nutt Valley High School in 1932. He qualified as an accountant for the Audit Department and served in the Wellington Scottish Territorials before enlisting. He met Linda some time before they were engaged and before he sailed for England in early 1942. He had been recruited in Scheme F, a system under which New Zealand sent regular drafts of men who would be commissioned and serve as pilots and observers in the Royal Navy's Fleet Air Arm.

Glen and Linda had so little time together. They were married in

Petone on April 28th 1945, and just five weeks later Glen returned to Sydney to rejoin his squadron on HMS Indefatigable.

Linda never saw him again. Glen, at the age of 27, the oldest member of the squadron, was lost over Japan on 16th August 1945. He died 5 days before Japan's surrender, the last New Zealander killed in action in World War II. Linda did not celebrate VJ day with her friends. She had not then heard of Glen's death, but somehow she had a premonition, a feeling that something was wrong. VJ was a Wednesday. The telegram saying Glen was missing was delivered to her the following Monday afternoon. Linda now lives in Lower Hutt. She remarried in 1949, raised a family and was widowed again when her second husband died over 12 years ago. She still has photographs of Glen, resplendent in his naval uniform and the small silver New Zealand Memorial Cross issued to the kin of all New Zealanders who gave their lives in World War II.

More than 1,000 young New Zealanders joined the air branch of the RNZVR in World War II, 738 achieving commissioned rank. More than 150 did not come home. New Zealand naval airmen numbered more than 10% of the FAA officers and the proportion was much higher in the aircraft carriers of the British Pacific Fleet. Among those in Glen's draft were Ian Darby, now living in Waipawa and the best man at Glen's wedding, and also Don Banks. Both Darby and Banks had scary moments; they survived and were lucky to do so.

Fleet Air Arm training was thorough and took a long time. Glen and the others were stationed at many naval establishments in Britain and had a long stint of flying training at an American airbase just outside Detroit. Back in Britain they were commissioned in late 1943 but Glen and Ian were not posted to their first squadron until the newly formed 1772 Squadron, equipped with Fairey Fireflies, was formed at Burscough on May 1st 1944. Even then it took a while to complete the training and working up.

In April/May 1945 the New Zealanders had long service leave at home and that's when Linda and Glen were married. On 3rd June, Glen, Ian and Burn O'Neill, Ian's pilot, were flown to Sydney. Here they rejoined 1772 and in no time the Indefatigable sailed to join the British Pacific Fleet. On 16th July the British Task Force joined the American Fleet, under Admiral Halsey. For the next month Glen was among the hundreds of FAA fliers who showered destruction on Japan. As the official history of the Royal New Zealand Navy records: 'Day after day thousands of aircraft from allied carriers and island bases bombed airfields, harbours, railway and industrial plants, causing immense havoc.'

Glen's luck ran out four days after the Americans unleashed nuclear war on Hiroshima. He and his pilot Glyn Roberts, were killed when their Firefly was lost while attacking Koriyama airfield, northeast of Tokyo: no one saw them go down, no one knows what really happened. Their bodies were never recovered.

Glen was first listed as 'missing' but at the war's end, it became clear that he was not a prisoner of war and in early November 1945, Linda got official word that her husband 'must be now presumed dead'. It was perhaps a coincidence that Ian and Burn were shot down on the same raid.

The above has been taken largely from an article of the 'Dominion' newspaper issued in August 1995. It was with some pleasure that it announced that Linda accompanied Ian and his wife, Ngaire, to the big 50th anniversary celebrations of Victory over Japan at Lee-on-Solent and Portsmouth in September 1995. It was the squadron's pleasure that Linda joined the 50th anniversary of the disbanding of 1772 in Sydney in September 1945, at Sherborne and Yeovilton. The article added; 'She

Mac with his best Man Ian Darby from the 'Dominion' Newspaper & Mac and his pilot Glyn Roberts.

may also meet a nephew of Mac's pilot who wrote to her recently. "... I know it doesn't bring them back, but I do think it's important that people of my generation who were not in the war, and later generations, realise the sort of sacrifices that were made". The nephew was Alan Gittins.

Teddy Key. 'It is a strange thing, how these premonitions do occur. The story of Glen and Linda above refers to Linda's innermost apprehensions. I remember one evening on the Indefatigable chatting away to Mac in my cabin and listening to his profoundly black thoughts about life. He was deeply 'into' religion and that is how our conversation had begun. By contrast I told him about my blind belief in the future and how on my last leave back in England I had laid the first preparations of a teaching course and that I was going to start at Oxford. I could see myself then, with my feet firmly placed on the steady surface of a classroom. Our evening chat was one of vivid contrast between the two of us. I think, that is why the memory of it has lasted so long. The war was full of comradeship, now the essence of the 'Friendly Squadron', but it was also abounding in hidden fears and doubts. Freddie Hockley of 894 Seafire Squadron was a similar chap at the end, though I did not see such depression myself. He was always a sunny and relaxed guy but on his last leave, with his arm in a plaster, he had visited my mother in Cambridge, on sick leave. His last words to her were that he would not see her again. I never did tell her about his death, he was very much one of her favourites. Mac was the last Kiwi to be killed in the war: Freddie was the very last Fleet Air Arm aircrew to be killed; and at the very time the cease-fire signal was hoisted on the mainmast of the Indefatigable.

ROY MELVILLE
Observer

Roy joined the Squadron about the middle of August 1944, and was assigned as observer to the CO Lt. Cdr. Gough. He replaced Monty

Baker who had been killed in the mid-air collision which also killed Jimmy Sloan, the Senior Observer. In retrospect, Roy deserved a medal. Like all of us Roy recalls the triple 'runway' prang and like many of us the memory has dimmed regarding some of the details, but shortly after both the CO and Senior Pilot received new postings. He recalls the night of the flight to Donibristle not long before we went abroad. 'Steve was obviously keen to see his wife who was expecting the young lass who became Merlin Stevens. It was arranged that a section would fly to Donibristle to swing the aircraft on the bronze compass base, "in the tail-up position". The day of departure arrived in typical Burscough weather but in spite of this we proceeded; if I am correct we were mainly Scots on this flight. We flew up the coast to the Firth of Clyde, along the Clyde to the Forth/Clyde Canal, then along the canal to the Firth of Forth and thence to Donibristle. I doubt if we were ever higher than 500 feet.' Roy recalls too, the Canungra Jungle fun in Queensland. 'You remember that we had to wander about the tropical rainforest for several days while soldiers followed us, letting off thunder flashes. After 3 or 4 days of this, with pouring rain making us wetter and wetter, we came to our final night camp. We were all so miserable and so completely fed up that we built a roaring fire, just to dry our clothes, despite the protests of the army wallahs.' Well Roy, you ultimately did drop a 'small clanger' but you'll have to read the book to find out who spilt the beans. All other reference to you in this story is very discreet.

Roy studied at Edinburgh University from October 1946 to July 1951, graduating and completing his medical studies. After house jobs around Edinburgh hospitals he joined the Colonial Service in Malaya in May 1954, moving to Sarawak in July 1957. 'We returned to this country at the beginning of 1971 and after a spell of 3½ years as a Deputy Medical Superintendent I joined the Civil Service as a Medical Officer in 1974, retiring in 1989.'

Roy was awarded the OBE for his services to medicine.

FORÊT MILLAR
Observer

What can be said of Forêt Primrose Millar? He was an outrageous character and a very 'party-man'. Is that a euphemism for a guy who perhaps drank just a little more than average? He was a lusty man and many a story exists of his amorous conquests and the consequences thereof. He didn't finish his days with us, for he was posted to 1771 Squadron on Implacable with his pilot Don Randle together with one other crew, Stu Jobbings and Rhys Heaven. Johnny O'Driscoll describes him as a 'pianist extraordinaire'; 'he could play almost anything from classics to rag. We always welcomed him to our parties because he made our sing-songs something above the average. He could improvise at will and had been known to be still capable of playing a piano when he'd fallen on to the floor'. Johnny believes that he did some arranging for Rawitz and Landauer, popular classical pianists, before he joined up. It is believed that he was Director of Music for Sutherland county after the war. Others in the squadron believe that his name was linked with the Hallé Choir in Manchester. Roy Melville, a fellow Scot recalls that he was a teacher of music in Sutherland and Roy met him in 1958 when he returned from Sarawak on leave. But no word since. And that is Dusty Millar. Did we call him 'Dusty' or 'Forêt'? There are so many holes in the story; what does one believe? Where are you Forêt?

Dusty with his Felix. Johnny O'Driscoll has said that many P's and O's had their lucky symbols. It is open to speculation why Dusty could not stand bright sunlight.

DES MULLEN
RNZNVR
Observer

Des came from New Zealand and Ian Darby describes him as 'an accomplished artist and architectural draughtsman'. It was Des who designed the original Squadron crest. This drawing had a pair of binoculars as its central theme but their Lordships of the Admiralty thought fit to eliminate this significant symbol of long-range vision. It is not wholly certain why he departed from us at Burscough but Ian

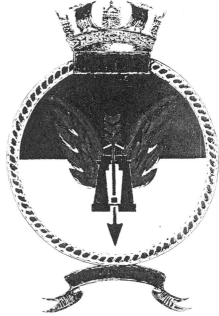

Des and His Wren Betty
Des's original Squadron sketch with the binoculars.

249

thinks it may have been acute sinus problems. Des seems to have gone to ground somewhere: Don Banks had seen him from time to time since he lives in Auckland. Geoff Rham remembers him because at Burscough he slept in the bunk opposite him. He remembers being awakened frequently by Des when he returned from late assignations with a very attractive Wren. His intentions proved most honourable because he married her and he asked Geoff to be his best man at the wedding which took place in Coventry. Judge for yourself the wedding picture of Des and Betty.

ROLLO NORMAN
Observer

'Rollo' Norman did not keep in contact with 1772 after demobilisation and therefore it is not possible to relate the story of how he came to join the Squadron in October 1944, with Bob Scott, Roy Hubble and Wally Pritchard as replacement crews. Suffice to say, he was with Wally Pritchard on the 65th Observer Course when he was given the opportunity to choose which aircraft type he wanted to fly. He settled for the best in the Fleet and was posted to 1772. In spite of his slight build he was more than a competent Rugby full-back and played for the Squadron team both at Burscough and Schofields. He also played for Leicester for a spell and had a number of representative games as well.

Throughout his time in the Squadron he was Bob Scott's 'looker' and Bob comments that, 'Rollo was a quiet competent observer . . . he even knew how to "wind-find" with smoke floats! His major attribute was that he could put up with me as a pilot', adds Bob. The team worked well, but Bob was to add, 'I must confess that carrying a married man in the back seat made a difference, particularly if, as I did, one knew his wife quite well!'

Rollo arrived in Sydney Harbour on the Activity and one of his first tasks was to go ashore and buy the largest bunch of bananas he could find, return and celebrate Wally Pritchard's 21st birthday. He enjoyed going ashore so much that it was not long before he fell in love and married Jill Patterson in Sydney Cathedral in April 1945. We got to know Jill very well as her mother, Bessie, a very delightful and hospitable mum, would give Branch Types invitations to her renowned parties at her South Huntville home. They lasted well into the early hours . . . never to be forgotten!

After the war Rollo and Jill went to Leicester for Rollo to acquire qualifications and to manage a shoe factory. Bob went to see them in Leicester during this period and found them flaunting a beautiful blue 1920's Bugatti. A little later they had a lovely daughter and later still went to South Africa where Rollo ran a shoe manufacturing business. Sadly after some years, Bob had a letter from Jill which bore a PS. 'By the way, Rollo and I are divorced'. Bob has not heard from either of them since.

JOHNNY O'DRISCOLL
Pilot

'I was born on 3rd February 1924 at Walton-on-the-Hill, Surrey. I was educated at Mere View School, Reigate Grammar School and the London Orphan School, which is now Reed's School, Cobham. I gained exemption from London Matriculation via the Cambridge School Certificate. I was School Vice-Captain, House Captain and I gained 1st XV Colours at Rugby Football. I left school in July 1940 and was employed by Wallace Brothers in the City of London. They were private bankers and East India Merchants. I joined the Home Guard and did fire-watching in the city. I volunteered for the Fleet Air Arm in February 1941 and joined the Navy at HMS Royal Arthur in July 1941, Course 232. My first major contribution to the war was guarding the East Coast at Skegness from the roof of Butlins, against the might of Germany. I was at St Vincent, Gosport on a TAG Course and then went to HMS Kestrel. Again I was involved in a major role of World War II. I was on Hangar Guard and aerodrome defence from a slit trench, all in the defence of the realm. A week in the Winchester Hospital with pneumonia was an apt reward for this selflessness in those inclement conditions. I remustered to a Pilot's course and so back to HMS Daedalus at Lee-on-Solent to wait for a course vacancy. Meantime, further guard duties at Shoot Farm and one week on the Isle of Wight defending the shoreline. HMS St Vincent followed and thence to Elementary Flying School at Sealand near Chester. I was shipped to Canada on HMT Beaverhill. My skills and keen eyesight were by now well known and I was placed on Submarine watch on the bridge . . . this time with blinding toothache. Senior Flying School at Kingston, Ontario was successful, I gained my 'wings' and was shipped home in the prestigious Queen Elizabeth, a reward no doubt for my unstinting devotion to many hours on guard duty. At HMS Heron at Yeovilton I joined 759 Squadron, No. 40 Course, Advanced Flying School. Before joining 1772 Squadron on 1st May 1944 I was posted for a spell to 771 Squadron at the RNAS Twatt, a Fleet Requirement Unit, doing air exercises with Royal Naval ships out of Scapa Flow.'

Johnny O'Driscoll teamed up with Geoff Rham, being 'the last two unattached aircrew in the crew room.' One has often wondered how the system of crewing worked under Gough. Johnny was on the 40th Pilot's Course at Yeovilton with Burn O'Neill, Maurice Goodsell, Rod Stevens and Jackie Ramsden.

Johnny's story is a delightful play-down of his true contribution . . . maybe due to a residue of the Irish in his bloodstream! He was and is a laughing guy, an upbeat fellow whose observations of pilot training in slit trenches and the development of a keen and watchful eye are a droll distortion of the main facts.

BURNIE O'NEILL
RNZNVR
Pilot

There was never any doubt that Burn was one of the really good pilots in the Squadron. It was generally accepted that Burn was one who had a natural flair for flying, had no fear, but knew how to couple it with plain common sense. Ian Darby always considered that he was one of the lucky 'O's in the Squadron, in having Burn as his pilot. There can be no better testimony to his skill and courage than to refer again to the story of their baling out over Japan. As an indication of Burn's wisdom in flying matters, it is interesting to read between the lines and see how they both tackled that ultimate problem in flying an aircraft by having a pretty clear idea of what they would do if 'the' problem ever did arrive. Burn was a good pilot; he had a passion for it. He wrote to us from New Zealand saying, 'My first wife died in 1965 and we had two boys. After two or three years I developed an urge to fly again, so I joined the local Aeroclub and qualified for my Private Pilot's Licence. I puttered about the Central Plateau skies with tourists, which was OK, as they paid expenses. One notable trip to the volcanoes took me to 9,000 feet and inside the crater of the mountain which was erupting. We flew around the inside of the crater and then across the crater again, a black, menacing smoking hole. Everything in the wee Cesna was quiet . . . until we eventually became clear of all the fury. I married again in 1969 and came to Waihi in 1970. She 'cleared out' in 1978. I married again in 1978, a diminutive Englishwoman; and as the old saying goes, 'He loves her as he's never loved before.' I spent all my working years in the building trade and although it cost some blood and sweat, I can walk about some areas, pointing out attractive edifices and saying, 'I built that back in . . .' Burn and Mary have never returned to the UK much as they would like to. They claim that neither of them travels very well; Burn in a message to the 50th Reunion said that he 'even gets jet-lag going to the supermarket.' He proclaims that they are very happy and comfortable in a cosy home in a small, friendly town, growing old gracefully. He concluded that he does think of us occasionally and that he grins to himself when he thinks of the things which happened; and just occasionally of those things, which had they not happened when they did happen, he would not be sitting where he was, writing to 1772. Never anything less than profound was Burnie O'Neill.

JOHNNY PALMER
Observer

Johnny has always been one of the Squadron's leading archivists and above all else he was a front-runner with Johnny O'Driscoll in getting the post-war reunions going. He is the man for accuracy and detail and one would suspect always the ideal guy to have in the back cockpit. Sadly one cannot ask his pilot because Gordon died several years ago, far too young. Johnny joined the No. 57 Observer Course in September 1942 in company with Knocker White at Lee-on-Solent. He went to Trinidad for flying training in January 1943 via Asbury Park, New York. He returned to the UK in December and was posted to 769 Squadron at Easthaven in January 1944 where Derek Fletcher who was due to join 1772 in May 1944 was killed in a Barracuda. His first pilot in 1772 was Rollo Moon and he claims to have flown with Teddy Key on a few occasions. His more permanent pilot was to be Gordon Davidson. He travelled to Australia on HMS Ruler and from the RNAS Station at Schofields was posted for a short while to 1770 Firefly Squadron with 3 other crews. After the war he was posted to Henstridge

for a spell and was demobbed in May 1946. He joined BOAC in June 1946 as a Radio Officer and he flew with BEA during the winter of 1946/7 before returning to BOAC at Hurn and flying in Yorks and Lancastrians. This was followed by Hermes, and then he was posted to Comets in 1952 until the crashes off the coast of Italy, before returning to Hermes. He was posted to Constellations in 1954 and he began pilot training at

Croydon during his stand-off periods. He did a Flight Navigation Course in 1957 and was posted to Brittania 102's as Navigator and continued his pilot training as before until 1958 when he obtained his Commercial Pilot's Licence. He was posted to Brittania 312's as a co-pilot and in 1963 posted to Boeing 707's as a co-pilot. In 1971 he passed out as Captain on 707's and then in 1978 posted to 747's and he retired in 1981 after 35 years . . . with a clean record. Not bad and not one A25! Eat your heart out you old prangers . . . Croose, Jobbers and 'Pranger' Pete. Johnny says that quite a few Observers became pilots after the war. There has to be a moral there – somewhere.

CROOSE PARRY
Senior Pilot
– after the loss of Rod Stevens

I was born on 3rd May 1923 at Long Ditton in Surrey. I spent my early childhood in Ireland, between Cork and Blarney, until I was 8 years old when my father died. I then returned to England and lived with my mother at the home of my maternal grandparents.

When war broke out I was at school at Marlborough and I remember the elder brother of a friend beating up the college in a Wellington bomber which may have influenced my decision to fly, so as the senior service appealed more than the RAF I found myself at Oxford being interviewed for the Fleet Air Arm.

In due course on 12th January 1942 I reported at Lee-on-Solent and stayed there for 2 weeks before moving on to St Vincent where my main memories were of the atrocious and inedible food. The fish was usually very many weeks past its sell-by-date and the liver was a rather hideous shade of green. As duty-hand one had to take the empty metal serving dish and wash it up under an outside cold tap which was a very proficient way of making residual fat and gravy congeal; it was then filled with the pudding, more often than not . . . brown duff.

From Gosport I went to EFTS at Sealand; eventually completing the course. Then on to Kingston Ontario in Canada. We sailed in an

American liner for civilians who were travelling to Canada and USA for safety. There were pretty girls on the Upper Deck which was out of bounds. As so-called sailors we were ordered to do duty as lookouts. I remember very clearly one night being on watch, on not quite the Upper Deck, when I saw two phosphorescent lines approaching the ship. I was terrified and speechless as they converged and passed under the ship exactly below where I was standing. I still do not know if they were torpedoes or some other fish.

Arriving at Kingston, the next stage of flying training began, this time it was Senior Flying Training School (SFTS) and here we flew Harvards and I must admit, ground-looping them as well. Memories of chipmunks and exotic butterflies, the end of summer, the beauty of the 'fall' and the severity of winter, come to mind. From Kingston, I moved to New Brunswick where it was even colder. I eventually boarded the M. V. Andes for the journey home. We met a gale in mid Atlantic; mess decks were awash with an extremely unpleasant mixture of un-mentionable ingredients. Back in the UK, proudly displaying my 'wings', I was commissioned, as Temporary Midshipman(A) RNVR. Then followed the conversion course at Errol flying Masters, Yeovilton followed and training began on Hurricanes. My first posting as a fully trained pilot was to the Ferry Pool at Donibristle which gave me an opportunity to fly various aircraft such as the Swordfish, Seafires and on one occasion at short notice a Hellcat which was to be delivered to Northern Ireland. In the hurry I failed fully to read up the handling notes and arrived over Aldergrove and realised I didn't know where the flaps lever was. Anyway the runway was long enough.

My next posting was to Easthaven, flying Swordfish, Fulmars and Hurricanes for trainee deck officers learning how to be batsmen. My last posting was of course to 1772 at Burscough.

After the war I spent over 20 years with a firm of colour printers in Croydon until they were eventually taken over and closed down. I then worked in the London office of a Mauritian Group of companies buying

 and arranging shipping for the companies within the group which acted as official agents for the Mauritian Government.

JOHN PRICE
Maintenance crew member

'I was born on 20th May 1924. My father was Irish, my mother was English and my name is Welsh, so I claim to be very British. I volunteered for the Royal Navy in May 1942 and was called up in September 1942. My initial training was at HMS Gosling at Warrington. I endured 6 weeks square bashing and 4 weeks land fighting. After aptitude testing I was sent to HMS St Vincent, Gosport to gain some knowledge of electrics, a 6 weeks course. I then was sent to RAF Melksham for training on aircraft electrics, gun circuits, engines etc. I was posted to HMS Vulture, St Merryn in Cornwall and attached to 792 Squadron. Their aircraft included Martinets, Defiants, Skuas and Gladiators. I spent a happy 10 months there from June 1943 to April 1944. After a brief spell at Daedalus I was drafted to HMS Ringtail, Burscough to join 1772 for 'working up'. We eventually sailed from Greenock in January 1945, on HMS Ruler bound for . . . Australia.

Prior to joining the Royal Navy I was employed in Royal Mail Lines Agency in Glasgow, as a shipping clerk. I was always interested in ships, two of my cousins were regular navy types, one on HMS Southampton, the other on HMS Fiji. Both were killed in Crete. Undeterred I was keen to get into the action. In retrospect I often wondered if and when we would ever get to sea. All things considered, despite living conditions, poor food, oppressive heat and the like, I enjoyed the whole of my life.

Joining the Indefatigable, to my way of thinking, put the icing on the cake. A big Fleet Carrier, action, flying off, landing on, joining up with the main fleet – what excitement, what a sight . . . what a memory! It was a tremendous thrill when we entered Sydney Heads on the Ruler. There was a thick white mist as we sailed along, and suddenly it lifted, and there it was. Breathtaking. All the small boats were hooting away and giving us a great welcome. We were all lined up on the Flight Deck and the band was playing. With the harbour bridge in the background, it was awe-inspiring. Those weeks at HMS Nabthorpe at Schofields

257

with the sun shining, fresh fruit brought along on a horse and cart in the morning were quite a different thing for us all. We would go 'ashore' in Sydney and Paramatta. There was the British Centre where we could obtain names and addresses of people offering hospitality at weekends. When my turn came for a ten-day leave, 'Bing' Powell (Petty Officer/Engines) and I opted for a trip to Orange, NSW and stayed with a sheep dealer, Mr Simpson and his wife and family. Mrs Simpson found out it was my 21st birthday and made me a birthday cake. Mr Simpson cracked his sole bottle of White Horse for the occasion. They gave us a wonderful time and we went shooting, exploring gold mining sites. They took us into Orange for the theatre, drinks in the 'Conobulus Hotel'. We had a great time. I can honestly say that the Aussies, whosoever and wherever, treated us royally.

After about two months on Randwick racecourse, under canvas, we were advised to pack our gear. We were taken down to the docks and were embarked on HMS Formidable, another Fleet Carrier. We slept in the hangar deck area on canvas stretcher beds, which had to be folded up and stowed away during the day. We left Sydney in early January and arrived back at Portsmouth in mid-February in an icy cold winter and after about 10 days we all shook hands and went our separate ways.

I applied to Royal Mail Lines in London for an interview and was accepted. They placed me in the Provedore (Victualling) Department Wharf. I did various jobs, ship's accounts, customs work, ships storage, etc over a period of 21 years. Furness Withy took over in 1967 and I left and worked for Italian General Shipping for 10 years and eventually for Cory Brothers Shipping. I was made redundant in 1987 after which a part-time job in a Patents and Trade Mark Agency. I finished with this job in January 1996 and am now properly retired. And glad of it!' His son is a teacher at Rutlish School in London.

WALLY PRITCHARD
Observer

In September 1939, 'on the day war broke out' I was at school at Southall, a somewhat different Southall from today. It was not long before I left school 'to make my way in the world'. The best careers for boys at that time were considered to be 'a job for life', in Banking, the Railways, particularly the GWR and the Civil Service. I chose none of these and in 1940 a company, managing rubber and tea estates in Malaya and India, with offices in Lloyds Building, Leadenhall Street, London EC, was the job that attracted me. The building which replaced the original Lloyds Building had just been bought by a German Company. At the same time I was made a 'messenger boy' for the ARP post at Norwood Green, Southall . . . and a 'fix lookout' for Lloyds Building. In September 1940 before starting work, I had a holiday with my 90 year old grandmother at Staplehurst in Kent where I had a perfect view of the Battle of Britain. On commencing work I had a front-row view of the London bombing raids and the resultant fires.

My grandfather was a sea captain from Deal and with this background and the desire to fly there was only one service to be in, the Fleet Air Arm. To ensure that I could achieve this I volunteered – under age and was eventually successful in being accepted on 9th January 1942 as a Naval Airman, Second Class, No. FX91660. This was a number never to be forgotten. My naval career started at HMS Royal Arthur, Skegness, on 25th March 1942, when I joined the 39th Telegraphist's/Air Gunner's Course.

Training took place at HMS Kestrel, Worthy Down, but was interrupted by an air crash in November 1942 and a spell in hospital. After that I joined 41st TAG Course and qualified as a Leading Airman TAG 3 in May 1943, obtaining first place in the examinations.

The reward for this was the choice of a pilot's or observer's Course which originally had been oversubscribed. I chose an Observer's Course and returned to HMS St Vincent at Gosport for initial training again, but this time as a 'Killick', a leading Airman.

In March 1944, I was promoted to Petty Officer and from then on enjoyed the facilities of an NCO's Mess. By August 1944 I had qualified as an Observer at HMS Condor, Arbroath, where I was offered a choice of aircraft. I opted for Fireflies and joined 1772 in October 1944, and was crewed with Roy Hubble; Bob Scott and Rollo Norman joined with me.

Chris Maclaren, Wally's pilot writes. 'I joined 1772 Squadron in June 1945 after my previous Squadron, 1770, had been disbanded and was immediately crewed with Wally Pritchard. Having Wally as my observer was one of the best things that happened to me. It is essential that a pilot and observer should be 'as one' and have complete faith in each other. When describing Wally, the word 'IMPERTURBABLE' comes to mind. To illustrate this point, whilst attacking an airfield on the Japanese mainland we received several hits from enemy anti-aircraft fire. The damage to the aircraft was such that I thought that it would be a case of having to bale out, so I told Wally to stand-by. One shell had blown off the cockpit hood and another had passed through the petrol tank between the two cockpits. The overload tank under the port wing was on fire and a large hole appeared in the starboard wing. I jettisoned the overload tank and repeated my instructions to Wally to stand by to bale out. The only response I received was a phlegmatic voice over the intercom. 'Steer course 260 degrees.' So as the engine was still firing on all cylinders and I felt compelled to 'obey that voice', I decided to try and make the carrier which was some 200 miles away. Seeing another Firefly ahead I joined up with him and it turned out to be Pete Kingston and Val Bennett, who described the amount of damage they could see. They escorted us safely back to the carrier.

I would like to put on record, that when later I was awarded the DSC, I considered that this medal was equally attributable to Wally Pritchard. We were a 'TEAM' and not individuals.'

The 'Andes' brought us home from Sydney in record time but we managed to learn the rudiments of bridge.

The return was an anti-climax; life in the peacetime navy was very 'pusser' and not at all like the 'Branch' we had left.

The job I left in 1941 was offered to me at 1939 rates of pay but with the opportunity to become a rubber planter in Malaya. This I declined and instead, started a career in Accountancy which Bob Scott was already following. I also declined the invitation of the Edgell family to join them in Bathurst, Australia. In 1951, with Bob Scott as my best man I married Heather and thereafter we attended every reunion we could.

A rider to the story of the 'big hit' on his plane was that Chris also added to his dismal assessment of a dodgy situation, 'Wally, we may have to bale out'. 'But I can't swim', responded Wally. Chris. 'I've thought of that; course 260° it is'. Wally had not been wholly truthful about whether he could swim or not, when he joined the Royal Navy!

DON RANDLE
Pilot

Don with his Observer Forêt Millar, together with Stu Jobbings and his 'looker' Rhys Heaven, were posted to 1771 Squadron, embarked on HMS Implacable, on 14th May 1945. They had been with 1772 for about a year. They flew to Jervis Bay and landed on Implacable on 23rd May. They sailed the following day for Manus in the Admiralty Islands. Before that 'we had the joy of joining the old squadron at Canungra in Queensland for jungle training, the course was "army-directed". What we wanted was "jungle survival".'

With 1771 he was involved in Operation INMATE, the assault on Truk. This operation was on 14/15th June, his first operation and his first take-off by catapult. These two old 1772 crews were with us on the final assault on Japan in that they were part of the British Task Force in June/July 1945. 1771 Fireflies were the first British aircraft to attack mainland Japan on 17th July. Stu Jobbings and Rhys Heaven managed to ditch safely during this spell of operations. Don also admits to a barrier prang while on Implacable.

In 1979, en route from Tokyo to Honolulu, Don did a diversion to Micronesia and stopped 48 hours in Truk. He snorkelled over the Japanese ships. It was a truly amazing experience for him. These ships had been sunk in 1943 by the devastating bombardment of the U.S. Navy.

Don spent his working life in the tobacco industry and was eventually the Chief Executive Officer of a major company. His work took him round the world by sea and air a dozen times and to virtually every country in the world. He covered 46 of the 50 States of the USA. He claims to have had a very full and fascinating life. He married Margaret in 1950 and he has two daughters and now seven grandchildren.

Don was hospitalised on return to Sydney in 1945 and then shipped back to the UK in the hospital ship MAJOLA. The reason was the need for a shoulder operation. He was demobbed on 7th May 1946 after a brief posting at Ternhill.

Don joined the Royal Navy on 5th October 1942 and was for a while a 'Spit' pilot at the end of his training. He did his spell of stooging.

One day, the thwarted trip in the back of the Historic Flight Mark 6 Firefly will be honoured. He won that seat in a reunion raffle, proceeds to the Historic Flight, but the little operation was stymied by . . . a taxiing accident!

GEOFF RHAM
RNVR
Observer

'My first contact with the Navy occurred on 8th September 1941 when I was ordered to present myself, together with 80 other prospective naval airmen, at HMS Daedalus Lee-on-Solent, to commence training on the 50th Observer Course. Having made our way to Gosport from various parts of the UK, a shuttle of buses transferred the new intake to HMS Daedalus throughout the afternoon. When finally assembled, a tannoy announcement was made ordering all course personnel to assemble on the parade ground. Somewhat unexpectedly we received a lecture from a Senior Officer on etiquette, a modified No. 11 punishment drill which involved doubling round the parade ground in our civilian clothes for what seemed a long time, and a three-day stoppage of leave. Most of us were unaware of the nature of the incident that provoked this reaction but, as we understood it, the CO's wife had also travelled on one of the ferrying buses and had not been offered a seat. This was duly reported and since it would have been difficult to blame anyone individually the whole course was made to suffer the consequences. As a result it was possible that we were in the running for some kind of first in naval history by incurring their Lordship's displeasure in such a record time. It is interesting to note that 50 years ago we realised that a breach of good manners had occurred and we had accepted the repercussions – not that we had a lot of choice in the matter. Needless to say, it created a big impression amongst the ship's company who had watched proceedings from a discreet distance with gaping mouths. It may also have caused some of them to review their own procedure when travelling in mixed company.

During our working-up period at HMS Nabthorpe in Australia, air-crew members were sent in two succeeding groups to attend an Australian Army Jungle Course at Conungra. We were transported to Brisbane in a Dakota and thence by narrow gauge railway to the Camp which was surrounded by tropical vegetation similar to that found in New Guinea.

The purpose was to familiarise us in ways of living and surviving off the land in the event of a forced landing. The first half of the course was taken up with rendering us fit enough to participate in the second half and, since in the Army's opinion the performance of the earlier group had left much to be desired in this respect, a more vigorous format was inaugurated. This involved a number of painful exercises which caused our muscles to seize up, but by the seventh day benefits began to emerge and we all made an uneventful recovery.

An incident which did much to enliven proceedings occurred in the early hours of one morning involving Roy Melville and the parade ground bell. The bell, which was used to summon the incumbents of the camp to meals and parades, was an object to which Roy had taken an obsessive dislike. In retrospect, I feel it was accorded a degree of reverence by the Aussies and had a significance beyond that of being just an ordinary bell – probably because of its food summoning function rather than any religious overtones. However, such veneration was far from Roy's mind when, having imbibed a little too freely, he embarked on a course of action which was to try relations between the Australian Army and the Royal Navy. At about 2 a.m. one morning he made his way to the parade ground and, seizing an iron bar which served as its clapper, beat the hell out of the bell until forcibly restrained. On hearing this thunderous noise the whole camp erupted into action convinced that a full scale invasion of mainland Australia by the Imperial Army of Japan was in full swing. When the dust had settled, and order had been restored amid a hail of adverse comments which featured frequent references to 'Pommie Bastards', we eventually turned in, mindful that consequences might ensue.

On the following morning, two of us were ordered to parade Roy before the Commandant. We were at a loss to offer much in the way of mitigation. Possibly we might have explained that Roy was a Scot and, in consequence could not be held responsible for his actions when affected by alcohol, but judging from the appearance of the Commandant's face, which began twitching horribly at the sight of Roy, it was unlikely that such a plea was going to be met with patient understanding.

As far as I remember Roy was given a monumental verbal roasting and we were all given stern warnings about any further breaches of discipline.'

In his post war years, Geoff was a Veterinary Surgeon, until his retirement.

GLYN ROBERTS
Pilot
Lost over Japan 10th August 1945
Awarded the DSC

Charles Birch, a Canadian friend of Glyn's recalled that on last seeing Glyn at Jervis Bay, south of Sydney, and just before 1772 joined HMS Indefatigable, Glyn had sewn two little red horns on his flying helmet.

As he said, nothing that he knew of Glyn had changed. Charles Birch's comments were recorded in Stuart Eadon's book 'Kamikaze'. He had added that Glyn had made a second and ill-advised run over Koriyama. For his bravery and other courageous incidents in his short time in the Pacific battle, he was awarded the DSC, but he lost his life.

Joan Wright writing to the squadron at the time of the 50th anniversary, told us how the reunion at Yeovilton and Sherborne together with the squadron video of the event had been a lovely way of 'retaining the memories, which for me were wonderful, sometimes sad but still wonderful. I learned so much about my brother – good and wicked, but so much in character. Always a daring rebel, dragging me into all kinds of trouble but always my Sir Galahad. I have always adored him. I thank all the members of 1772 for adding to my memories.' Joan Wright was Glyn's sister.

When it came to the challenge of writing the 1772 Story, Joan was most willing to provide the story of Glyn.

Glyn was born on 10 February 1922 and educated at Gwersyllt School near Wrexham Clwyd and also at Grove Park Grammar School at Wrexham. Glyn had two friends throughout his years at school and the years that followed on from school. They were Glyn Williams who joined the Royal Air Force and Joe Cash, a Rear Gunner who was killed in action. They were an inseparable trio until war dictated otherwise. Following Joe's death in the early days of the war, Glyn wanted to get to Joe's funeral, but for security reasons Glyn Williams could not get permission to go. Glyn Roberts then borrowed his father's car and persuaded/cajoled me to be his passenger. We got into the camp under some pretence, hid Glyn Williams in the back seat, drove to the funeral and back into the camp the same way. They were both determined to say 'Cheerio' to their friend.

The two Glyns both had motorbikes, a BSA and a Norton and later Glyn Roberts bought a Morgan sports car, faster and noisier. Everyone in the village recognised the sound of the bikes and the car. That car was great fun; no wipers, the door permanently tied up. If it snowed or rained the passenger, (me), was kept extremely busy keeping the windscreen clear. People used to wonder why my hand was permanently blue, but we always arrived and returned safely.

For holiday work Glyn was with Holland, Hannen and Cubitts Construction Co at Saighton Camp, Chester. This company constructed airfields. Glyn remained on the permanent staff, round about 1938, and this was his first contact with air traffic. It was here that he waited out his time for conscription.

About 1940–41, Glyn joined the Bolton Police Force, (maybe a change from 'chased', to being the 'chaser'). He enjoyed his duties and feedback suggested early promotion.

Glyn joined the FAA in 1942. He went to Sealand where he trained on Tiger Moths. All the surrounding villages recognised his plane on his training flights. For example he flew over Llay Colliery to wave 'hello' to his Dad; with lots of aerobatics. He'd then go to Johnstown with a wave, a wing-wiggle, more aerobatics and 'Here comes Glyn' from all the neighbours.

I last saw Glyn when I was serving in Ack Ack on the East Coast. I was summoned to the Battery Office. 'Oh, not again'. I had just completed 3 days CB, but there stood Glyn, resplendent in his Naval uniform. What a joyous sight for me and for several other AA girls. He was in time to join us for an impromptu Fancy Dress Party. What a night! I shall never forget that evening; he had come miles to say, 'duty calls, see you sis.' 'See you broth.'. Now I know where he was going – it really was 'goodbye'.

Among my childhood memories I remember that he led, I followed. No questions asked. He was not a complicated character. How we survived his suggested adventures I do not know, but then as in later days, his view was that life was for living and not for vegetating. He was fearless, many times taking great risks. He was intensely loyal, stubborn, devilish, gung-ho, Robin Hood and a swashbuckler type, all rolled into one. He was though, a very loving son and brother. 'WAR' was just his time to be alive? Was the 'excitement', if one can call war exciting, his natural milieu, one in which he excelled? We shall never know.'

Glyn was an original member of 1772 Squadron, joining on 1st May 1944. He was always in the forefront of any 'action'. He, like many of us, was classified as 'a steady and sober drinker'! He loved the parties and all the squadron photographs which bear evidence of those parties, show his sense of profound enjoyment and commitment. There was never any doubt about his skills in the air and several of us have in retrospect wondered why their Lordships could not see things as we saw them. Surely here was the natural 'Spit' type: he should have been in a Seafire Squadron. Glyn followed the usual route to his 'Wings' which he received on 14 May 1943. He progressed via HMS Daedalus, St Vincent, EFTS at Sealand, 31 SFTS at Kingston Ontario in Canada and in July 1943 promoted to Temporary Acting Sub Lieutenant(A). According to Seedie's list of FAA Awards Glyn Desmond Roberts was noted in the 'London Gazette on 21st August 1945 for air attacks on targets in Japan whilst serving with HMS Implacable.' It should be pointed out that whilst the 1772 Squadron was finishing final training, two groups were seconded for brief service with 1770 and 1771, then involved in operations over the Sakashima Islands. During that spell on Implacable and flying with 1771 Squadron, Glyn won his DSC. Teddy Key wrote in 'Kamikaze', by Stuart Eadon, 'In life Glyn was the essence of the more-than-courageous fearless FAA pilot. The incident when he kept his Firefly in the air, mixture weakened, pitch coarsened to 'hover' around a downed pilot in the sea may have been forgotten but I bet Glyn must hold the record for the length of time a Firefly ever stayed airborne on a tank of fuel. Glen 'Mac' MacBride I think found Glyn's fearlessness difficult to fly with. I hated flying as a passenger.'

Alan Gittins, Glyn's nephew: 'When I first discovered the possibility that my uncle had been executed by the Japanese after crash-landing on 10th August 1945, I resolved to try to find out the truth.' Alan has spent a great deal of time and emotion in correspondence, trying to reach that truth. The origins of Alan's research were in Stuart Eadon's books, 'Kamikaze' and 'Sakashima', which contained statements by Ian Darby. Ian's facts had originated from letters from Major E. H. Powell of the U.S. Army, who had investigated Japanese War Crimes just after the war. Major Powell had discovered facts about a Rolls Royce engine which had been sold to a fishing company in Japan. There was evidence that certain men had been involved in Glyn and Glen's execution and Glen's brother, in Japan, had made efforts to locate the bodies which had been buried in shallow graves. The Firefly had been buried and attempts seemed to have been made to burn it. However Ian Darby never learned the final outcome of Major Powell's investigations nor is there any current record of the graves. Investigations for a number of reasons switched to the UK and Alan's research involved the Naval Historical Branch in London, the Public Records Office at Kew, the Commonwealth War Graves Commission, the Fleet Air Arm Museum at Yeovilton, the Imperial War Museum, the U.S. Embassy and the Ministry of Defence. None came up with any new information. Robin Henderson, Senior Observer, had been adamant that Glyn and Glen did not survive the crash. Ian Darby and Burn O'Neill had baled out on the same raid on Koriyama airfield, so two Firefly aircraft had crashed more or less at the same time in the same area, but only one was reported to have exploded. War Crimes trials in Japan in early 1995 involved Alan in correspondence with the Daily Mail and the solicitors of the claimants, ex POW's. Again, no lead.

Further communication with Ian Darby seemed to come up with the one conclusion, that the 'aircraft which seemed to explode' was the Firefly of Darby and O'Neill. Ian was convinced in his letters to Alan, that Glyn and Glen had force-landed. Alan was convinced after research assistance from a Commander Hobbs, that there was an investigation of their deaths in Japan. Alan still pursued several other avenues and eventually discovered that Major Powell had died in the 1960's. Since then Alan claims that the trail has gone cold but he continues the enquiries.

To support Robin Henderson's log book entry, which stated that, 'Glyn and Glen had bought it', contact with Pete Kingston in New Zealand produced the fact that in his log book he had written, 'Glyn and Mac (Glen and Mac were used as his name) shot down in flames,' Pete, was by then in poorly health and his answer to Alan stated that he had 'no personal recollection of what happened to Glyn and Mac on the day in question'. Alan, with his aunt, Glyn's sister Joan Wright, did meet Linda Gillingham, Glen's widow, at the 50th Reunion, but they had little information to offer either way, other than the huge doubt which surrounded the whole story. Alan says that he and Joan were very pleased to meet Linda but it was a meeting tinged with sadness because of the circumstances and memories. The McBride family had virtually all died off and there was never any detail following from Glen's brother's visit to Japan, to find his last resting place.

Teddy Key: 'With the organisation of the reunions, I had been in contact with Alan and I was therefore the go-between for all this information. Robin (Hank) Henderson is certain that the crash was of such a nature, that neither of the aircrew could have survived. Pete Kingston's log book entry says that 'the aircraft burst into flames'. A document from the Admiralty addressed to 'Minor War Crimes' (sic) Tokyo' listing details of a number of FAA casualties, including 1772's Maurice Goodsell, Mike La Grange, Rod Stevens, states, '– (they) did not return from the attack on Koriyama at about 1400 hours, 10th August 1945. The pilot who was shot down in the same attack and who has since been liberated by the Japanese stated he saw a Firefly dive into the ground. He did not see any parachute.' Ian's descent, in his own words, does pose the question of how accurate he could have been in separating the paths of the two aircraft. I do tend to believe Ian, however.'

Major Powell had certainly done a great deal of work on the investigation of the remains of a body and an aircraft, both of which bore evidence of burns . . . by the Japanese or by the fiery crash. Unfortunately only one letter has survived from his correspondence with Ian Darby and that does not make it absolutely clear whether the grave for Glyn and Glen had been discovered or whether Major Powell was referring to another aircraft and crew. Ian Darby maintains the missing correspondence confirms that Major Powell did locate Glyn and Glen's grave and their aircraft. There was evidence that serial numbers had been eradicated from the plane. Men covering a criminal act of murder or trying not to be accused of making profit from war remains? This is entirely a personal conclusion and perhaps a frail analysis of the tragedy.'

Glyn was a dare-devil character and that perhaps is just part of his fascination for Alan, Glyn's nephew. Ian Darby claims that he flew as Glyn's observer on nine occasions. Ian had been subjected to some hair-raising aerobatics on one occasion over the home town, Wrexham, in Wales. He was sure that he had aged 70 years in that one flight. Other observers tell the same sort of story. In Alan's letters to Teddy Key, he tells why finding out about his uncle's death has been so important to him. He felt that members of the Squadron might want to know a little more about Glyn.

Glyn's father was an engineer in the Wrexham area and he died a few years ago, aged 103. He was a very determined and fearless character. Glyn was the 'Darling' of his mother, 'a beautiful child with long curly locks'; she died at the age of 60 in 1948; Glyn's death had destroyed her. Alan says that he was born 8 years after the death of his uncle and Glyn was always an outspoken presence while Alan was growing up. Photographs existed but many had been destroyed by Glyn's distraught mother. Glyn was adored by all his family, his mother, father and two sisters. He was the youngest one, a happy carefree child and as such, quite possibly indulged by his elders. Joan says, 'Glyn was a happy carefree child, the youngest and 'a boy at last'. It was so easy to adore him and indulge him because he gave so much joy and laughter; I would like to emphasise 'the laughter'. The word 'scamp' describes him, no malice, just no fear.'

He was a leader and always unthinking of danger. Alan's young and developing interests had centred on things military, his father had been in the 8th Army in the Western Desert and therefore war stories existed in the family, but somehow in the case of his uncle he was hesitant about asking questions. For 40 years Glyn was a picture on the wall, a row of medals and the tankard with all our 1772 signatures on it. Years passed and Glyn lived in Alan's mind. Sometime about 1994, Charlie Birch, an old FAA friend of Glyn's made contact with the family. Charlie knew of stories about Glyn; the meeting in Australia when Glyn faced him wearing red horns on his flying helmet and that perhaps Glyn had spent a night in gaol over a low-flying incident. Alan had asked about the vagueness regarding Glyn's death – Charlie said that he knew the answers – but did Alan want to know? It was then that he told him that Glyn had been decapitated by the Japanese after crash-landing. The shock was of course enormous and there followed the heart-searching question of whether to tell Joan. Joan's family and Alan decided they should. Joan accepted the news with great courage and promised Alan that she would help all she could to find the truth.

Alan has lived in the post-war years when those of us who knew something of the horrors of war lived alongside generations who relied on stories only. Alan came to terms with those emotions but for him there remained but one emphatic message, 'GLYN AND GLEN SHOULD NOT BE FORGOTTEN, NOR WHAT THEY DID'. Those of us who remain in 1772 have never forgotten them. This book is a tribute to them and those who have no known resting place . . . except perhaps in the pages of this book. Here the memory resides, with affection and admiration for:–

GLYN
GLEN
STEVE
MAURICE
MIKE

A signal of Admiral Halsey at the end of a particularly hot period of action in July seems relevant to what happened in August, for Glyn and Glen; 'For the great flying fighters who fought it out over Japan to a smashing victory, I have no words that I can add to the glory of the

Val Bennett's sketch of Glyn

GLYN.

28 August 1945.

Sir,

I am commanded by My Lords Commissioners of the Admiralty to inform you that they have learned with great pleasure that, on the advice of the First Lord, the King has been graciously pleased to award you the Distinguished Service Cross for determination and devotion to duty in air attacks on targets in Japan.

This Award was published in the London Gazette Supplement of 21st August 1945.

I am, Sir,
Your obedient Servant,

Sub-Lieutenant (A) Glyn Desmond Roberts, D.S.C., R.N.V.R.

Glyn was noted in the London Gazette on 21st August 1945, 'For air attacks on targets in Japan whilst serving on HMS Implacable.'

factual record they wrote, with their courage, their blood and lives.'

I hope that Alan will approve my summary of a complex investigation which he undertook. Perhaps he will allow me to quote from Lin Yutang, a Chinese philosopher, of our time and youth.

'The scamp will be the last and most formidable enemy of dictatorships. He will be the champion of human dignity and individual freedom and will be the last to be conquered. All modern civilisation depends entirely on him. Probably the Creator knew well that when He created man upon this earth He was producing a scamp, a brilliant scamp it is true, but a scamp nevertheless. The scamp-like qualities of man are, after all, his most hopeful qualities. This scamp, that the Creator has produced is undoubtedly, a brilliant scamp. He is still a very unruly and awkward adolescent, thinking himself greater and wiser than he really is, still full of mischief and naughtiness and a love of a free-for-all. The world can be a more peaceful and a more reasonable place to live in, only when men have imbued themselves in the light gaiety of the spirit.'

Glyn's parents and sister Joan, receive Glyn's Distinguished Service Cross at Buckingham Palace.

271

The Friendly Squadron

LT. CDR. (A) L.C. WORT. R.N.U.R.
R.N. AIR SQUADRON 1772.
c/o G.P.O. LONDON.
10th September. 1945.

Dear Mr. & Mrs. Roberts.

I am writing to express to you the sympathy of my Squadron and myself in your great loss. I don't know what details you have been given but the circumstances were as follows.

Glyn was pilot of one of a formation of aircraft attacking Koriyama Airfield in northern Honshu, Japan. This target was heavily defended and we lost two Fireflies as well as some aircraft of other squadrons. I haven't written before because the other Firefly crew, S/Lts. O'Neill and Darby, were seen to bale out and get down safely, and I hoped when they were sent back from the Prisoner of War Camp, that they might be able to give me some information of Glyn and his observer S/Lt. McBride.

They have now got back to us, but I'm afraid they have no news. An American pilot, who was shot down on the same operation, returned with them, states that he saw a Firefly crash into the ground on the airfield. This must have been Glyn's aircraft as the other one crashed about six miles away.

Several pilots and observers who were taken prisoner around the same time were sent to the same camp and all came back together. I think therefore it is only fair to tell you that I do not think there is much hope of Glyn having survived the crash, as I feel sure we should have heard something by now.

Glyn was one of the most popular officers in the Squadron. He was especially liked by the ratings with whom he came into closer contact than anyone else as a result of his divisional duties. He was a good pilot and very keen on his job and on the Squadron. As divisional officer he was exceptionally efficient and the greatest possible help to me.

We all feel that we have lost a fine messmate and a good friend. Words are inadequate to express feelings in matters of this nature and I can only assure you of my very deep personal sympathy.

Yours sincerely,
L. Wort

The CO's letter to Glyn's parents, written on 10th September 1945.

272

ALAN ROWLINSON
Observer

I was born on 7th February 1925 at Woodford Green, Essex and educated at Bancroft's School. I achieved limited academic success but did reach 1st XV status in Rugby Football, Cricket and Swimming. My ambition at that stage was to be either an Admiral or a Farmer, though closer to 1939 I wanted to fly.

Having tried special entry to Dartmouth, but failed Physics, I passed through the portals of Gosport under the sign, 'Join the Fleet Air Arm . . . but be a sailor first.' The date was 1st May 1943. That same day Sammy Samuelson and Ken Neuschild joined me on the 61st Observers Course. All three of us were to become observers in 1772 though sadly Ken Neuschild was to die in a flying accident at Burscough. During our flying training course at Arbroath we were at one stage taken to Rosyth to 'go over' a new Fleet Carrier being built there. Over 2 years later, I realised that the ugly beast, covered in wires, compressors and masses of other paraphernalia, we had 'inspected', was indeed our very own HMS Indefatigable. One year after that, having qualified as Midshipman(A) RNVR I was posted to RNAS Easthaven for flying control duties. Then about 6 weeks later their Lordships of the Admiralty transferred me to RNAS Burscough as an Observer in 1772 Squadron. Geoff Gill was my pilot and I was part of Green Section. At a later stage in 1945, Les Wort, The Boss, appointed me, '1772 Sports Officer.' I'll never know why he did that but the task involved me in deck hockey, various games, even tournaments on the Flight Deck when on board the Indefatigable. Deck hockey was played with sort-of-hockey sticks and coiled rope grommets. I cannot possibly recall any serious or famous victories, but someone at a fairly recent Indefatigable reunion in Birmingham (1995) happened to say, 'I remember you . . . you played a very dirty game of deck hockey.'

As a very young Sub Lieutenant for the three months when I was part of 1772 on the Indefatigable in the British Pacific Fleet, I was made to feel a very small cog in a very large machine. Only a few memories stick in my mind.

The first was when Dave Hebditch, my pilot by that time, and I were heading for the Japanese mainland and had to turn back because of an oil leakage problem. Because of the Kamikaze threat, any aircraft heading towards the fleet from the direction of Japan was automatically regarded with the highest suspicion . . . and fired upon. Therefore all Allied aircraft headed back to a picket of 3 or four destroyers or frigates, stationed several miles north or south of the Fleet. The final approach therefore was from a totally different bearing. When Dave told me we had to return to base I gave him a course and Estimated Time of Arrival (ETA) in order to arrive at the approved point over the destroyer picket. When we arrived at the ETA position, not a single ship could be seen. I gave Dave another course and ETA to return to the Indefatigable. I was more than a little worried that I might have been wrong in the first place, but at least, the Indefatigable was exactly where I said it should be. After landing on I reported to the Commander(O) that the picket was not yet 'on station', but I didn't hear any further explanation and I didn't dare ask. The second was a slightly less than perfect landing, when Dave bounced on touchdown and we went over the first barrier and landed with a splat into the second. The normal treatment for shock was an invitation to drink about a tumblerful of brandy after which of course nothing seemed to be seriously wrong. But . . . maybe, I exaggerate. This was on 24th July 1945.

After about 2 to 3 days of operations over the Japanese mainland the Fleet retired several hundred miles to meet the Fleet Train to take on board oil, supplies, replacements etc. This was a time for relaxation for the aircrews and my third scrap of memory relates to the peace of a collapsible safari bed on the cool quarterdeck in the afternoon listening to classical records. I can recall even now two of my favourites: Rachmaninov's 2nd Piano Concerto and Beniamino Gigli, singing 'Panus Angelicus'. There were others of course.

The remaining memories mainly concern VJ Day, splicing the mainbrace (three times); sailing into Tokyo Bay with almost full naval Pomp and Circumstance. I can remember the party when Burn O'Neill and Ian Darby returned on board followed by the 'fire-work' display, as we bade farewell to the visiting aircrews from USS Ticonderoga. After that we returned fairly fast to Sydney, but because there was no beer left, the gesture was made of lowering the price of whisky in the wardroom from 3 pence to 2 pence and gin from 2 pence to 1½ pence.

Nearly two years later when their Lordships said, 'Thank you, but Goodbye' and when I realised that I would not fulfil my ambitions of being an Admiral, I applied to and was accepted by Reading University. Three years later I was able to put B.Sc. (Agric) after my name. Then followed six years as a farm manager, (learning how little I knew about farming) on farms, in Sussex, Essex and Hampshire, before it dawned on me that there wasn't much money, nor much of a future for me in that line I decided on a career change. I went into the world of commerce specialising in animal feeds, becoming eventually a specialist in ruminant nutrition with particular emphasis on a liquid feed supplement, which at one time contained alcohol, fed on an ad-lib basis and capable of balancing the quality of whatever feeds are available to the farmer . . . fascinating! Early retirement nearly 10 years ago, led me to restore the derelict first house ever built at Harlyn Bay on the North Cornwall coast. This was a very enjoyable two years. Now in Farnham in Surrey Ann and I have had further enjoyment and leisure together with our family extending down to 4 grandchildren.'

In the last decade, Alan has assumed nay, been appointed to the role of 'Reluctant Chairman' of our Duke of Wellington 'happenings', which has steered the reunions along a happy course. His throaty and sensual laugh rules every 1772 occasion and others too, one supposes, except when his very young grandson thrashes him at golf!

SAMMY SAMUELSON
Observer

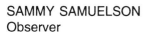

I was born a rebel. My father was in the Army in WW1 and my elder brothers and my cousins were all WW2 Army. So why not be different and join the Navy? A passion for cars, indulged in by by my family, turned to one for aeroplanes, and therefore, based on a mixture of logic and stroppiness, my decision had to be the Fleet Air Arm. I countered my luke-warm interest in the school OTC by joining the newly formed ATC and with the help of a bicycle, another love, I found myself visiting aerodromes and learning to glide! After my first interview and medical I was sent off with three shillings, to advance to the age of 18. My first night away from home was in Oxford, spent in some sort of servicemens' dosshouse, the horrors of which I remedied by dining at The Mitre. I now faced the main interview and medical. The usual question of 'Why?' produced the answers, 'Because I want to fly' and to the question of 'why not join the RAF?' I answered, 'I thought it would be fun.' Obviously the wrong answer, because the questioner changed colour. I had listed my sports on the application form and they seemed to have escalated to about 20 activities including Beagling. A rugged two-and-half striper from some front row, said, 'You seem to have played quite a lot of games.' I replied in total honesty, that I had not been any good at any of them and considered that it was a good idea to keep on trying new ones because some sport might eventually be to my liking. I had completely beaten him because all he could say was, 'Ah'. I was in.

St Vincent at Gosport was like heaven after the sadistic discipline and appalling food of boarding school. The rigours of square-bashing and the learning were easy for me and I rapidly became proud of the sailor's uniform. I had made few friends at school but now I was making new ones; one has lasted to this day . . . thank you Alan! The family farmhouse was close by and leaves were easy. Soon I was to become Acting Leading Airman and my pay trebled.

A spell at Chatham Gunnery School, learning the secrets of sleeping in a hammock and as a future observer, discovering how to fire a 4" naval gun, was followed by a signals course at Eastleigh. It was an interesting place because there were aircraft about, a delivery of fresh milk every morning by a Steptoe-like pony-cart, fun and games and I had a very 'tiddley' suit made by an ex-East End Tailor-turned-sailmaker. It cost me £3!

I was next posted to HMS Condor at Arbroath for Observers' Training. On Kings Cross Station I met an Auntie who was with a Belgian officer. Not monumentally significant in itself but it did fit into the pattern of events at home, in the farmhouse. There always seemed to be a clandestine atmosphere of spies there, close to Tangmere and the mysterious black Lysanders. The family had had connections with Belgian and French Resistance organisations. The family had always been fluent in French. Arbroath was cold and we flew in

Swordfish and Albacores though I loved the old Walrus. Trips to Dundee for tea, buns and boogie-woogie on an old upright piano were a great relaxation. Arbroath was isolated but there were lots of things to do in one's off-duty moments. There were Wren parties, amateur dramatics and a little church on the airfield which was infinitely better than the gymnasium sing-song type of service. Soon it was time to be measured up for officer uniforms and in Rosyth I was to walk under 'The Indefatigable': 18 months later I would be on top of it, for another reason.

The Naval College course at Greenwich followed and here I started my 6 months as a Midshipman. It was a fabulous place for food and we could get to the West End very easily. One night in an air raid I was told to investigate a naked light. I tapped on the offending window and a small elderly man appeared clad in a dressing gown. I gave him a wigging and he apologised profusely. Next morning that gentleman appeared at top-table resplendent in medal ribbons and gold braid up to his elbow! Alan Rowlinson, Ken Neuschild and I were interviewed for appointments and Ken and I were duly appointed in May 1944 to 1772 Squadron. No sign of Alan.

Ken became observer to Harry Garbutt, a gentle smiling type who played 'Honeysuckle Rose', badly, on a clarinet. I became observer to Teddy Key and we flew together from beginning to end, of the life of 1772. In between times I had to fly with other pilots but one or two could scare one to death. Many of us will have told stories of life at Burscough. There was so much to do and the Midshipman's pay just didn't balance with the range of outgoings.

Tragedy soon took over from the mounting fun and games and the excitement of flying in a potentially operational squadron. Ken and Harry were killed when Teddy and I were flying on a paired exercise with them. They crashed into the sea just off Blackpool. I was devastated because Ken and I had been real oppos for so long. The irony was that Alan replaced Ken in 1772. I was later to witness the tragic accident which killed our two most senior officers, below the CO.

The Boss, Les Wort, improved life so much and in the remaining summer months I enjoyed the countryside on my bicycle, visiting country pubs and playing dominoes with the locals. As winter approached we visited afternoon concerts by Malcolm Sargent in Liverpool. We flew to Donibristle to 'swing the compasses' and because of bad weather we were stranded on Christmas Day at the aerodrome. We left Greenock with the aircraft and all the gear in January 1945; I was on HMS Activity, a rather crowded escort carrier loaded with Avengers. We stopped at Port Said and Colombo and on the way picked up some survivors. Time was spent watching the flying fish and albatrosses, playing Liar Dice and drinking port.

We settled down quite quickly in the unfinished and primitive accommodation at HMS Nabthorpe, Schofields, NSW and learned to live with other squadrons stationed there. I made friends with a very friendly Mrs MacMaster and that friendship lasted many years. Another friendly family was the Robinson family. The frogs and the crickets of Schofields reminded me of the family's considerable fascination for France. We had been in France about the time war was to be declared. Father had a friend in high places in the War Office and he had agreed to let us know if war was imminent. In due course our 'coded' telegram arrived, 'Delighted to see the children'. We raced back to the UK in father's 4½ litre Bentley and got the last boat from Dieppe to Newhaven. I remember at the time of Chamberlain's speech, seeing a Puss Moth, to the sound of our first air raid sirens, screaming at a great rate of knots from across the channel. Many others must have made the last minute dash. Anyway, the frogs and crickets reminded me of that moment. Canungra jungle training was another event altogether. We learned how to rid ourselves of leeches and dig latrines. We were fed up with Maurice for doing his washing in a part of the river we had set aside for drinking water. Shaving in ice-cold stream water was no joy. It was here that the young man rode up on horseback to tell us that the war was over. 'What war?' was the answer I remember well.

For some reason I can remember very little about the actual conflict. Some things like having to get up very early in the morning to fly and struggling across the flight deck with my chart board, flood back. I took several cameras with me to give myself something to do. There were two Army officers who used to brief us about targets and what sort of anti-aircraft fire to expect and then de-brief us when we returned. The Indefatigable was VAST. I never really found my way about the place. Accommodation was cramped but the food was good. The Japanese countryside was surprisingly beautiful from the air; all grey hills and green trees. I could see trains and people cycling to work. Once we had to descend through cloud on the way back and when we came out we were somewhat scattered about the sky and there were some U.S. Navy squadrons in the distance all in beautiful formation. We soon reformed! The Americans in their Superfortresses used to 'invade' our R/T wavelength and chatter all the time, so we didn't stand much chance if we did need to break R/T silence. I remember watching other squadrons landing-on, from the 'goofers'. I shan't forget the dreadful crash in which a Seafire caught fire and a South African pilot lost his life. Also a less disastrous one when a U.S. Navy Hellcat went through the barriers and wrote off 3 Seafires. The pilot was unhurt and climbed down from the wreckage, looked at the Seafires and said, 'Gee, I'm sorry.'

When we sailed into Tokyo Bay after the war ended I was furious that we were not allowed ashore but I enjoyed sitting on the flight deck watching a film projected on the 'island' coming back to Sydney. It was rather like a cruise. We used to sleep on our little folding camp beds on the quarter deck at night, to keep cool. One night I was awakened by shouting. It seemed that a Petty Officer had fallen overboard and I believe he was picked up by a following destroyer. On Sunday afternoons we listened to classical music played over the ship's tannoy system. It was relayed by a Claude Jackson, a ship's writer officer. We still meet in Petersfield.

In Sydney we waited patiently for a ship to take us home. I stayed in the notorious Kings Cross area where we had a murder opposite, used cigarettes as taxi fares and four shilling bottles of whisky as presents for our 'grippos'. I came home on the 'Andes'. I was immediately redundant, learned to drive a car, Mother's Morris Eight, and eventually learned to drive lorries at Henstridge. I taught Wrens and sailors how to drive, but really, I was quite useless at the job. After demobilisation I did an Art course at Manchester Art School and linked up with Eric Bramhall and family. I was in civilian rig by June 1946 and learned to fly. I was taught by Cecil Pashley at £3 per hour – and I soloed in 8 hours!

So, as my father's favourite sport had been since 1910 and still was, motor racing, I got into the business somewhere below the bottom rung of the ladder, and there began, ANOTHER STORY, ANOTHER BOOK, MINE.

Teddy Key. 'I doubt if he will; he always professes to being too busy. That is to say that his contribution to the 'Friendly Squadron' has never been less than considerable. He was always one of the great enthusiasts, a magnificent patriot and world champion talker on almost anything.

"Whither goeth Sammy? The Squadron would have been the poorer without him because he was a character . . . in the nicest sense. He still is. He was a very fine navigator because he was bright, observant and very much one point in front of the game. Sometimes his style was misleading and confusing but he had a very deep sense of 'Royal Navy' pride; he moaned about being a Midshipman but quite honestly, I do believe he enjoyed the role. He was a 'bon viveur', despite his capacity for describing some navy food as palatable. With his family background and School he could never have been a mongrel like many of us; he loved the good life. But he loved the simple things in the mad world of navy flying, like disappearing into the countryside and meeting 'folk'.

He would wander off to little churches and find sources of good music. He was a great party man; he was a 1772 man and again I add – he still is. Sammy is a very loyal guy and he loves to surround himself with good chat, a jug of ale and a good measure of laughter. Lest I forget, 50 years ago he was a damn good 'looker', the guy in the back seat. He didn't flap, he knew his job and we had some fun. We brought each other home to a good life since and we are still good pals . . . aren't we, . . . you nutty free spirit!"

JOE 'BOB' SCOTT
Pilot

I was born in Leeds on 13th November 1924. In 1940 I saw the newsreels of the Battle of Britain and I longed to fly a Seafire. Perhaps just schoolboy dreams, but I wanted to fly. In 1942 I saw my first Spitfire flying off a carrier. It coincided with my awareness of the existence of the 'Y' Scheme entry into the Royal Navy. I was hooked.

In 1943 I went to Sealand for my EFTS and in 1943/44 I was at SFTS at Aylmer, Ontario, Canada. Back in the UK, it was a brief spell at the Advanced Flying Unit at Errol, Perthshire. From June to August 1944 I was at NAFS Henstridge and 719 Squadron at St Merryn. FLYING SEAFIRES! On August 30th and 31st I did my first deck landings on HMS Ravager. In September 1944 I joined 1772 Squadron at Burscough.

With me were Roy Hubble, Wally Pritchard and Rollo Norman. Rollo became my 'looker'. After the war between 1946 and 1949 I was articled to a firm of Chartered Accountants. On 27th March 1947 I was married and in 1950 I became a Chartered Accountant. Between 1951 and 1986 my career was in industry firstly as a chief accountant and then as a director of public companies.

On 21st December 1963, Deborah was born and on 21st September 1964 Michael was born.

I married for the second time on 4th November 1982, to Anne. From 1986 to 1994 I was a Consultant at DTI in the East Midlands. On 31st August 1994 I retired as did Anne from teaching and her post as Headmistress.'

'Joebob' and Anne have now emigrated to Western Australia. Bob a refreshing extrovert with strong Yorkshire overtones has been rather reticent about his adventures in FAA and the Squadron for with the best will in the world one cannot believe that this friendly and adventurous spirit managed to avoid trouble. Some have been mentioned elsewhere in the story. He remarked that he has failed to be 'light and amusing'. A pity because Bob always radiated good humour and with such a sunny nature he fitted into our Squadron with consummate ease. Bob was never dull.

It is only right that having worked so hard on the very early and rough proofs produced by Teddy Key, Anne should claim a little space for Bob. She says that under some duress, 'Bob allowed me to add a story or two to the above account of himself.'

'By his own admission he was a harum-scarum and had plenty of escapades for which he ought to have been severely dressed down. Low flying over Leeds and 'beating up' his own street ('There's our Joe!') is one which is remembered by Frances his 'kid' sister. Another time, he was, for whatever reason, flying through a canyon in the beautiful Blue Mountains west of Sydney. Suddenly he was confronted by a fast-approaching wall of rock – the canyon had no way out. Unlike a jet the Firefly could not climb out, but it had marvellous flaps and could turn on a sixpence. With the adrenalin pumping Bob turned, almost grazing the mountainside, and lived to tell the tale. Who was with him on that occasion? Bob cannot remember.

Another moment when he nearly bought it occurred at the very end, off Sydney, when he was leaving the Indefatigable. He was ranged on

the flight deck, waiting for the signal to take off. He explained to me: 'These deck officers are very experienced and can see much more of the picture than you, so you obey them implicitly. They wait for exactly the right moment, and time it so that you take off when the bow is going up. On this occasion I obeyed the signal, but as I took off the bow was *going down!* I only just made it. The guy came up to me in the bar that evening and bought me a drink!' Bob's response to him is not recorded.

GEORGE TROLLOPE
Pilot

George should by every right be the architect of so much material for this story. Here was one of the great extroverts of the squadron for George was never short of a word or two. His mind was the liveliest of the lot and throughout his successful business career in the city of London he was involved deeply in the Stock Market and particularly with Gilts. George had great energy, applying it to many aspects of life not the least being education, in which area he became a school governor in Hornchurch, Essex. He was a great companion, a very typical 'Branch type'. George unfortunately says that a ropey old memory related to the years of the war prevents any serious recall of the happenings of that marvellous time we shared.

Teddy Key. 'He was a great and loyal friend and with Johnny O'Driscoll the three of us were a mildly wicked trio. Our triple Fancy Dress Ball act of the 'Three Musthavebeers' was fun. I think I could recreate those costumes even to this day – but where did the green curtains come from?'

It is a great pity that George is denied some of the great memories of the Fleet Air Arm days for there were so many of them. This book is a testament to them and even then, between all of us, there are gaps; the collective memory is not 100%. Nevertheless, the present is with him in terms of contentment and the voice and brio . . . 'élan vital', still remain intact. No doubt the joys of 3 children and 7 grandchildren add to those present pleasures and Joyce one presumes remembers all the birthdays! It is understood that he is still very adept with both Times and Telegraph crosswords; one completed with the left hand and the other with the right . . . simultaneously?

282

There were of course others in the Squadron with whom we have lost contact. Some maybe have run out of steam in their retirement. ERIC BRAMHALL was Johnny Coles' pilot. He was a cheerful rogue, in the nicest sense. He was an ardent Manchester United fan, an extrovert Lancastrian who loved 'beating up' his family homes. He has died.

GORDON DAVIDSON was a Scot and a most talented flyer. He was a first-rate athlete being a swimmer with an outstanding representational record in Scotland. He was a powerful looking and fearless man. Johnny Palmer was his observer. Gordon died at a young age.

ROY HUBBLE joined the Squadron at the same time as Bob Scott, Rollo Norman and Wally Pritchard. He was Wally's pilot until deck-landing exercises in Jervis Bay in Australia, when it was thought that he had bent too many aircraft to continue with the Squadron and he was posted.

DAVE HEBDITCH joined the Squadron in Australia and became Alan Rowlinson's pilot. They flew together until Tokyo Bay. They lost touch with each other after the return to Sydney. Prior to 1772 Dave was in 1770 Squadron. In the Sakashima operation he had to ditch his aircraft due to oil feed problems. Dave has died since the war.

PETE KINGSTON. It is a pity that Pete could not be persuaded to add something to our story but he has suffered cruelly from ill-health. He lives now, quietly, in Napier, New Zealand. He was a pilot of great talent and 'odd' carelessness. He was good company, loved the girls; a very relaxed Kiwi, quieter than most, but capable of a great deal of mischief. He was 'one great colleague'.

JOHN PRINCE joined us so late that very few remember him and his pilot –

– VIN REDDING. They arrived with a flourish and also nearly became our last prang. (Cleverly. 'Pranger Pete' stole that accolade from them by ramming a concrete block when he landed, on his last flight at Schofields when the Squadron was 'flown-off!') They bent an undercarriage on landing-on, transferring from 1771 but they managed to join us on a couple of POW runs. John Prince claims one distinction in that he served in all three Firefly Squadrons. 1770 he loved, 1771 he hated and 1772 he would have loved, if the war had lasted longer! John was on the same course as Sammy Samuelson, Ken Neuschild and Alan Rowlinson.

We hardly remember some of our colleagues. 'They had their entrances and their exits.'

A postscript. DEREK GREEN of Castle Bromwich is a late 'emergence' – through the pages of 'Navy News'. Now a widower and suffering the misfortunes of a stroke 8 years ago, he was an airframe mechanic of 1772 from the beginning to the end of the Squadron. He says he was a fitter on Croose Parry's Firefly and 'he was a busy man'! He recalls flying with Gough on one occasion whilst at Burscough on a maintenance trip after some work on the machine. Ground crew always enjoyed these airborne perks. On this occasion, approaching the coast near Blackpool from the sea, Gough announced that they 'may have to bale out'. No real reason was given and Derek says that he doesn't remember being scared. It occurred to him at that point that he had no idea of how to leave a rear cockpit of a Firefly and then there was the matter of very limited knowledge about taking to a parachute. Derek mentioned these points to Gough but by that time all seemed to be in order. He remembered when on the Indefatigable, they used to collect bottles for the aircrews to stuff down their flare chutes. Was that something they got from Ian Darby?

MICHAEL QUINN was a member of the Squadron we have yet to meet. Disenchanted with civilian work, closely attached to the Royal Navy, he longed to join the sea-going Royal Navy. After enlisting he had a brief spell at HMS Heron, Henstridge, (a satellite of Yeovilton):

Jimmy Haslam

Pete Kingston

Shiner Wright

'Knocker' White

Rollo Moon

he joined 1772 at Burscough in September 1944 as a Naval Airman. Michael enjoyed his time with 1772 and especially the Australian period. He has twice returned to Australia, partly to trace old shipmates. He was one of the few original 1772 members who stayed on board the Indefatigable to 'show the flag' in New Zealand; 'a wonderful experience'. He was drafted to HMS Implacable and was billeted in Hyde Park, Sydney, 'very handy for the Randwick Racecourse'. He then returned to the UK on Indefatigable, by then, doing troopship duties, via Cape Town and Gibraltar. He was demobbed from Lee-on-Solent in April 1947 and whilst at Daedalus, he shared a cabin with Sir Malcolm Sargent's son. He claims to have had no regrets about his service days – he enjoyed it all very much.

HARRY RUSSELL was for a long time a regular member of our reunions, always cheerful and outward going. He seems to have retreated from us in recent months and perhaps one can assume, either disenchantment with 1772 or personal and family problems. It is a pity because he was so well liked. He was a member of our ground maintenance crew, specialising in the Griffon engine. His technical training was completed at the RAF Hednesford school and he served for a time at Worthy Down. He remembers that the task of unloading the equipment of the Squadron from Squadron Stores at Burscough and again unloading from HMS Ruler to RNAS Schofields in Australia was a very big task. He remarked to us on one occasion how the whole operation was a great team effort and consumed a great amount of the ground crews' time, but that it was all in the cause of duty and really good fun.

The Young Harry Russell.

EPILOGUE – A REVIEW OR EVEN A REVUE

Our revels are now ended; these our actors,
As I foretold you, were all spirits, and
Are melted into air...
We are such stuff
As dreams are made on; and our little life
Is rounded with a sleep.   *Shakespeare (The Tempest)*

Good words shall gain you honour in the market place,
but deeds shall gain you friends among men.
                                  Old Chinese saying

This has been a modest tale, a tale told by a number of people which covers a period from the early Forties when some young men decided to join an elite service, the Fleet Air Arm. The story has concentrated upon the core of events from mid-1944 up to the Japanese surrender in September 1945. In their individual stories they tell of how they came to terms with civilian life in the next 50 years. Their contribution to the real action of the war was small in the context of the length of the war and the amount of time spent in the teeth of action by many other serving men. Most of them would claim that, even in that time, there was enough excitement to last them a lifetime. 1772 was in at the kill and in close attendance when the final curtain came down. Those lives which were, for a while, very closely linked come together, even until the present day, in a series of reunions. On these occasions they now meet the relatives of those who did not survive or who have died since the war.

We wonder about the truth. Have our memories deceived us over the years? But, it did happen though the mind sometimes is a little obscure, sometimes quite clear and some events are unforgettable. Like the history we struggled with at school, maybe, and the news items we endeavour to comprehend in their awfulness today, we find that reportage differs with each story teller. But, here in this story, 'not a lot'.

We have used the theatrical metaphor as the broadest of outlines to this story so why not 'play on' in a cheerful, optimistic, yet musical way. Why did we join the FAA? Simply because it was and is an elite service. COME FLY WITH ME. We loved being sailors. ALL THE NICE GIRLS LOVE A SAILOR, ALL THE NICE GIRLS LOVE A TAR. There were lots of girls, maybe a few; won and lost; or even, just one. UNFORGETTABLE YOU. We had our fearful times as well as being, very sad and homesick. WHENEVER I FEEL AFRAID I WHISTLE A HAPPY TUNE.

I KNOW WHERE I'M GOING AND I KNOW WHO IS GOING WITH ME. We rarely did and even when we settled into our final act as 1772, uncertainties prevailed.

ONE MORNING IN MAY this story really began; 1772, 'The Friendly Squadron' was born on the first. It had been conceived as the third, wanted Firefly child of their Lordships and RNAS Burscough became the cradle, a really significant part of that mould which was to fashion our lives. Burscough was ideally planned for us with a public house neatly placed between the 1772 aerodrome dispersal and the Wardroom. Proof of this planning came to light only recently when a piece of scrap paper was found in an old naval file. It had been a mere discarded slip, confined to the bin and never shredded. The document

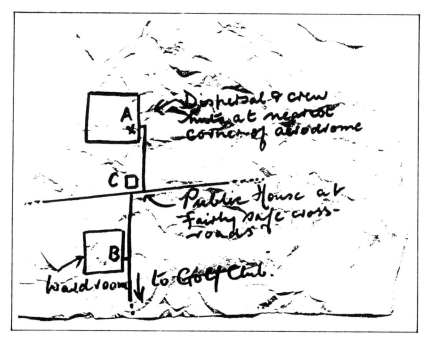

can be reproduced above as it is no longer an official secret. The Bull and Dog became a shrine and 1772 became an endangered – or was it a dangerous? – species. The friendships of a lifetime were begun. Some were to die in action or after the war. Some we have lost contact with. The odd one has lost the 1772 feeling and is too busy being elderly or babysitting the grandchildren. But aren't we all?

There was LOVE AND MARRIAGE. Life was DANCING IN THE OLD FASHIONED WAY and of course CHEEK TO CHEEK. The melodies of the day spanned the emotions from IN THE MOOD to JEALOUSY. It was all very lovely and there were the Wrens – BLESS THEIR BEAUTIFUL HIDES. You see, once even the ageing Branch mind arrives in the lighter vein, his head spins with song. Steve and Agnes were married and lived in a little house near the aerodrome. Johnny O'Driscoll married his Wren, Madge. She AIN'T MIS-BEHAVING because she was a Wren Steward at RNAS Yeovilton. The local press enjoyed their 'reunion' at Yeovilton in 1994 when we celebrated the 50th anniversary of our 'forming up'. Teddy Key was their best man and this was a responsibility enjoyed by many guys in the squadron during and after the war. Other 'best men' included Bob Scott for Wally Pritchard, Jackie Ramsden for Steve Stevens, Geoff Gill for Alan Rowlinson and Alan Rowlinson for Geoff Gill. Dancing and dining out at romantic venues or just drinking at the local – and even a slow walk through the woods – were but part of the lighter pattern of life. Young love blossomed and faded when the next posting came. But not in every case. Des Mullen married his Wren. The Blue Pyjamas mystery is but a part of squadron mythology. They were lost, left somewhere, one can only assume. Handsewn they were, so the story goes, by a Wren in the Wrennery, with love in her heart. It is known that they were treasured, but the mystery ends there. Did they perish under the pillow during a fire at say the Adelphi in Liverpool? IT COULD HAVE BEEN THE START OF SOMETHING BIG.

There still remains a huge imbalance in writing this story when considering the contribution of former members of the ground crews. There is little more that one can do to redress that balance. We cannot, however, reiterate enough the gratitude we had and still feel for those guys who tended to our planes. They did a super job and it was good and reassuring to have SOMEONE TO WATCH OVER US. The Pacific Ocean was a huge space and the Japanese mainland spelled unbounded horrors. The Boss was always there, caring; and Captain Q. D. Graham got us home to Sydney, more or less in one piece, short of food and booze after a record-breaking time at sea.

SEPTEMBER SONG was a happy time. Short of fuel, food, (one

ration item was 1 dessertspoonful of dehydrated potato per day) and overburdened with a sense of anti-climax, we sailed home, never turned to face Fujiyama, and, broken by a Yankee Hellcat, we tied up at Sydney. We said 'farewell' and in indecent haste and were bundled into digs in the red-light district of Kings Cross. All very humbling, forgotten already maybe, and probably without exception we escaped to our friends in Australia until our ships, Andes or Stratheden, signalled to us that we would soon to be on our way home – real home. PARTING (WAS) SUCH SWEET SORROW.

DON'T FENCE ME IN was, one supposes, the feeling of us all when we had to cast aside the wild side of life and settle into 'civvy street'. WHEN THIS BLOODY WAR 'WAS' OVER we were enclosed by a whole new set of strictures. We had to live with the reality that FINGS 'WERE' NOT WHAT THEY USED TO BE. Like every soldier, sailor or airman, friend or foe, the individual man who had lived dangerously and had lived with a bitterness in his soul, departed to begin a new life, each in his own separate way. As they grew into their mature and later years, perhaps wiser, probably more compassionate, they all must have asked the same old question: Why? Who among us came up with a definitive answer? Whatever we did in the war or since, WE DID IT OUR WAY – CRAZY PEOPLE!

Major 'Cheese' Cheesman, the CO of the first Firefly Squadron 1770, one of the great Fleet Air Arm Squadrons of the war, wrote to us referring to our article in the News Sheet of the Fleet Air Arm Officers' Association.

'You sound somewhat dismayed but I do not go along with that. Every Squadron goes through a bad patch so let's deal with the good parts.

1. I seem to remember that you had a great Squadron Commander in Les Wort, right?
2. You served in the Indefatigable.
3. You were the first Firefly Squadron, or rather British Squadron, to fly over Tokyo Bay and Japan itself.
   (Not quite true. Two of our crews had been seconded to 1771 Squadron: Stu Jobbings and Rhys Heaven, Don Randle and Forêt Millar. 1771 Firefly Squadron therefore claims this honour, with the help of our original guys.)
4. You have memories and stories to covet in this respect.
5. You did all you could to achieve the objectives in all these operations.
6. You and your ship first flew the signal of: 'Cease operations against Japan.'

7. You sailed into Tokyo Bay.
8. You formed an association in which to relive all this in the years ahead.
9. You've kept the spirit going for 50 years – well done!
10. All your members have been most loyal to the cause.
11. Think of the enormous joy and relief you brought to our POW's.
12. Keep that one thought to the fore and think positively – *WE ALL PLAYED A PART IN BEATING THEM.'*

He rounded off another letter to us by saying: 'And so to Sydney, where 1770 handed over to 1772 Squadron. WE started it, YOU finished it – in Tokyo Bay. Well done the Firefly, and 1772.' THE VERY MODEL OF A MODERN MAJOR . . .

On September 6th 1996 a small group of us made a sort of pilgrimage to The Bull and Dog at Burscough. We had been in contact with four local people through a letter in the Ormskirk Advertiser, which 'warned' them that 1772 would be around on this date. The 'sessions' on the Friday and Saturday of that weekend attracted so many of them. There was a little man, well into his eighties, who used to cut the grass between the runways for feeding to his goats – or was it rabbits? A couple who live now in the 'Admiral's Cottage' just inside the non-existent main gate, showed us the deeds of the property taken over by the Admiralty in that area which was our dispersal area. One of those landowners was Walter Gorst, venerable publican of The Bull and Dog in the war years. His daughter, Monica who served in the hostelry and is now 83 years old, came for lunch with us and, looking at photos asked, 'How was Mike?' When asked what the 21st Birthday round of 32 pints would have cost then, she came out with the answer 13/4d, or today, £1.60 – 5 pence per pint! QUE SERA SERA.

There were residents who wanted information about local histories they were writing and just folk who wanted to talk about the old days. They had memories, too, often vague because they sometimes belonged to their parents. Mrs Riding, a resident of Burscough, remembers a story of her mother, regarding the chatter in The Bull and Dog, when aircrew would talk about the death that day of a colleague in a flying accident. She tells how they drank their beer and there seemed to be no tears. AH, 'WE' REMEMBER IT WELL and we do remember THEM, the guys we lost. This story is humbly dedicated to the Boss and all of them no longer with us. 'Today at The Bull and Dog we'll raise a glass to you. "Today" is Friday, 6th September 1996.'
WE'LL GO NO MORE A-ROVIN'

No action, whether foul or fair,
Is ever done, but it leaves somewhere
A record, written by fingers ghostly,
As a blessing or a curse.

Longfellow

ACKNOWLEDGEMENTS

*'If you must tell me your opinions, tell me what you
believe in. I have plenty of doubts of my own.'*   Goethe

'The best thing we get from history is the enthusiasm it rouses.'
                                                              Goethe

The stories of 1772 Firefly Squadron have spanned our lives from callow teens to mellow retirement. Many people have contributed and we hope we will have said our 'thank you's' to all of them. They have not suffered too badly under the scalpel of the editor; for the most part what they have had to tell is unexpurgated, warts, whinges, wishes and all. Some contributed at length, baring almost all, with words and pictures. Some have displayed uncharacteristic modesty and some have taken their time. There have been a few 'pikers' who have gone to earth: a pity really because it would have been desirable to have had a full muster.

The tale is told; the breakfast 'threat' in September 1995 has been fulfilled, the deed is done. It is now time for others, our peers and posterity, to judge the worth of the opus. By 'others', we mean those who were not privy to the antics and activities of once-young men, as it happened. 'Others' have added their 'penn'orth' and we thank them. Agnes, Steve's widow in Canada, has always given 'a fistful of dollars' to the squadron and we remain grateful to her for her enthusiasm for 1772 matters. Alan Gittins and Joan Wright, loving kin of Glyn Roberts, have been most keen to help, believing that the book not only preserves the memory of those who died, but in particular, records the brief lives of Glyn and his observer, Mac. They would like it to be recorded, that what they died for must not be forgotten. Les Wort's widow Dorothy has supported us well, along with her two daughters. We wish to thank her for permission to use a photo of the young 'Subby' Wort. Ian Darby has kept us in touch with the Kiwi contingent; he has been the self-appointed spokesman of the excellent and distant band of colleagues, Burn and Pete and the late Don Banks, as well as Mac's widow Linda. A trio of Wrens, Jackie Cockrill, Sue Tonks and Joan Hanson have contributed. No offence to their married mates, but we would only wish to remember the Burscough lasses by their maidenly names!

Our thanks are due to Major Cheesman, George Birch who bravely taught postwar 'sprogs' to fly the Firefly and Graham Mottram of the Museum at Yeovilton, for his early encouragement and preserving for all to see, our dismal record of prangs. Our thanks to the Royal Navy Historic Flight are on hold, until they complete the exercise to get a member of the Squadron off the ground . . . without mishaps, with overtones of 1772! Ray Sturtivant put us in the right direction, via the Public Records Office at Kew, to discover the truth about the Squadron Crest and uncover some of the 'strike' reports of our raids over Japan. Ken Hughes corrected the errors in Latin translation and spelling of our crest. Without him, none of us would have known the difference! Glyn Manning designed the letter headings we have used for a long time in our correspondence and he has kindly tackled other artwork.

A number of journals have spread our pleas for information, namely, the Association of Wrens, Navy News and the Fleet Air Arm Officers Association, where Mick Lawrence has always been a good friend of 1772. Even the landlord of the Bull and Dog at Burscough has spread our gospel with the help of the Ormskirk Advertiser.

Some local folk of Burscough and Ormskirk have been rallied by that local newspaper. We thank the Baxters, Maureen Riding, Monica Gorst, Philip Pearson, Beryl Arkwright and Bob Lea for their interest. There were others whose names were never noted but they came to say 'hello' despite the fact that we helped to ruin their countryside.

We have all once again, gone through the several books written about the Pacific War, the Indefatigable and the Firefly. We are grateful to their authors for their permission to use some of their material and pictures. Much of our story is of course first-hand and several of us have contributed to these other books. Most of the photos in our book belong to the squadron members. Photographs such as the classic picture of the Firefly by Charles Brown have been reproduced by kind permission. In most cases these books have been valuable in cross-checking dates and placing our events in a wider context. The books are as follow:

'Sakashima – and Back.'	Stuart Eadon	Charity Books
'Kamikaze'	Stuart Eadon	Square One Publications
'The Forgotten Fleet'	John Winton	Douglas Boyd Books
'Fairey Firefly'	Bill Harrison	Airlife Publishing
'Memoirs of a Reluctant Batsman'	A 'Cappy' Masters	Janus Publishing

HMS Indefatigable Fleet Aircraft Carrier	P. Bonney and B. Briggs	Peter Bonney
'My Dad, My Hero.'	Michael Bentinck	Print-Out. Histon.

Regarding the latter book, the extract is but a small one but it was chosen to illustrate a major aspect of our time fighting the Japanese, namely the consequences of being caught and subjected to the squalid mind of a squalid enemy. From the publication of this humble praise of his father and his sufferings at that awful centre of allied suffering, Changi, Michael Bentinck received such a response that he has since produced two other books about those who suffered at the hands of the Japanese, 'Forgotten Heroes' and the latest, 'A Will to Live', compilations of the horrors of Japanese captivity. Honesty must now prevail in our minds and we have to admit that a small corner of our young brains was cognisant of that terror.

Having put it all together there had to be the need for it to be read carefully, in order to eliminate the gaffs, poor choice of words, the hopelessly wrong phrases and of course the bent facts. To this end, several friendly people must be thanked. Eve Trowbridge laboured and though she admits to never coming within a nautical mile of a sailor's collar she came to grips with the task with, 'a bit long-winded in parts and could do with a little pruning'. This we did. Marion Street applied her charitable side and her insight for order, and expressed her views with characteristic candour. So we ironed out some of the 'howlers', at this early stage.

A very early copy found its way to Western Australia via Wally Pritchard where no doubt Bob Scott added his rusty aviation knowledge to the literary skills of his wife, Anne.

To Anne Scott we owe a special debt of gratitude for the considerable reading and re-reading she did. She re-shaped some chapters in order to give a greater impact to the material we had. She completely re-vamped the Epilogue because it had become a trifle top-heavy. She gave a lot of attention to the style of the piece and made many suggestions and corrections which have improved the quality of the book a great deal. Now as a result of a number of readers who have added their criticism, we can be grateful to Anne, Eve, Marion, Wally, Johnny Coles, Monica and Alan. There is now a carefully nurtured 1772 Story.

Wally Pritchard and Alan Rowlinson read the rough proofs and were most helpful in correcting a number of points. Alan searched diligently for the split infinitive and was delighted to find a small catch . . . or to delightfully find! Wally's accountancy 'eye' and imperturbable nature were ever to the fore in reading the script.

We are grateful to Roy Johnson, Marketing Manager at the Yeovilton Museum, for the title of the book, though he may be unaware of this fact. It came about at the end of the 50th Anniversary celebration, we at the Museum, of our 'birth' in 1944. He was asked if we would be welcome the following year when all the celebrations for the end of the Japanese War and the return of 'The Forgotten Fleet' would be held. He replied that we would be most welcome because 'we were one of the friendliest squadrons to return to Yeovilton for reunions.'

Our grateful thanks are due to Desmond Wilkey, former Senior Observer of 1770 Firefly Squadron, who did his best to help us find the Squadron Diary, which has been 'lost' for over 50 years. Whilst the Public Records Office at Kew had a copy of their squadron diary on file, 1772 had no such luck.

Agnes Stevens did some valiant work in contacting the Canadian Naval Aviation Museum in Ottawa. They provided a lot of useful information leading to the eventual rebuilding of one of the few remaining early marks of the Firefly. We are very grateful to the Museum.

More than 95% of the photographs have been submitted by the squadron members as they ripped into their precious albums. Many thanks to them.

Dick Allen via Johnny Palmer and Dennis White via 'Jabberwock' provided material on 'The Boss', Les Wort.

Apologies have to be made for the problem of Japanese spelling . . . in English! Jack Freestone of Ormskirk sent us some good aerial shots of Burscough airfield and the camps and we must say thank you to Commander Bissett of the South African Naval Museum at Simonstown for his efforts in trying to find information about Mike La Grange.

Those who answered our pleas for help were the Royal Air Force Museum, the Imperial War Museum, the Society of Friends of the Fleet Air Arm Museum, Frank Ott and the journal 'Jabberwock', and the Telegraphist Air Gunners' Association. We are grateful for the use of John Winton's metaphor of the Good Samaritan and Lin Yutang's 'Scamp' in his book 'The Importance of Living' published by William Heinemann, firstly in 1937.

Many sources were contacted in the cause of politeness and correctitude and sometimes there was no answer. Some of our sources were as old as ourselves!

In an attempt to make certain that the chapter on the Firefly was as accurate as possible, a copy of that chapter was sent to Westland Aircraft in Yeovil in the hope that it might find some Fairey archivist who would be interested in corresponding with us. That envelope must have fallen on stony ground.

Any errors and omissions in the above acknowledgements are entirely unintentional. Everything possible was done to recognise those who added to this compilation and to respect copyright and ownership of material referred to and used.

There was one final task, the reading and correcting the galley proofs. To this end Monica Hart, Wally Pritchard and Johnny Coles put in a great deal of hard work. The editor was determined to find some scapegoats as 'we put the book to bed' and was delighted to find yet again that special spirit of 'the friendly squadron'.

> If you your lips would keep from slips,
> Of five things have a care:
> To whom you speak, of whom you speak,
> And how, and when, and where.
> An old Maxim.

THE EDITOR

'Please do not shoot the pianist . . . he did his best.'   *Wilde*

There was once an author/compiler who set about publishing a book of funny sayings and anecdotes. The exercise proved to be a disaster when he realised that he had no sense of humour! I sincerely hope that I have succeeded, using the material at my disposal, in attaining a right sense of proportion in this story in that it finally conveys the true and genuine facts of a very small part of the 1939/45 conflict, together with the right mixture of the humour of the times; 'men behaving badly' sometimes, in a violent and cruel war, and young impressionable men committed to the serious and dangerous processes of learning to fly and applying those ultimately deadly skills in a Royal Navy Squadron. I feel that with the help of my excellent colleagues, a sense of the values by which we lived then, has been committed to the humble story of 1772 Firefly Squadron.

My sincerest gratitude has to be extended to the Duke of Wellington gang who sustained my morale with the occasional flash of flattery. Alan Rowlinson fulfilled the role of 'Reluctant Chairman' with consummate ease and his other, self-inflicted duty of 'kitty minder and sandwich orderly' was carried out with characteristic good nature. I have been most appreciative of his good humour and generous nature, which has helped to spur me on. I am most grateful to Wally Pritchard for the work he did on the commercial side of publishing the book. His expertise in manipulating numbers in his 'sums' and the small print, were indispensable and in the company of Alan, a cheerful trio negotiated the unchartered waters of publishing. Here we had the good fortune to choose Mary Wilkinson of Square One Publishing out of nearly ten publishers we contacted. To quote one of her other 'Militaria' authors, 'she was a gem'.

The others in the Duke of Wellington gang at East Horsley were, Johnny O'Driscoll, Geoff Rham, Croose Parry, Sammy Samuelson, Johnny Coles and Gordon Macrow. For a brief while Harry Russell and John Price attended our 'happenings' . . . a rough appreciation of a 1772 meeting. Those gatherings are surviving the ravages of time and I firmly believe that they will be the final resting remnants of 1772 reunions . . . zimmer frames and all. They have remained to date a most amusing group of gentle tipplers, heavily impregnated with the 1772 spirit.

Stuart Eadon was one of the first I contacted when the first blank sheet of white typing paper glared at me – challenging me! Stuart was most encouraging and friendly, as always, and one significant piece of advice, among several, was 'to keep everything in an orderly manner'. How right he was! We were to meet him again in Upton upon Severn when the publishers took over, early in 1997 . . . to receive his blessing?

The task of stirring the squadron to 'shake off dull sloth and joyful rise', was a fulsome, but most enjoyable task: such an activity concentrates the mind, hones the memory, keeps a lone widower on the straight and narrow path to virtue and dampens alien thoughts. It was a task well suited to an outward-going introvert! I hope that all who cared about the book had 'their space' but what an editor hasn't got he cannot include.

The wonder of survival and the overcoming of very profound fears has been present most of the time. As Alan Rowlinson reminded me at the time of the 1996 Cenotaph Service, 'there is still time for weeping'. The doubts I had as a young flyer in a modern war, about the 'purpose of war', have long-since gone. It had to be fought, like all evil; problems of such dimensions can only be resolved by a forthright attitude. I have had doubts too about recalling it all; why not let it rest? It has however been more than interesting to put it all together in one place, for I have felt that what we did, relatively small though it was, received scant praise. In the end I had no qualms, it was worthwhile and in any case; why be fearful of memories whether they be trivial or profound, sad or happy, virtuous or wicked, dull or exciting? Unashamedly, we have spilled our beans!

Teddy Key

A postscript

Searching for some link with the Americans with whom we shared a part of the war, Wally Pritchard suggested a well-known American Naval pilot, George Bush. With some presumption we wrote to him, asking him to send his blessings. His spokesman in Houston, Jim McGrath, answered our letter saying: "Please be assured that the request is not a presumptuous one on your part. President Bush sends his respects to you and your fellow squadron mates, and he congratulates you for your efforts to tell your story of service to your country".

When I was a lad I served a spell
As Subby on the ocean swell,
I flew Fireflies in the Fleet Air Arm
And I polished them off without any harm;
I polished them off so thoroughly,
That now I am retired from the Queen's
Navee.

With apologies to W. Gilbert

Almost the end – all that is left of the Control Tower at RNAS Burscough September 1996.

Here between these covers lies,
The solemn remnants of our lives.
Many yarns and stories told,
Of courage, fun . . . and not so bold.
We've told them all with honesty;
Kept quiet about . . . impropriety!
Here between these covers rests,
A tale of mem'rable conquests.

Anon

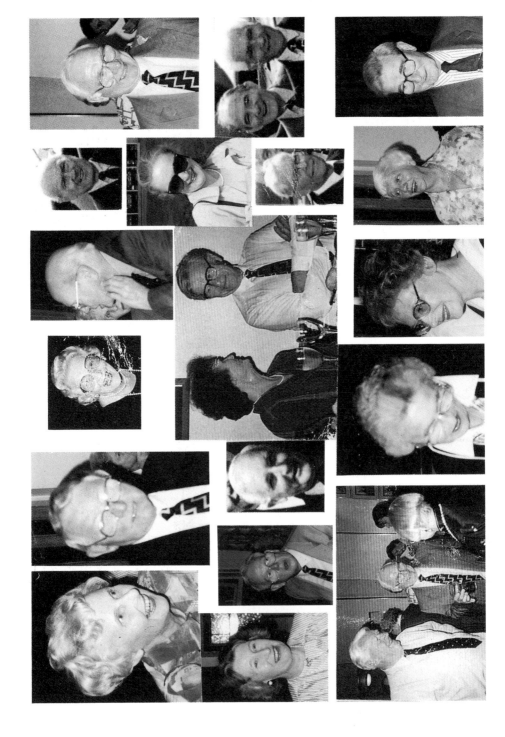

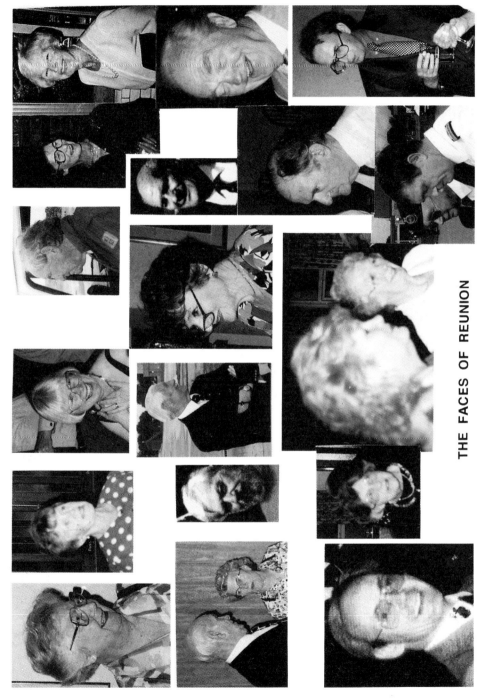

THE FACES OF REUNION